D0787042

CLASSICS IN PSYCHOLOGY

CLASSICS IN PSYCHOLOGY

A NOTE ABOUT THE AUTHOR

WALTER B. PILLSBURY, eminent American psychologist and educator, was born in Burlington, Iowa, in 1872. After receiving an A. B. from the University of Nebraska in 1892, Pillsbury went to Cornell, where he studied with E. B. Titchener and received his doctorate in 1896. Pillsbury soon moved to the University of Michigan where he taught for many years, becoming Chairman of the Department of Psychology in 1929. Pillsbury held many editorial positions, conducted research in nearly every area of psychology, and was elected to the presidency of the American Psychological Association in 1910. He belonged to no school of psychology, though, broadly speaking, he was sympathetic to the Titchenerian approach and suspicious of psychologists who departed from concrete and commonplace experience. At the same time, however, he was very interested in the nature of logical reasoning and wrote an influential *Psychology of Reasoning,* published in 1910. Pillsbury's most famous work was his investigation of attention, which resulted in the first scholarly monograph on this subject, and one of the first attempts by a psychologist to bring the whole range of psychological experimentation and theorizing to bear upon a central concept in the field.

ATTENTION

W[alter] B[owers] Pillsbury

ARNO PRESS

A New York Times Company
New York ★ 1973

Reprint Edition 1973 by Arno Press Inc.

Reprinted by permission of
George Allen & Unwin Ltd.

Reprinted from a copy in
The Princeton University Library

Classics in Psychology
ISBN for complete set: 0-405-05130-1
See last pages of this volume for titles.

Manufactured in the United States of America

———◆———

Library of Congress Cataloging in Publication Data

Pillsbury, Walter Bowers, 1872-1960.
    Attention.

    (Classics in psychology)
    Reprint of the 1908 ed. published by Sonnenschein,
London, and Macmillan, New York, in series: Library
of philosophy.
    Bibliography: p.
    1. Attention. I. Title. II. Series.
III. Series: Library of philosophy.
 [DNLM: BFP642a 1908F]
BF321.P5 1973   153.7'33   73-2982
ISBN 0-405-05154-9

ATTENTION

ATTENTION

BY

W. B. PILLSBURY

JUNIOR PROFESSOR OF PHILOSOPHY, DIRECTOR OF THE PSYCHOLOGICAL
LABORATORY, UNIVERSITY OF MICHIGAN

LONDON

SWAN SONNENSCHEIN & CO., LTD.

NEW YORK: THE MACMILLAN CO.

1908

TO

PROFESSOR E. B. TITCHENER

AS A TOKEN OF ESTEEM

AND AN ACKNOWLEDGMENT

OF HIS INSTRUCTION

PREFACE TO ENGLISH EDITION

THIS volume was published in 1906 in the "Bibliothèque internationale de psychologie expérimentale." In the present edition I have taken advantage of the greater space to make numerous additions. I have added chapters upon measurements of attention, upon the relations of attention to the feelings and to the self, and have appended a chapter on the educational applications of some of the conclusions. Moreover, the short chapter in the French edition on memory, will, and reason has been expanded into three. New material has been introduced here and there throughout the work. I have endeavoured to make full use of the suggestions offered by my numerous reviewers, and have taken advantage of all that seemed practical. In a topic with so many ramifications as attention it is difficult to decide just where to stop. One is always tempted to extend discussion to topics not directly connected with the main theme, and to discuss them for themselves, not for their bearing upon the subject in hand. I desire to thank M. Vaschide for his courtesy in connection with the French edition, and I wish to express my gratitude particularly to the editor of the "Library of Philosophy," Professor Muirhead, for the care he has given my manuscript and for numerous valued suggestions.

Considerable portions of chapter xiii. were published in the "Philosophical Review" for July, 1907, and are reprinted by permission of the editors.

W. B. PILLSBURY.

UNIVERSITY OF MICHIGAN

PREFACE

IN the present chaotic condition of attention theories an attempt, however modest, to harmonise the known facts with one another needs no apology. I have endeavoured in the present volume to bring together in an orderly way the results of the different researches, and the theory that results is, I hope, nothing more than a general statement of fact. It has been my aim to exclude rigidly all tendencies towards hypothetical constructions, and to give all explanations in terms of observed phenomena. Where this has been impossible through the limitations of knowledge, I have been satisfied with the simple statement, "We do not know."

In criticism of the different theories, I have striven to show the relation between the theory and the facts, to show what interpretation of the facts has led to the theory, and to make use of the theory in my own.

For the sake of completeness, more emphasis has been placed upon the higher mental processes than is usual in works on attention. This seems desirable, both because it enables one to note how close is the relation between the factors that control attention and those that determine the more complicated intellectual processes, and because an important part of the simple perception can be understood only if treated as a mental construction.

The pleasant duty remains of acknowledging my indebtedness to friends for the assistance they have rendered in the preparation of the manuscript. To my colleagues, Professors Lombard and McMurrich, I am grateful for suggestions as to literature in physiology and neurology. Professor Lloyd has read the entire manuscript, as has Professor James R. Angell, Professor Lombard the physiological parts, and each has made numerous corrections. But particularly I desire to thank my teacher of former years, Professor Titchener of Cornell University, who not only has read the completed manuscript, but who encouraged me to write it, and to whom I owe a more general debt for the inspiration I received from his guidance and friendship during four years of personal intercourse.

CONTENTS

ATTENTION

CHAPTER I

THE MENTAL EFFECTS OF ATTENTION

THE manifestations of the state that we commonly call attention are protean. No part of the individual is untouched by them. They extend to every part of the physical organism, and are among the most profound facts of mind. So numerous and varied are the ramifications of attention, that we find it defined by competent authorities as a state of muscular contraction and adaptation, as a pure mental activity, as an emotion or feeling, and as a change in the clearness of ideas. Each of the definitions can be justified from the facts, if we put the chief emphasis now upon one phase and now upon another of its varied expressions. Each of these aspects must be discussed in turn, but for the purposes of the present chapter we may confine ourselves to the immediate changes in conscious states, since these are most open to observation and seem to be fundamental for all the others.

Perhaps the best general description of the effect of attention is afforded by Wundt's comparison of consciousness to the field of vision. As in the eye there is a point of clearest vision, where all impressions are very distinct as opposed to the vagueness of the objects seen with other parts of the retina, so in mind there are always a few processes which stand out clearly, while the others are blurred and indefinite. And as the eye can wander over the various

B

objects before it, bringing first one then the other into the most favourable position, so the sensations, of which we are conscious at one instant, disappear from consciousness at the next. Attention may wander over the mental field as the eye may wander over a surface in the outside world. Omitting the metaphor, we may say that attention increases the clearness of the sensations attended to, but it is very difficult to describe what is meant by clearness in a way that shall make it any more easily understood. Every one knows what is meant by the term and has experienced the change which actually goes on during attention. It means largely that some one element of consciousness is picked out from the others, and given an advantage over them. It is more fully conscious, more adequately a part of our experience than are the others. Clearness is then purely a relative matter. All mental processes affect us in some degree, but those processes to which we attend affect us in a much higher degree than those to which we do not attend. Increase in the degree to which an impression is conscious and increase in attention to that impression are synonymous terms.

There are many similarities between attention thus regarded and the intensity of a sensation, and it has been suggested that attention really has the same effect upon a conscious content as that which results when the intensity of a stimulus affecting us is increased. There are, however, serious objections to this view, and there is probably no other phase of the attention problem which excites so much dispute as this one of the relation of attention to the intensity of the mental process affected. There are two rival views as to how the attention might affect the sensation. The first and most direct, held by Mach, and in a certain degree by Stumpf among others, is that the sensation attended to is directly and immediately increased in intensity; the other, favoured by Wundt, is that there is a relative increase in the intensity or effectiveness of the sensation, due to the fact that all the remaining content of consciousness has its intensity decreased by the attending process. The strongest objection to the assumption that there is an actual increase in the intensity of the process attended to is one that we owe to Külpe, derived from a technical argument based upon the facts of Weber's law. The statement of the law in simplest terms is that one notices absolutely equal differences of intensity much more easily when the sensations compared are faint than when strong, and that the keenness in discrimination of absolute difference decreases as the intensities increase, while the relative discrimination is constant. One is more likely to overlook changes of the same amount in the intensity of a cannon shot than in the buzzing of a bee. If there were an actual increase in the intensity of the sensation when attended to, it would become more difficult to notice small differences when straining the attention than when not attending at all. This is of course entirely out of harmony both with the facts of daily life and the results of technical experiments. Judgments of difference are always more accurate when the attention is good. There is one possible flaw in the argument. This is that it is not at all certain that attention may not produce an increase in the intensity of the sensation proportional to the intensity of the stimulus, rather than an absolute, arbitrary increase. If the increase were thus relative one would find that loud sounds are increased in greater amount than faint sounds. This harmonises with what we know of mental states, and is fully as probable as that the increase should be absolute in amount. The only lack of harmony in that case between the facts of the attention and the results obtained from the experiments on Weber's law is that the attention decreases the fraction of the stimulus which can just be noticed instead of leaving it unchanged—a fact which can be explained only on the assumption of some other influence than the change in intensity. It is probably as easy to assume that this other effect, whatever it may prove to be, explains all of the results of the attention as well as those which are manifested in connection with experiments on Weber's law. While then the a priori objections to the theory are sufficiently strong to make it improbable that the change in intensity is sufficient to account for the effects of the attention, they are not positive enough to decide against any concrete facts which may have a bearing on the question.

The great difficulty in settling the matter on the basis of fact is that it is impossible directly to compare an object attended to with one not attended to. There is an unavoidable impulse to attend to both before the judgment is made, and any results that should claim to be accurate on this point would be open to grave suspicion.

The men who have formed an opinion from introspection, and who have had experience enough to make them competent judges, are hopelessly at variance. An interesting instance of this is offered by the difference of opinion between Stumpf [6] and Mach with reference to the effect of attention upon sounds. Stumpf holds in his second volume that weak tones in a group of other tones, whether weak or strong, are increased in intensity when attended to. He denies, however, that there is any increase in tones of moderate intensity even when sounding in a chord or clang. Mach, under the same circumstances, with the same complex of tones, is equally positive that the tones increase in intensity as attention turns upon them. It should be added that Stumpf holds that there is no increase in intensity even with faint tones beyond that which they would have were they sounding alone with no physiological hindrances in the way of their coming to consciousness. As he rightly argues, were attention to increase tones indefinitely, one could never be sure whether a change were objective or subjective. The same divergence of opinion exists among other authorities equally entitled to an opinion. Evidently no help can be obtained from this source.

Lehmann [4] settles the question in favour of the independence of attention of intensity by reminding us that when we are gazing at a sheet of white paper there is no difference in shade between the part looked at directly and the surrounding parts which are not attended to. Again, there are two objections to this summary settlement of the question. In the first place, it is frequently denied that the intensity of the visual stimulus is accompanied by corresponding change in the intensity of the sensation, but rather that the series of grays that we find on the sensation side are differences in quality. In that case we should expect no change in colour to come with the attending, for no one has claimed that quality changes with degree of attention. In the second place even if there were a difference in the shade we would not expect it to be noticed, as it is well known that an evenly-coloured red area seems red over its entire extent, although we know that we can only see the red in a limited field in the centre. And finally, the objection would hold here also that it is impossible to compare the portion attended to with the other parts of the field, because with the comparison there comes at once and involuntarily a change of the attention to the parts of the field hitherto not directly observed.

The experiments that have been devoted to the question by Münsterberg, [5] Külpe, [2] and Miss Hamlin all rest upon the assumption that distraction decreases the amount of attention. This may or may not be true, as will be seen in a later chapter. Even granting the general principle, we are no better off, for results vary between proving that attention increases the intensity of a sensation and that it decreases it.

A careful consideration of the facts seems to give no definite proof in favour of either side in the controversy. We are left with the mere fact that the weight of authority is in favour of regarding the effect of attention as different from the effect of an increased intensity of the external stimulus, but with no convincing proof in favour of that position. One other factor demands consideration in this connection before we can turn to other phases of the problem. That is that many of the writers who insist that attention does not increase the intensity of sensations of moderate strength, also assert that it does increase the intensity of very weak sensations. The fact upon which this statement is based is that in many cases we can by attending bring to consciousness sensations so weak that they ordinarily pass unobserved. If you will attend fixedly for a few moments to any point on the external skin, you will find coming into consciousness a number of itching, tingling, or prickling sensations which you had not previously noticed, and would in all probability not have observed were it not for the increased attention to that part of the body. In the same way attentive listening will at any time bring to consciousness noises which for the most part would pass unnoticed under ordinary circumstances. It may be the gentle rustling of leaves, the rippling of a distant brook, the droning of insects, or in case these and all other external sounds are lacking, there is still left the sound of the blood as it pulses through the ears. The same principle could be illustrated from any of the senses. In these cases it is still a question whether we have to do with a phenomenon of a new sort rather than an application of the principles earlier considered to a new intensity. Were it certain in any case that the sound which came in with the attention had been entirely without effect upon consciousness up to the time that the attention was turned toward it we might have a clear case of the influence upon intensity. But in nearly every instance we can assume that the faint sensation was contributing its share to the total impression received, and was merely picked out of the mass for increased emphasis. All the noises of a summer day in the woods undoubtedly contribute their part to the woodland impression, although they may not be heard in isolation. The complex of sensations from the skin, it has frequently been suggested, unites with the sensations from the internal organs to furnish the background of our consciousness. They are probably always present in varying degrees, but yet with sufficient constancy to constitute one of the marks of our personal identity. All that attention does then is probably to bring to greater prominence one of these elements. It is merely an increase in clearness, as was the other, and there seems no evidence for regarding this case as different from the other. If there is no increase in intensity at the basis of the gain in clearness in the one instance, there seems no reason to assume it in the other. Nowhere do we find an example of attention in which we may be sure that an impression which was entirely unconscious becomes entirely conscious owing to a change in the attention. In all cases, apparently, there is a mass of sensations which unite in some one group, and it is possible to select relatively smaller bits from the mass, or to combine them in even larger wholes, but in any case each part is contributing its share to the total effect. The intensity of the sensation makes no difference in principle. It matters not whether the tones of a single violin are made to stand out from an orchestra, or whether an overtone is heard out from the compound note of a single violin string. In both cases we are analysing a whole into its parts, and there seems to be no reason for assuming that the analysis is accomplished at one time in a way different from that in which it is accomplished in the other. If intensity is what changes in one case, there is no reason for assuming that it is not also at the basis of the other change. Nowhere do we find an instance in which a sensation comes to a sense organ which has not been just previously stimulated, or in which we can be sure that there is not another stimulation that is at work at the same time which serves as a background from which the previously unnoticed impression is picked out by the attention. Nowhere then can we be sure that we have a case of mere increase in intensity, rather than an increase in clearness, which gives one of several equally intense sensations an advantage over the others.

Another closely related explanation has been suggested to account for the prominence given to one at the expense of the other elements. This is that all the other mental processes have their intensity decreased, while the object attended to remains at its normal intensity. This theory is open to all of the objections to which the first was subjected. It would not account for the phenomena of Weber's law any more than the other, and all the results of direct introspection would have the same bearing upon it as upon the other. We could not distinguish by observation between the results of increasing the intensity of one element and decreasing the intensity of all the others. It has no advantages over assuming directly that attention increases the intensity of the impression attended to. And there are many difficulties that are peculiar to the more complicated theory from its theoretical side. The only picture that we could have on this assumption would be that the difference in level between the mountain peak of the attention and the plain of the ordinary consciousness would be produced not by elevating the peak, but by depressing the plain. With a very insignificant exception all the elements of consciousness would be held at a level much below that which they would ordinarily attain, and to which their inherent energy would raise them. On any analogy with physical energy it would be impossible for consciousness to have sufficient force to neutralise so much more than half of its entire energy. If it is denied that the analogies from energy have a place, it is at least opposed to the general law of parsimony in science to choose the more complicated explanation when the simpler is equally in harmony with the facts. Furthermore, as will be seen later on in the discussion, this explanation is entirely at variance with what we know of the physiological processes.

On the whole then there seems to be no very satisfactory outcome to the discussion of the relation between clearness and intensity. It is impossible to accept any of the arguments on either side as conclusive. There are a number of points in which intensity and attention have the same effects, and it will perhaps help us more to enumerate them than to delay longer with the apparently insoluble theoretical problem of their ultimate relation. To begin with intensity as the simpler and better known phenomenon, we can perhaps best define it as a change in sensation due to a change in the amount of physical energy which affects the sense organs. From the subjective standpoint it is a change that affects one conscious process alone, and is not accompanied by a corresponding change in any other conscious process. The change in degree of attention on the other hand, although it may be very similar to the change in intensity, affects not only the one element of consciousness, but all the other elements that are present at the same time. When one idea becomes clear and distinct all the others lose in distinctness. And again the degree of attention is limited by the number of objects which come into attention at the same time. If a number of objects are attended to, each stands out less clearly than if it alone had held the field. While then the intensity of a sensation is practically independent of any other sensation, and one or any number of sensations may increase or decrease without affecting the intensity of any other, the amount of attention is practically constant, and cannot be applied to one object without affecting the clearness of others.

But intensity and attention cannnot be readily isolated in practice. We must always abstract from one to consider the other. In comparing intensities we always think of each as at the maximum of attention, and we also think of the intensities as identical when comparing the efficiency of attention. There is no doubt, as will be seen in the next chapter, that intensity makes attention easier on the one side, and that the effectiveness of an intensity in consciousness depends very much upon the state of the attention. From this standpoint we might define the intensity as the degree of efficiency of a sensation in consciousness due to the energy expended upon the sense organ, attention as an increase in efficiency due to subjective conditions alone. We may summarise the concrete differences between them in the statement that, while they are alike in that both increase the clearness and distinctness of the elements which they affect, they are different in so far as increase in the intensity renders discrimination more difficult, while increase in the attention renders it easier, and that intensity is an individual thing affecting only the one sensation, while attention is general in its results and has an influence upon consciousness as a whole.

It has been suggested that an important characteristic of attention is that it holds in consciousness for a longer time than usual the sensation to which it is applied. This was early held by Stumpf to be the only influence of attention. Later, however, he withdrew the suggestion on the ground that one sees the influence of attention in mental states that persist for but a brief period. It is probable that there is some influence, but it is relatively unimportant. Even if true, it might be a subordinate influence of increase in intensity, for we know that in single sensations increase in intensity often has the same effect as increase in duration. In rhythm intensity and duration are almost interchangeable. If we could assume increase in intensity, persistence in consciousness must follow immediately.

One other aspect is, however, peculiar to attention, and that is the analytic function. When we attend to a process we break it up into its elements, and many times into elements which we did not know to be present before the analysis took place. An object is given in a chaotic mass without any particular form, and it is only under the influence of the attention that it takes shape. First one bit or aspect of the process stands out, and then another, as the attention plays over it, and we get a real conception of the object only as the result of many different acts of the attention. It is hardly fair to say, however, that the function of the attention is always analytic, for just as frequently it partakes of the nature of a synthesis. It is just as possible for the minute elements to be seen first, and for them to suggest the whole, as for the whole to come first and be followed by the parts. And in many cases neither happens, but the attention selects first one, then another, of several co-ordinate aspects. What is selected is not so much a part of the given whole as a phase of the whole—a point of view from which to observe the total mass. The function of analysis then is not essential to the attention—in fact most cases of attention do not result in analysis. Rather may we say that attention is fundamentally a change in clearness of some one phase or aspect of a mental process. And while analysis depends upon that, it is not, as has been suggested, the prime effect, but is merely incidental to other functions, is, in fact, a result of the one thing which is characteristic of attention—the increase in clearness or prominence which it produces in some one idea, or of some aspect of that one idea. Increase in clearness is the only change which can certainly be affirmed to be the result of attention.

SUMMARY

1. The essence of attention as a conscious process is an increase in the clearness of one idea or group of ideas at the expense of others.

2. Whether the change in clearness is identical with, or dependent upon, change in intensity is as yet open to controversy.

3. The analytic function of attention is dependent upon the change in clearness, and so must be regarded as subordinate, not primary.

CHAPTER II

THE MOTOR CONCOMITANTS OF ATTENTION

ONE of the most striking facts in connection with the attention is its close connection with bodily movement and posture. The ordinary objective measure of attention rests upon the attitude of the man's body, the direction of his eyes, and other bodily signs. There is no act of the attention that is unaccompanied by some motor process, and it is our problem in this chapter to classify, and so far as is possible to explain, the different changes that take place in the body during attention.

It is possible to divide the motor manifestations which accompany attention into four great groups :—

I. Movements of adaptation in the sense organ which prepare it the better to receive the entering sensation.

II. Correlated movements in the organism in general whose nature and direction depend upon the nature of the particular stimulus.

III. General overflow effects upon the voluntary muscles which do not depend upon the nature of the stimulus.

IV. Effects upon the involuntary or semi-voluntary mechanisms of pulse, respiration, and vaso-motor activities.

Of course, there are subdivisions under each of these heads that could almost as justly be given a separate classification, and several of the groups made come very near together, but the classification will suffice as a basis for discussion.

That the sense organs adapt themselves to give the

fullest possible amount of each impression is a commonplace of our daily life. That adaptation and attending are concomitant processes is a fact of which each can convince himself upon the slightest observation. When an object in the field of vision catches the attention, seems interesting, the eye at once turns toward it ; when a vague sound is heard at night the head is adjusted to the source of sound to give the most favourable condition for listening. These observations of the daily life are confirmed and extended by the experiments to which they have been subjected. Not only do we turn the eyes toward the object, but before it is possible to obtain a clear image there must also be an adjustment of the crystalline lens and a convergence of the eyes which shall bring the object in question upon the centre, the spot of clearest vision, of each eye. The first is accomplished by the relaxation of the ciliary muscle, which by flattening the lens or permitting it to assume its normal rotundity gives the adjustment necessary for obtaining a clear image upon the retina. The convergence takes place through a relaxation of the external recti muscles and contraction of the internal, or vice versa, if the new object is at a greater distance than the one just looked at, until the image falls upon the centre of each retina.

It can easily be seen from introspection that these adjustments follow the attention in order of time. If while reading a book there is a sudden desire to learn the time of day, it will be noticed that remembered images of the clock come into consciousness before the movement begins, and that there is a considerable interval between the instant that the eyes are adjusted upon the clock before the accommodation is complete and the image is distinct enough to permit of telling the hour. All of these movements are reflexes of the attention. The only condition for their occurrence is that an object catches the attention, and as soon as it attracts the attention the movement which is necessary to give the most favourable condition for its entrance follows at once. As you look out of the window, the direction of the line of sight, the accommodation of the lens, and the convergence, change constantly and spontaneously as, one after another, the objects in the landscape attract you. If a moving wagon come into the field at a distance from you and from the object at which you are looking, it will at once catch the attention, and immediately the complex series of movements that result in bringing it into the best relations for clear vision will begin. So close is this connection that there is no other way in which it can be brought about except through the attention. If the photographer should ask you to lower the eyes thirty degrees below the horizontal plane, and turn them twenty degrees to the left of the median plane, with the eyes focussed and converged upon an object at a distance of forty feet, you would have great difficulty in carrying out his directions, and could do it then only by selecting one object after another in the field of vision and deciding which one fulfilled the conditions most closely. When, however, he asks you to look at some object that he places before you, you can do it at once without the least difficulty, and almost without knowing how the movements are brought about.

The mechanism is purely reflex, but of a high degree of complexity. When the object attracts attention, the nature of the double images which it casts upon the two retinas, the size of its retinal image in comparison with its known real size, and other similar marks of distance, combine to form a stimulus which produces an excitation of the oculo-motor and ciliary nerves, and these in turn bring about the proper adjustment. The effect of the attention is merely to choose and emphasize one of the many sets of stimuli which are all ready to determine the movements in one way or the other. Similarly each object that affects the retina seems to exert a reflex influence which tends to turn the eyes so that the object will fall upon the point of clearest vision. Each impression is a stimulus for both sets of movements at the same time.

So strong is this physiological tendency to look at the object attended to, that it is only with the greatest difficulty that one can attend to one object and have the eyes directed to another, and even when successful there seems to be a divided attention between the object mainly attended to and the object upon which the eyes are fixed. The difficulty of attending to an object without turning the eyes upon it can be seen clearly if one studies some imperfection of the media of the eye, which is a little to one side of the line of sight. Unconsciously, and in spite of the fact that the movement is of not the slightest value in aiding observation, there is a turning of the eyes towards the object, and as that movement carries the imperfection with it, there is still another movement, until the object has been followed through the limits of rotation of the eye. These vain movements in search of the will-o'-the-wisp imperfection will result as often as the eye is brought back to the central position and the attempt to observe the imperfection is continued. There is no change by the degree of practice that one can obtain in ordinary experiments.

Heinrich has shown that there is not only a special adjustment for each object in the field of vision, but that there is also a characteristic attitude for cases of strained attention to impressions from other senses and for attention to remembered impressions. In the latter case the lens is flattened and the axes of the eyes are parallel, as in looking at distant objects, and in some cases he tells us that the adjustment for distant objects may be exceeded, so that the lens becomes even flatter than for seeing objects on the horizon, and the eyes actually diverge instead of converge. There is also under these circumstances a marked dilation of the pupil. In attending to impressions from other sense organs the eyes are adjusted to receive the same impression even if it is dark, or there is some other condition which prevents the object from being seen. An excellent instance of this can be obtained by watching a man trying to attend to two tuning forks held one before each ear. As the attention turns from fork to fork there is an accompanying movement of the eyes from side to side in the most striking manner, in spite of the fact that the forks are held in such a position that it is impossible to see either.

How far there may be an analogous adaptation of the ear in hearing it is difficult to say. It has been suggested that the *tensor tympani*—the muscle attached to the malleus, through which it can exert a tension upon the drum of the ear—might be of influence in adjusting the drum to tones of different pitch. That it plays some part in the hearing process is made evident by the fact that it degenerates when the auditory nerve is destroyed. Opinion as to whether its function is a tuning of the drum is still divided. Experiments of Ostmann [12, 13] make it probable that the function is merely to protect the ear from very intense and very high sounds. He found that the muscle was contracted only during very intense and very complicated noises. Pure tones, no matter how high or how intense, seemed to have but very slight effects. Heinrich, on the other hand, has convinced himself by recent experiments that the muscle has a definite influence in accommodating the tympanum to receive noises even of moderate intensities. [6] Evidently, then, it is still a matter of doubt as to the exact part that this muscle plays in preparing the ear for hearing. Whatever it may be, however, the movement is undoubtedly of a reflex character, and follows the turning of the attention to a particular tonal element. There is no agreement as to what may be the action of the other small muscle, the stapedius, which might also have a part in adjusting the auditory mechanism.

There are certainly definite adjustments for touch. As the question whether a surface is rough or smooth, hot or cold, comes into mind there is a movement of the fingers toward the surface, if it is within reach. This movement takes place almost as reflexly and with as little conscious intention as do the movements of the eyes. In the blind, who are largely dependent on touch for their knowledge as a whole, movements of contraction and relaxation of the finger tips have been noticed as the accompaniments of the attentive examination of any surface. These are of great value in giving an idea of the form and nature of the surface. A moving finger will notice differences which would be entirely unobserved by one at rest.

Smell, too, has its reflex adaptive movements. It will be noticed that one carefully testing any substance by its odour will take long breaths almost involuntarily. They are the direct result of the desire to attain certainty of the nature of the substance, and not due to any distinct intention of the man making the test. This reflex can probably be observed to best advantage in the lower animals, who depend upon smell most completely for their protection and food, but it is undoubtedly present to a large extent in man as well.

In much the same way a substance to be tasted is rolled over the tongue and pressed against the roof of the mouth in an endeavour to bring it as completely as possible in contact with the tongue. This movement is also accompanied by movements of the lips and the external facial muscles, which probably play little or no part in making the tasting more accurate, but are merely survivals of associated movements. They indicate to the observer that close attention is being given to the sensations of taste.

Estimates of weight are also accompanied by a number of slight lifting movements, which serve to bring into play the more delicate sensory endings of muscle and tendon in addition to the sensory endings of the skin. They thus bring about the same increase in the accuracy of the comparison as accommodation in vision, and in so far are to be put into the same category.

In all but the strictly organic senses, then, there are movements that serve to adjust the organ to give the impression its greatest effect in consciousness. These move-

c

ments are all initiated as a result of attending, and many, if not all, of the movements can be made in no other way than by attending to some stimulus. It must also be emphasised that the movements are not made as the result of a distinct purpose, but come as an unforeseen accompaniment of the attending itself. Another point which it may be well to emphasise because of its bearing on a theory to be discussed later, is that the movements seem in every case to follow the attention and never to initiate it.

II. The second series of bodily movements which accompany the attention process is unlike the preceding, in that they have no influence upon the efficiency of the attention, and have little or nothing to do with the sense organs involved, but they are like them in that the nature and direction of the movements depend upon the object which is attended to and the degree of the attention. These movements consist of changes in the position of the limbs, of the general posture of the body, and of changes in the conditions of contraction and relaxation of the voluntary muscles generally. It has been very clearly demonstrated that every act of the attention is accompanied by a movement which is different enough to mark that particular act of the attention off from every other. Popularly, this is perhaps best shown by some of the parlour mind-reading games. A very common instance is that in which some member of the party volunteers to leave the room while the others choose some object, and then will tell what object has been chosen if those present will only keep their minds upon it continuously. If you will watch carefully a company as it "thinks," you will notice that there are frequent furtive glances of all the members toward the object, that hands unconsciously drift toward it, and the position of the body as a whole in some cases becomes a tell-tale of the object. These movements, together with the awed hush whenever the object is approached, and the slight exclamations when the wrong direction is taken, are a sufficient guide to the seeker as to the whereabouts of the desired object. Often the person who takes advantage of these movements is as unconscious as the persons who give him the hints as to the nature of the guidance, or that there has been any guidance of this kind at all. His usual statement is that he merely felt that he was right, but could not say in what the feeling consisted. He is just as sure that he has received no assistance of this simple kind from the spectators as the other members of the company are that they have given none. What has happened is that he has unconsciously inferred his goal from a number of slight separate indications, no one of which is noticed in itself, but which together are convincing.

A more extended and complicated use of this fact, that the movements are directed as well as called out by the attention, is to be found in the professional exhibitions of mind, or more properly muscle, reading which are given in many parts of the world. Nearly all of the feats of the well-known mind readers are to be explained as shrewd inferences from slight movements of this kind to the mental states which must have been present to occasion them. In many cases the person whose mind is being read and the person who reads it are equally ignorant of the way in which the information is given or received, but the fact that even the most skilful operators insist upon receiving the "spirit influence" by direct physical contact is sufficient to raise a suspicion that there is some transfer of mechanical impressions. When a performer opens a safe blindfolded while holding the hand of the owner, who knows the combination, he is undoubtedly directed when to stop by involuntary movements of the owner, for whom the sight of certain figures under the pointer had been for years the signal to turn backward or to stop. There are similar movements in large number which accompany every other act of the attention, and even mental processes not so closely connected with the senses.

Scientific experiments made by Professors Sommer, W. Jastrow, and others, confirm the statement that there is an actual movement of the hand that corresponds to the nature and direction of the attention. They have devised apparatus that records on smoked paper all the movements of the members, and enables them to compare the records with the nature of the mental processes that were going on at the time. Extended experiments show that there is a very close connection between the movements and the direction of the attention. If the subject looked attentively at an object in any direction there was at once a movement of the hand toward that object. When listening to a man walking across the floor behind him the hand would swing backward and forward in time with the movements of the walking, and also usually tend backward in the direction that he had from the subject. While watching the swing of a pendulum there is a rhythmic swing back and forth in time with the pendulum.

A more striking illustration of the same fact is offered by the movements of a crowd in watching any game or contest that involves movement. If you have ever stood upon the side lines during an exciting football contest, you will have noticed the marked tendency of the whole mass of observers to follow the movements of the players with their bodies. In some moments of excitement the entire body will move forward in complete unconsciousness of the fact that any movement is being made until it is very difficult for the individuals to regain their equilibrium, and in most cases the whole crowd will have changed its position very considerably without being conscious that a step has been taken.

It is evident from these results that every act of attending is accompanied by movements of some kind that are of a nature related to the position of the object attended to, and in some cases to its nature and intensity. It would be possible to cite innumerable other cases, but these seem sufficient to confirm the statement.

III. The third class of movements are neither useful nor

symbolic; they do not make the attention more effective so far as can be seen, and do not vary with the changes in the object attended to or with its direction from the observer. These it seems simplest to regard as mere overflow phenomena, and to think of them as due to a spread of nervous energy from the centres of the brain involved in attention along the paths of least resistance to the various motor centres. They are analogous in their origin to the diffused motor excitations which come out during strenuous physical exertion. It will be noticed when lifting a heavy weight, for instance, that in addition to the muscles directly involved, there are a number of apparently unrelated muscles in a state of contraction. Careful observation will show that the teeth are firmly set, the forehead is wrinkled, and the body as a whole is braced for the effort. The motor impulse seems to spread from the nerve centres directly involved to others only remotely connected. In attention exactly the same process goes on, and much the same muscles are affected. One who is studying intently has a wrinkled brow, and in extreme cases the hand may be clenched and the greater number of the voluntary muscles be in a state of contraction. In addition to its general excitatory effect, attention seems to have a tendency to inhibit movements in general. One who becomes suddenly interested in a train of thought or line of argument with a companion will frequently stop and stand still until his interest is decreased. A woman engaged in knitting or some other mechanical task while listening to a conversation or lecture will suddenly stop as she becomes interested in what is being said, to resume again when some less engrossing subject is reached. It is possible and usual to measure the attention of an assemblage by the quiet of the room. When the programme is uninteresting there is always the noise of rustling garments, of books and programmes in motion, and the other accompaniments of slight movements. When the audience is interested all these movements are inhibited, and there is quiet. This inhibitory effect of attention can hardly be classed as purposeless, but it belongs in this group because due to immediate overflow effects which vary only with the degree of the attention, and not at all with its nature or direction.

This entire series of immediate overflow effects is accompanied by a consciousness of strain, which in part serves us as a subjective measure of the degree of attention. It is one of the most marked conscious concomitants of the attention. Its function must be discussed in a later chapter.

IV. No less widespread, and equally important from the theoretical standpoint, are the changes of the involuntary and partially voluntary activities of the body during attention, which have been brought together for consideration under the fourth head. There is no process concerned in circulation or respiration that is not profoundly modified when attention is prolonged or intense. Much ingenuity has been spent by many investigators in devising apparatus to record the various movements, and in collecting and interpreting the data obtained. We must omit all mention of mechanical methods, and devote ourselves to the main results that have been so far established.

We may for convenience divide the phenomena connected with circulation into three groups : the pulse rate, the tonic condition of the arterial walls (vaso-motor phenomena), and blood pressure. The latter undoubtedly depends in part upon the two former, but as there is also involved the strength of heart-beat, we must treat it separately.

There are two ways of studying the rate of the pulse. The simplest is merely to count the number of beats in the minute during a resting condition, and again when the subject is attentive. A comparison of the two will give a rough measure of the change due to the attention. The more delicate method involves recording the separate pulse-beats upon a revolving drum or other moving surface. After the record is made the length of each pulsebeat may be measured and a curve plotted from the results that will show the changes during the periods in question. The first method shows roughly that the heart rate is considerably quickened during attention. The second method shows that the rate is nearly always changed, but there is no very definite rule as to the direction of the change. Often the first change is compensated for by a second in the opposite direction. In general, we may say that any activity of the attention is accompanied by a slowing of the pulse rate, followed by a more prolonged acceleration.

The effect upon the muscles in the walls of the blood-vessels is even more marked. It is known that the walls of the arteries contain smooth muscle tissues, which are connected through the sympathetic system with a centre in the medulla. It has been shown by experiments that nearly every mental process is reflected in the condition of contraction or relaxation of these muscles. The attention forms no exception to this rule. Every act of the attention of any considerable degree or intensity, or of appreciable duration, is accompanied by a contraction of the arteries and a consequent diminution of the volume of the members. This contraction seems to increase continuously throughout the entire time that attention is strongly active, even when that period may cover half an hour or more, and recovery is quite slow.

This question takes two different forms as we consider different parts of the body. The effect upon the volume of the brain is probably not the same as that upon the capillaries of the limbs. Mosso and Patrizi, who have studied the changes in the volume of the brain upon individuals suffering from injuries to the skull, have found that during the process of attention there is an increase in the volume of the brain and a dilatation of its capillaries as opposed to the constriction of the vessels of the limbs. This was shown both by directly recording the changes in volume on individuals whose cerebral cavity had been brought into connection with the outside air through some injury, and also by balancing the person to be experimented upon on a delicately adjusted board and noting the change in balance as the blood rushed to the head in prolonged attention. There is also as an accompaniment of the increasing blood supply a rise in the temperature of the brain. Tracings taken at the same time from the arm and leg would show a contraction of the blood-vessels, if any change was noticed at all. As we have seen, there is in normal individuals a decrease in the volume in nearly every case if the attention be of sufficient degree. There has been some discussion among the different investigators as to whether the effect upon the circulation of the brain were direct or merely an acompaniment of the decrease in the volume of the peripheral vessels, and there is as yet no general agreement upon this point, in spite of the tracings of Mosso, which show that the volumes of the arm, the leg, and the brain may change independently of each other.

Measurements of blood pressure are not so numerous as those of changes in volume and in heart rate, but the results so far obtained are quite constant, and show that during attention there is a marked increase in the pressure in the peripheral vessels. The change in blood pressure is probably in part the result of the contraction of the arteries and in part due to the increase in frequency of heart-beat, but there is also probably a change in the strength of heart-beat that adds to the total effect.

The changes in the respiratory processes during attention are perhaps the most decided of all. They are certainly most evident to the casual observer. It can be noticed without special means of observation that the breath is held or considerably checked during strained attention, and it is to this fact that we owe the phrase " breathless attention." The period of checked respiration is always followed by a very deep breath—the sigh that is so frequently noticed as relief from prolonged attention. Records taken of movements of the chest wall confirm and extend common observation. During attention the respiratory movements are considerably more frequent, and are also much shallower, than in normal breathing, and are followed for a considerable period by deep and slow respiration.

All of the changes are probably the result of overflows of the nervous processes in the cerebrum that are involved in the attention process upon the medullary centres, and through them upon the particular mechanisms involved. The question of their utility in the attention process must be discussed later.

As a whole then it seems that the physiological effects of the attention are as widespread as they well could be. There seems to be no muscle in any part of the body that may not be affected in some degree by a sufficiently strong attention process. There is at the time a motor disturbance that extends through the entire nervous system. It is no wonder then that the physiological aspects of the problem have attracted so much notice, and have been given such an important place by the theorists, although we must postpone a discussion of the problem of the place of these movements in the general theory to a later time.

SUMMARY

Attention to any stimulus is accompanied by widespread motor phenomena.

1. The muscles of sense organs contract to give the greatest possible effect to the stimulus.

2. The voluntary muscles of limbs and trunk undergo contractions that have previously been found useful under stimulations of the same kind.

3. There is a diffuse contraction of many voluntary muscles without reference to the nature of the stimulus.

4. The respiratory and circulatory processes are profoundly affected.

5. The bodily processes succeed, or at most accompany, the attention. They do not precede it.

CHAPTER III

THE CONDITIONS OF ATTENTION

BEFORE we can attempt any theory of the attention, or even any more extended treatment of the effects of attention in consciousness, it seems well to give an unprejudiced statement of the conditions under which attending takes place. By condition in this connection we mean not so much to imply a final cause as merely to enumerate the antecedent and concomitant states of consciousness, and to select those which seem more than accidental to the state of attention. In order to obtain a complete list of the relevant processes we shall have recourse in part to introspection, in larger part to conditions which have been enumerated by others, and in part to experimental results. It is hoped that by collecting all the conditions that have been suggested it will be possible by eliminating and combining them to obtain a more complete list than would be possible in any other way, and also to prepare the way for an adequate theory of the processes involved much better than if the theory were constructed for itself with reference to but one aspect of the problem.

We shall not attempt to discuss the physiological processes in this chapter, but shall confine ourselves entirely to the conscious states. While the results of the different theories that have been offered will undoubtedly modify the statement of the conditions, there will be no specific mention of theories in the chapter. All that must come later, when we can utilise the material which is to be gathered here. The present chapter then must be looked upon merely as a collection of facts, not in any sense as a theory of the attention. Its purpose will have been fulfilled if we can state under what conditions one is likely to attend to a particular event, and do not here concern ourselves to discover the reason for the conditions.

In order fully to comply with the ideal we have set, it may be well to mention that all the physiological changes mentioned in the last chapter have by some authors been regarded as among the conditions of the attention, if not as the conditions. If we accepted that theory it would be well to combine both chapters under the one heading. But as the facts are also susceptible of a different treatment, and one that we believe to be truer, we shall pass them over for the time being with this mere reference.

We may roughly divide the conditions of the attention into two great classes—the subjective and the objective. The line is not always sharply drawn. One class gradually shades off into the other, and there is a border-land of considerable extent in which the processes may be brought, now under one head, now under the other, as you change the point of view. The classification will serve fairly well for practical purposes, however, and it is not difficult to point out the reasons for the divergencies when the phenomena are not to be assigned with certainty to any one class.

In a general way we may define the objective conditions as those qualities which belong to the entering sensation alone, regarded in isolation from the environment in which it was received; or in the rough, those characteristics which depend upon the nature of the external world at the time. Those conditions which depend upon impressions received through the senses, retained in some way to be again active at a later time, we may call subjective. We may say, if we care to, that they depend upon the nature of the mind at the time; but as we can know what the nature of the mind is only from the impressions which have affected it at some earlier time, or from the different ways in which it responds at the present time, it is more convenient and truer to the limits of our knowledge to say that the subjective conditions consist of the earlier impressions that the individual has been subjected to, including, of course, the influences that have affected the ancestors and have given the individual in question his hereditary bent. They include what Professor Huxley calls the nature and nurture of the individual. It is the group of hereditary tendencies which offers the most difficulties in the way of classification. Here where the tendencies are common to many individuals, it is very difficult to say how much belongs to the stimulus and how much is due to the common heredity of mankind. The details of the difficulty may be postponed for the present.

The most important of the objective conditions is probably the intensity of the sensation. A loud noise, a very intense odour, or a brilliant light will force their way into consciousness in spite of all the subjective forces which may attempt to oppose them. Hegel in the Napoleonic wars, and Archimedes at the taking of Syracuse, are the exceptions which prove the rule. Ordinarily if a cannon is fired under your window, or a bright light is thrown into your eyes, there is immediate attention given to it, no matter what the incentives may be to hold the attention upon the duty of the moment. The effect seems to depend entirely upon the brute force of the stimulus and as little as may be upon the nature of the organism at the time.

However, it is not the mere intensity of the stimulus which is effective in attracting the attention, so much as it is the change in its intensity. The noise of the train upon which we are riding passes unnoticed after a short interval, while the whirl of the train which passes on the parallel line, although it does not add very greatly to the din, will be noticed at once. The lighting of a candle in a dark room has vastly more power to attract us than the continuous glare of the sun to which we have been long exposed. And other instances could be cited indefinitely.

Not only is a positive change an important condition of the attention, but a negative change as well will have the same general effect in attracting the attention. The miller who has become entirely unconscious of the noise which his mill makes is at once aroused by its stopping. A lull in the conversation in the adjoining room is more effective in rousing one from work than doubling the intensity of the tones. This is very well illustrated by the sudden stopping of the clock on your desk. Its ticking may have been entirely unnoticed up to the moment it stops, but with the stopping there comes at once not only the knowledge that it has stopped, but the last ticks are distinctly heard. Sounds are heard that would have passed entirely unnoticed if they had not ceased, and they are not heard until they fail to be followed by others in the regular rhythm. Of the same nature are the explanations of the frequent stories of men who go to sleep in battle from excessive fatigue and are awakened by the cessation of the firing. It is also a very common experience for one who has gone to sleep on a moving railway train to be awakened by the stopping of the train, or for the passengers on a boat to be disturbed by the quiet that follows the slowing or stopping of the propeller. In general then it seems that it is not so much the intensity of the sensation as it is the change in the intensity which is effective in calling the attention.

Dr. Knight Dunlap found that if a faint noise from a telephone receiver be interrupted, it would be noticed, when the constant tone itself would not be perceived. In fact one is more likely to notice the disappearance of a tone than its appearance. It is possible for a tone to begin and to remain unnoticed until it ceases, and then to become noticed for the first time.

There is also evidence of a summation effect when several successive stimuli, each too slight in itself to attract the attention, act upon a man. If, for instance, you desire to attract the attention of a man absorbed in some occupation, it will be found that while he will not hear his name the first time it is called, he will be aroused from his work if the same sound is repeated several times at the same intensity. We have an analogous phenomenon in the so-called " staircase " phenomenon of muscle-nerve physiology. If a stimulus be repeatedly applied to a muscle-nerve preparation, the earlier contractions are seen to be considerably smaller than the later, and for many stimulations each contraction is greater than the preceding.

Another factor of importance is the rate of change in the intensity. A sudden change is much more effective than a gradual one, no matter in which direction it takes place. This seems to be a general law of nervous excitability. Preyer succeeded in destroying the life of a brainless frog, without producing the slightest reaction, by increasing the temperature of the water by very slow degrees. Professor Stratton, Dr. Stern, and Dr. Goldscheider have shown in various sense departments that it is very much easier within wide limits to detect a rapid change of intensity than a slight one.

Another objective factor which is very closely related to intensity in this connection as in most others is extensity for sight and touch. A large object is more likely to attract the attention than a small one, other things being equal. A large object in the field of vision is noticed if there be nothing else about that is particularly noteworthy. A tall man, a high building, a large expanse of meadow, will each scarcely escape notice when in the field of view, while smaller objects no more striking for themselves will be overlooked under the same circumstances. This is almost the universal rule in vision, although here again there is a large part played by contrast just as there was by change in intensity. A comparatively large object among many small ones affects us as much as a very large among medium-sized. It makes no difference what the object may be.

There is apparently an exception to the rule in the tactual sensations where a small object is the more startling. A pin-prick will attract one when an equally intense pressure from a large blunt object would pass almost unnoticed. This is an exception which can very evidently be explained on evolutionary grounds. A large object in contact with the body means on the average, a support and a source of benefit rather than of danger, while a small object is very likely to injure the skin and may prove disastrous. It was therefore necessary if the animal were to survive that the small object be attended to and avoided, while attention to the broad surface was largely a matter of indifference.

Change is as important in attracting the attention in extensity as in intensity. When an object in the field of vision suddenly changes in size attention is at once drawn. The same thing is true for touch. It need not be considered at any length, however, for change in size in every day life is a comparatively infrequent phenomenon.

The effect of duration upon attention is very hard to state. Up to a certain point increase in duration has the same effect as increase in intensity, and serves to call attention to the stimulus. Weak stimuli of short duration will pass unnoticed, while if long persistent they may come to consciousness. On the other hand, a considerable duration even of comparatively intense sensations blunts the sense organs and makes it easy to distract the attention from them. There has been no determination of the limits within which duration is a favourable condition, or of the time at which it becomes unfavourable. We can only make the statement, based entirely upon rough observation, that moderate duration is favourable, prolonged stimulation unfavourable, to attention.

These complete the list of objective conditions favourable to attention. It might be possible to include in the list such factors as newness and variety of stimulation, the presence of contours, and the effect of movement, but as all of these can be shown to depend for their efficiency upon inherited or acquired modifications of consciousness, they can best be treated under the head of the subjective conditions. Their explanation is to be found in the past history of consciousness, not in the present nature of the nervous system. It is only their widespread appearance that makes them seem to fall within the class of objective conditions.

A study of the subjective conditions offers more difficulties, because it is not so easy to interpret the results. We cannot say at once what the conditions are here that make a given object stand out. We can only say that certain objects do attract the attention, and then study the previous circumstances in the life history of the individual which brings about that result. We can in this chapter merely enumerate the objects that are interesting, and give the results of as many investigations as possible that serve to explain the interest which attaches to them. The group of subjective conditions must be treated abstractly and in masses rather than concretely in terms of specific instances, because there are too many different groups and too many details in the phenomena to make it feasible to give anything more than typical illustrations of the nature of the effects.

One of the most satisfactory ways of studying many of the phenomena of the attention is by means of a simple stereoscope. If you replace the pictures of the ordinary parlour instrument by a card having upon one side a square of red paper, upon the other a square of green, and adjust them so that each square entirely fills one half of the field of vision, it will be found that there will be a constant fluctuation from one colour to the other, and neither will be seen all the time. As you have two fields in themselves equally likely to attract attention, and neither with any advantage of position, the triumph of one or the other must depend upon the attitude of the mind toward it, upon the subjective conditions. Unfortunately, from the standpoint of the experiment, there tends to enter a regular alternation between the two fields, so that the immediate effect of determining to attend to one or the other is very slight. However, subjective conditions decide which colour shall be seen first, and in so far the method throws some light upon our problem. One of the determining factors is the idea which is in mind at the time the cards are first presented. If you expect to see the red, and have a distinct memory image of the red, you will see it first, and will continue to see it until fatigue for that process sets in, when the green will supplant it. This alternation will then continue at regular intervals, and at a rate which depends upon the nature of the general stimulation, as long as the instrument is held before the eye. The general explanation of the alternations must be left over to a later chapter. We are concerned with them now only as a means of studying the conditions under which one colour is preferred to another. Other factors may be studied by this method on the assumption that the object favoured in any way will persist longer than those not so favoured. It is only necessary to compare the times that each colour holds the field, as conditions are varied, to determine the relative strength of the different influences at work. So Dr. Breese [2] found that if you draw straight lines upon each coloured field, and count the lines upon the one colour, you will keep its image more continuously before the mind, and also make it persist a considerably longer period than the other. That the memory image will be more easily kept in consciousness under these conditions is due to the earlier experience of the individual in a way that will be discussed in chapter vii.

Another instance of the importance of the idea in mind just before the stimulus to be attended to is given by Helmholtz. [5] In determining the part played by eye movements in the perception of depth, Helmholtz had occasion to make a number of experiments on the influence of successive illuminations of the field of vision by the electric

D

spark. The two halves of an ordinary stereoscopic view were placed on the wall of a dark box, with their centres separated by a distance equal to the distance between the eyes. The centres of the cards were pierced to admit a light just strong enough to permit the centre of each picture to be fixated by the eyes with axes parallel. By this arrangement the two halves of the picture were united in such a way that the same effect was produced as by the stereoscope ordinarily used. The spark lasted far too short a time to permit of eye movements, or of seeing the whole picture during any one illumination. Helmholtz found under these circumstances that he could at will fix upon any one part of the field of vision, and make that part stand out in clear relief. The selection was accom-plished, he says, by picturing to himself the part of the field of vision which he desired to see. This is the more striking from the fact mentioned above that it was impossible to bring any one part into a more favourable position of the field by moving the eyes, for any eye movement would have disturbed the stereoscopic vision and have shown all the objects in double images. The process of turning the attention to any one part of the field consisted of nothing else than having in mind before the spark came a memory image of that part. When the flash came the part imagined stood out predominant in consciousness, and impressions were received from it alone.

Another important discovery in the same experiment was that what was seen during one exposure helped in the perception of the next impression. At first only a very imperfect image of any part is received. With each succeeding spark a greater amount of detail is perceived, until a clear image of that region is obtained. Here the explanation is that each image calls up by association some connected image, and if that really is present it is seen distinctly because of the aid from the image already in mind; and if the suggestion was not fortunate it is excluded from the next preparatory image, and a second and perhaps more fortunate possibility succeeds, to be confirmed or rejected by the next glance. Both the attention to the object and its interpretation are facilitated by the idea in the mind at the instant the impression is received.

Another classical example of the influence of ideas in the mind at the time upon other ideas that are just entering is seen in " hearing out " overtones. It has been found that if the sounding of a complex note is preceded by sounding alone the overtone it is desired to hear, it is very much easier to assure oneself of its presence than if the tone is not sounded. It seems to be essential to hearing the overtone at all that there be an image of the tone to be heard in mind, and Stumpf suggests that the greater success of musicians over ordinary persons in hearing these tones is due to the fact that they have in mind a greater number of remembered tones, and when listening can more easily call up the image of the tone desired. They do not escape the general requirement for accurate listening, but are able to satisfy it much more readily and certainly.

Picking out the separate tones of the different instruments in an orchestra follows very much the same laws. If you have in mind the visual picture of the instrument which you are listening for, it is more easily detected than if there is no such aid. Looking at the instrument will also have the same effect. Probably in this case too the visual impression helps mainly because it calls up the tone of the instrument by association. For it is certain that having a memory of the tone is more effective than the mere visual impression.

We might extend the illustrations to each of the other senses. As you think of an itching sensation on any part of the skin you bring out impressions before unnoticed, which may become disagreeable in their intensity, and, apparently, they owe their origin entirely to having held the expected sensation in mind for a considerable period of time. It is possible that the tactual impression is complicated by the vaso-motor changes which attention induces, and that the impression is actually produced by attending rather than that a sensation already present is brought into clearer consciousness. But making all allowances, there is a large part of the experience, particularly that which comes early, which is due merely to the reinforcing influence of the idea upon the sensory stimulus which is ready to come in. In taste and smell we could find cases that would illustrate the same point, but there are none striking enough to warrant special mention.

Everyday life offers very many instances of the same principle. It is much easier to see any lost article if you have a definite picture of what is sought. In fact, searching for anything consists ordinarily of nothing more than walking about the place where the object is supposed to be, with the idea of the object kept prominently in mind, and thereby standing ready to facilitate the entrance of the perception when it offers itself. It is for that reason too that it is much easier to find an object again after finding it once, because you can look with a more definite image and can apply it more accurately to the right place in the environment.

All these instances, then, go to show that one of the important conditions of attending to an object is to have in mind at the time it is received an image of the object, and they seem sufficient in number and diversity to entitle the principle to rank as a general condition of the attention. Given any idea in mind and a corresponding impression offered to the senses, that impression will be preferred over the others. [6]

Not only do ideas that are actually present in consciousness at the moment have an influence in determining what impressions shall become conscious, but other experiences, which are much more remote in time and not in consciousness at the moment, also play a part. We can trace these other conditions backward in time, and as they become farther distant they also become more general and are harder to trace as individual influences because combined

with others in a total complex. We shall roughly endeavour to classify them in point of remoteness and generality,
and again give illustrations of the effect of each class. Many
of these influences do not affect the single act of the attention immediately, but only indirectly through their influence upon less remote conditions. Still they must all
be considered to be conditions, for if they had not existed
this particular mental process would not have taken the
form which it did. For instance, many of the factors
which we must consider are effective in determining what
idea shall be in mind at the moment of perception, but
through that they will also have an important influence
in determining the direction of the attention. To be compelled to stop our explanation with the statement that
the idea in mind at the moment would determine the next
idea to be received, and not be able to give the conditions
for that idea, would be no explanation at all. These latter conditions then might be looked at as merely conditions for tracing back the train of conditions to an ever-
increasing remoteness. In many cases, however, these
more remote influences seem to act immediately, and not
through an idea. In such cases the attention attaches
not to some impression that is in mind, but to something
entirely different or only remotely connected with the
idea most prominent at the instant. At these times attention seems spontaneous, as there is no foreshadowing of
the object attended to.

The most important of these more remote conditions
is the general mood of the moment—the attitude toward
the world in general that the individual has at that time.
This mood or attitude varies with the occupation of the
hour and with every change in the train of thought, however
it may be induced. After a portion of an hour spent in
a lecture-room with a class in mathematics, words and
figures will be noticed that would not be observed, or if
observed would be interpreted in an entirely different
way, in a class in literature. The mood, the general atti-

tude toward the world, is changed by the surroundings and the things that are said, and with it the object liable to become prominent will be entirely changed. In the same way a business man will notice events in his office that would pass almost unnoticed while at home. If a man has several occupations he will change his attitude toward the world as he changes his occupations, even if the changes take place at short intervals, and with the attitude there will be a variation in the object which is likely to catch his attention. Let a botanist turn amateur gardener, and he notices plants that he would not have been the least interested in as a scientist, or which would have looked entirely different to him in that capacity. The only varieties which he distinguishes are vegetables and weeds, without reference to the different forms that they present. The only characteristics that strike the attention are those that mark the entire group as corn or not corn, whereas when he looks as a botanist the minor differences are all clearly noticed, and the usefulness or harmfulness is not in the least considered.

Similar instances can be drawn from any profession. A flash of light in his laboratory will be at once noticed by the electrical engineer, while a light of the same intensity in his home would pass entirely unnoticed. The tick of the telegraph key in his office will be heard by the operator above very much more intense sounds, whereas in the street or in a place of public assembly it would be heard much less readily. The environment in which the impression is received seems to predispose the mind for the reception of one set of impressions, and it matters not if the impression be expected or not, or what the conscious mental attitude toward it may be. When the sensation is received under these conditions it at once assumes the chief place in consciousness. There are also negative effects of the same kind, in which it is rendered more difficult for impressions of a certain class to enter the mind. An odour will pass unnoticed in a chemical laboratory that would be noticed at once in a church or a dwelling-house. A corpse in a dissecting-room will pass unnoticed, while on the street it would strongly attract attention. In fact we might add that a positive adaptation to one set of stimuli in itself acts as a negative adaptation to all others, with varying degrees of intensity. But whether positive or negative, one of the factors which plays an important part in determining that a certain object shall be attended to at a given time is the mood of the moment, and this mood is determined partly by the external environment at the time, and in part depends upon still more remote subjective factors, which we must consider in their turn.

Professor Külpe [7] and his students have, in recent years, devoted a large amount of work to determine the influence of these moods—or, as they call them, tasks or purposes—upon the influence of mental processes of several kinds, including attention, thinking, and action. The task may be set by a definite question from another, or as an experimental requirement, but whatever the method, when the task dominates consciousness it has the same effect that we have assigned to the mood. So nonsense syllables of different colours were shown for a moment in a dark room, and the observer was asked to look at them at different times with the purposes in mind : to give the number of of letters visible, to give the colours and their positions, and to name the letters and their positions. It was determined that the best results from looking were obtained when the statements that were made coincided with the task that had been set in advance. Colours could be given more accurately when the task had been to name the colours and their positions. In general, observers were relatively blind to those phases of the experience that were not represented in the antecedent task.

The first of the factors which control the mental attitude of the moment is the general training of the individual. Under this head the conditions cover so large an extent of

time, and the number of influences which have been at
work is so great, that it is not possible accurately to mark
off one group from another. Any division must be more
or less arbitrary, and, do the best we can, it will never be
possible to carry one through completely. There will be
many conditions that might as well be classified in one
place as in another. The list of determining factors which
must be considered in the remaining groups covers practically every influence that the individual has been subjected
to from birth on, and includes also many hereditary influences that complicate the situation already sufficiently
difficult to disentangle. We may perhaps for convenience
divide the influences into three great groups : the training of
the individual, the social forces which have acted upon him,
and his inherited characteristics. It is no more impossible
to say just how much depends upon one of these groups
of influences and how much upon another, than it is to say
how much of any act of the attention depends upon objective and how much upon the subjective conditions ; or
how much depends upon ideas in mind at the moment,
and how much upon the mental attitude. In any case
the classification will serve as well as any other as a basis
for the enumeration of the empirically-given conditions,
and besides, has the advantage of following the traditional
lines of division.

1. The effects of training and of past experience cannot of
course be shown experimentally, but illustrative instances
can be drawn in great number from daily life. Every
large group of the community that has had a peculiar
training—has been subjected to a distinctive set of experiences—shows the effects of them in the peculiar way in
which individuals of the group will react to the various
stimuli of life—in the impressions which attract their
attention at any given time. Nearly every trade and
profession has given its members a mind adapted to receiving impressions that would not be received by the
great mass of men. Much of what passes for extreme

acuteness of some special sense is nothing more than the result of a special training of the attention to greater efficiency in one particular line.

There is a popular belief, for example, that the eye of the savage is much keener than the eye of civilised man. It is true that he will notice a footprint where the civilised man will not be able to see the slightest disturbance of the ground. He can follow game when the white companion is entirely without a clue to the direction of the trail. He will also detect the approach of an animal by the ear when another would not be conscious of any sound, and so on. Instances of his peculiar perfection of sense could be drawn from each class of sensations. It is not that the organs are more perfect, however. The results of the tests made on savages in different parts of the world by recent scientific expeditions go to show that their senses are no more perfect than those of Europeans, in fact on the average are even less sensitive. It is merely that all of their training during their lifetime has been concentrated upon recognising and interpreting the particular objects and differences which have a meaning for the chase, and in adult life no element of the perception that can have the least bearing upon this point can escape him. His civilised companions have no such special subjective preparation, and consequently lack the peculiar readiness in noticing the slight marks. The acuteness of vision of the sailor is to be explained in the same way. For him every mark upon the horizon is correctly interpreted, and every small object is seen, because there are images in mind ready to be called out by any impression that is likely to appear there. The passenger by his side sees the same impressions, but there is nothing in the mind to favour the entrance of the important phases as opposed to the unimportant, and he will notice one as readily as the other. That it is the special training rather than the keenness of sense that makes the difference can best be shown by repeating the test with some material for which there has been no special preparation. If you ask the savage to describe the characters upon a printed page he will not see as much as a boy of six ; or compare the sailor's perception of a microscopic preparation with the trained biologist's, and you would find him placed at a greater relative disadvantage than was the passenger at sea compared with himself.

The ear of the musician is probably not more delicate than the ear of the untrained man in the recognition of differences of pitch or of intensity, it is only that his training has prepared him to notice combinations and shades that will escape other men. The education of the tactual and auditory senses in the blind is probably due to a similar change in mental disposition and acuteness of the attention rather than to any increase in the accuracy of perception in the sense organs themselves. The blind can, it is true, recognise differences in stimuli of the most rudimentary kind, such as the distance between the two points of a compass, much more accurately than the normal man ; but the normal man can also increase the accuracy of these same discriminations by any practice which furthers attention to them. So that it seems probable that the education of the blind is also due to a development in the adequacy of the attention rather than to any development of the sense organ. The extraordinary acuteness of sense developed by tea-tasters and others who rely upon one sense almost exclusively for complicated determinations is to be traced similarly to mental rather than to sensory training.

Another instance of the effect of training upon the attention is to be seen in learning a foreign language. When first heard the spoken words are a jumble of confused sounds ; nothing is heard for itself, although all the tones strike upon the ear. As time goes on and practice is continued, the mass is broken up into its component parts and each is heard. The feeling that the speech is unusually rapid decreases with familiarity, and the different parts stand out for themselves. There has been no change in the ear ; it is merely that training has increased the facility with which attention can be given in this particular field. The effect is central rather than peripheral—mental, not physical.

Besides the influence which practice has upon increasing the adequacy of attention, it has an almost equally marked effect upon determining the direction of attention at any given time—of determining the object that shall be attended to. This can perhaps be best illustrated by considering what two men of different education would see under precisely the same objective conditions. Suppose a geologist and a builder to take a walk through a rocky country new to both of them. Ask each what he has seen on his return, and the replies will be as different as if they had traversed an entirely different region. The geologist will be full of discussions of topics in connection with his science. He will tell you of glacial scratches, of drift from northern ledges, tilting of strata, and of faults. The builder will have seen none of these. His report would be of granite and of sandstone, of the colour and friability of the stone, and of the means of quarrying and transportation. You would imagine from the conversation that the two men had traversed an entirely different country. And the same difference would appear if any two men of dissimilar training were exposed to the same stimuli. It has been said that it is possible to judge a man's occupation by his answer to a single question ; much more is it true that you can tell pretty accurately what his training has been from a statement of what he has seen during a certain interval provided only that the situation in which he is placed is complex enough, and he be not too polite to mention the things which he has really been interested in, rather than those which he thinks will interest the listener. The world is presented in almost infinite possibilities of perception, but each man takes from it only what his previous training has prepared him to receive. What he has seen at one time is very largely instrumental in determining what he shall see later, each experience prepares the way for another.

We can obtain a good proof of the part which more remote experiences play in determining attention from the experiment with the stereoscope on retinal rivalry, which we cited in discussing the first group of conditions. If one of the eyes be offered an unbroken surface while the other is diversified in any way, it will be found that the one marked will ordinarily hold the field of consciousness against the other, no matter how strongly we attempt to see the first. Dr. Breese found that if one surface had figures of any kind upon it, it would hold the attention for from 64 per cent to 79 per cent of the time against 21 per cent to 36 per cent of the time for the other homogeneously coloured field. The variations were for different arrangements of the lines and for different experiments. That the contours should hold the field is probably due to the fact that in our experience contours have always meant objects, and so something that must be attended to for procuring food or for avoiding danger, while the homogeneous surface is comparatively meaningless from every standpoint. An educated man, too, will always see a printed page when it is offered at the same time as a field of straight lines. This again is due to the fact that the words have acquired a greater meaning for him from the use to which they are put and the frequency with which they are used—another expression of the general rule that a man attends most easily and frequently to the objects most closely related to the great mass of his experience.

Usually education influences attention secondarily only, through the mediation of the earlier mentioned conditions. Training serves to evoke and direct the purpose of the moment, that arouses an idea, and the idea in turn determines what shall enter consciousness. The zoologist, e.g., is led by his earlier knowledge to expect a definite form of life in the cold and darkness of the depths of the ocean. This gives a purpose to his examination of the contents of the dredge. The purpose gives rise to a definite premonitory image of minute shells, and the corresponding beings at once take shape among the grains of sand. Most seeing is the result of a similar self-conscious purpose. But far from lessening the importance of education, a recognition of this fact serves rather to emphasize the wide range of its action. And there are innumerable instances, too, in which education acts directly without premonitory purpose or idea. A telegrapher, imprisoned or in some other environment where nothing suggests his occupation, will recognize the Morse code in faint taps, while another would overlook the very sounds themselves as well as the order in their recurrence.

2. The social factors in determining the attention are also of a very general nature, and take us even farther back in time than any of the others so far considered. They might for the most part be almost as well discussed under the head of the training, but as they usually appear most fully during the early years of life, and before training has advanced very far, and are most important elements of training, a separate treatment offers numerous advantages. Only in recent years has there been any adequate conception of what the individual owes to his fellows in society for his stock-in-trade and for impetus to effort. Partly through tradition, including the printed book, partly through immediate contact with his neighbours, every child comes into touch with the experience of the race already prepared for assimilation. A large part of the knowledge acquired in the process of training is drawn from this source. In so far, the social factors may be said to have been considered in the preceding discussion.

But another and more distinctive side of the social influence is to be found in the pressure that society exerts to force its standards upon the individual. Its standards are enforced in part directly through the respect that is felt for the opinions of others, and in part indirectly through physical force wielded by the parents, and in rarer instances by the officers of the law. Much of what we know popularly as duty resolves itself on careful examination into the fear of public opinion, to the fact that mankind in general looks with favour upon certain forms of action and disapproves of others. Were it not for this set of conditions the training of the child would be largely a matter of chance, and the attention of any moment would conform to no general law. As it is, the child is impressed with the importance of adapting himself to the social order from the very beginning. There is unconscious pressure in the attempt to learn to speak. The interest which the child feels in the speech of parents and others about him—the first incentive to speech—is undoubtedly a case of social pressure. These beings are for him the source of food and of all good things of life, and an important part of the total series of impressions that results in the acquirement of the comforts is the spoken word, passed to and fro as the preliminary to most actions which benefit him. Attention to the people about soon irradiates to the spoken word which is so frequently associated with them. With attention once fixed upon the word the only further condition necessary for speech is that some chance movement of the child's vocal organs should produce one of the sounds that have already attracted his attention. With the coming of this sound it too is attended to, and there follows a frequent repetition which establishes the connection between sound and movement, until it becomes so close that thereafter it is only necessary to have the picture of the word come up in consciousness for the word itself to follow. The social impetus helps indirectly at each stage of the process. The exclamations and general excitement which greet the first word, and the advantages which accrue at a later stage from communication with his fellows, are all strong incentives to make every effort to perfect the process.

As the child grows older the pressure from society becomes ever stronger. He is held to most of his tasks, after the first interest which comes from their novelty has worn off, by the desire of approbation or by the fear of blame. His early attendance at school comes from parental desire or from a liking for the society of children of his own age, and once in school approbation of the teacher and of his mates are the strongest incentives to further progress—particularly to continued application in the less congenial tasks. Gradually there comes from the frequent repetition of the pressure the feeling that to be inattentive, to do nothing, or to waste time, is not in accordance with social tradition, is wrong. It is this habit once formed that brings him to hold himself to some one line of work until the end is attained, without much conscious reference to that end or to the passing pleasure that comes from the work itself. What the line of work shall be is also in large measure determined by family or neighbourhood traditions, and the standard of excellence that he shall aim to attain in that line is fixed very largely by the ideals of his community. In short, the impetus to attention which leads to training, as well as the direction which that training shall take, are both very largely derived from social influences, and the rewards which come from attainment of the ideals of training and the punishments which follow failure are almost entirely social in their nature. Without these elements no man would give prolonged attention to any one thing—education in the present sense would be an impossibility. And as without preliminary training the natural attention would not attach to anything above the commonplace, and there would be no continued attention even to that, there could be no advance beyond the stage of barbarism.

Finally, we must consider the most remote set of conditions of all, those which are derived from heredity. It is again very difficult to distinguish between hereditary conditions and those which are due to the more general experiences. There are certain circumstances which attract the attention so universally both in animals and in men that it seems safe to regard them as due to the common experience of the race, rather than as acquired during the lifetime of the individual.

Most striking of these is the influence of movement. It is true of both the spatial senses that any moving object holds the attention against almost any other form of stimulation, and there are analogous facts that might be mentioned in the non-spatial senses. An object in motion in any part of the field of vision will at once attract the attention, and will hold it as long as it continues to move. Many an object that can be seen perfectly easily as it moves across the field of view, is lost to sight when it comes to rest. A distant golf ball is plainly visible so long as it continues its course, but seems to disappear utterly when it stops, even if it is not hidden by any intervening object. An after image again is never seen while the eye is moving, although it again becomes visible as the eye stops, and this in spite of the fact that the image is fainter at that time than it was before. The shadows of retinal blood-vessels which we have overlooked all our lives because they do not change their position with respect to the retina will suddenly become visible if the source of light changes its position rapidly enough to throw the shadows into pronounced movement.

This effect of movement in attracting the attention is common to many different grades of animals. The kitten pricks up its ears as soon as the ball starts to roll across the floor, a horse shies when a bit of paper blows across the road, while both animals would remain unaffected by the same objects at rest. Wild animals are startled by the movements of the hunter, while they fail to notice him under the same conditions if he is perfectly still. Dr. Breese, in his experiments on retinal rivalry, also obtained striking experimental proof of the importance of movement. He found that with one field of vision in movement, the other at rest, the moving field was seen 53 per cent to 60 per cent of the time instead of about 50 per cent in the normal experiments. And so, from the lowest animals which possess eyes upward to man, any object that moves in the field of vision will attract the attention, even if the object in itself be inconspicuous and the attention be claimed by attractive objects of other kinds.

On the skin the same law holds. It is much easier to perceive a moving object than a resting one. A weight too light to be felt while at rest becomes easily felt when drawn across the surface. The distance that an object must be moved before the movement is noticed is considerably less than the least distance between two resting points which permits them to be felt as two. And the moving object also will attract the attention here as in vision when there has been no preparation for attending to the stimulus, and attention to a moving object is also more effective when it occurs.

The fact that change in general is a condition for the attention might have the same explanation, and even be made a sub-head under the law. Motion may be regarded as a form of change in intensity. It consists of an increase of intensity at some point, accompanied by a decrease on the place last stimulated. Owing to the inertia of the sense organ the stimulus appears gradually at one point and dies away just as gradually, so that all parts stimulated are undergoing a change in the intensity of stimulation. On the other hand, it is quite usual to speak of changes in intensity and quality as movements through different degrees. So we have in music the statement that the moving part is attended to in spite of a low intensity. Advantage is taken of this to make the relatively weak solo part stand out above the accompaniment by giving it a different direction on the scale from the orchestral parts. In this particular case the change impresses the hearer as very much like a movement. And there are other changes both in quality and intensity that make the same impression. In a similar way anything that is new in our experience tends to attract us. A new picture on the wall, a new face at the table, will draw all eyes, whether there be any other striking feature or not. And

E

also a tree in a plain, or a black face in an audience of Caucasians will be noticed at once.

At first sight this seems to be out of harmony with the statement in the earlier part of the chapter, that ideas which had previously been in consciousness facilitated the entrance of the corresponding sensation when presented again. The opposition is only apparent. Both statements are true, but in different connections. The new thing will draw the attention, but not to hold it for long, while the known both attracts the attention and holds it. We see the new as easily, perhaps, but we certainly see more in the old. The child or savage is more astonished by the locomotive than the engineer, but the latter sees infinitely more in it than the former. Furthermore, when the attention is held by the new thing it is frequently because the new is not entirely new, and the familiar serves with the new to attract the attention. The two principles do not conflict, as has been asserted, but are complementary. Either the new or the old will attract the attention, but for different reasons.

That movement and these related changes attract the attention is very evidently to be explained from the evolution of the race. A moving object means either a bit of food or an enemy. In either case it must be observed if the animal is to survive. This tendency must have become ingrained in the animal series at a very early age by the process of eliminating the unfit, and its wide distribution throughout the animal kingdom shows that none of the animals above the most rudimentary has escaped it. The same evolutionary explanation that applies to movement will also apply to change and the effect of the new or unknown in attracting the attention. A sudden increase in the intensity or even change in the quality of a stimulus, means that a new adaptation to the environment is necessary, and that failure to adapt oneself may be disastrous. The unfamiliar is in the same way a possible source of danger, and attention must be given if there is to be survival.

When we are dealing with an inherited tendency that is as widespread as this among animals and men, it is difficult to decide whether the condition is to be regarded as objective or subjective ; whether its explanation is to be historical, or whether it depends upon the general nature of nervous tissue. The basis of settlement is to be found in the fact that there seems to be no purely physical reason why a moving or changing stimulus should have a greater effect upon the nerve than a constant or stationary one, while there does seem to be a historical reason for its effect. In this it differs from intensity, which can be seen to have a greater effect in disturbing the chemical equilibrium of a nerve.

In addition to these very general hereditary conditions of the attention, there are undoubtedly certain elements in each individual which are peculiar to him, on account of his descent, which he has inherited from his immediate parents, and which make him attend more readily to one set of stimuli than to others. Galton, in his " Hereditary Genius," shows that sons tend to follow the professions of their fathers, and excel in the same directions. This would depend in the last analysis very largely upon attention. The whole question is clouded, however, by the fact that it is very difficult to decide in any case whether we have to deal with heredity pure and simple, or with the social factors of family tradition. In nearly every case fathers educate their own children, and it is therefore equally easy to assume that the similarity in taste and ability is due to the inheritance or to the training. With man there are so few instances in which environment can be distinguished from heredity, that it is impossible to give an example of attention that can be clearly shown to be due to heredity alone. That some part even of this level is derived from heredity is probable from the innate characteristics of animals. A setter dog, for instance, has its attention drawn at once by a game bird, while a pug or a Saint Bernard would hardly notice it at all. A kitten will be attracted by the odour of a dog on the hands of the person who fondles it before she has seen anything of a dog. Other instances to the same purpose might be given in great numbers. These seem sufficient, however, to indicate that the attention is in part determined by heredity in the animal series, and probably the same circumstances are at work in man.

Altogether, then, it seems that the conditions of the attention are as widespread as the conditions of consciousness itself. Every event that has at any time affected the individual in any way is at some time likely to determine in some degree the direction and efficiency of his attention. Not only, moreover, must we regard all the experiences of the individual as determining any given state of the attention, but also through heredity and social environment everything that has helped to select for survival his ancestors or the race at any time will play some part, great or small, in deciding between the many stimuli offered on any occasion.

SUMMARY

1. The conditions of any act of attention are to be found in the present environment (objective conditions) and in the past experience of the individual (subjective conditions).

2. The main objective conditions are the intensity, extent, and duration of the stimulus.

3. The subjective conditions are to be found in the idea in mind at the time, in the mood of the moment, the education, previous social environment, and heredity of the individual.

CHAPTER IV

INTEREST AND FEELING OF ACTIVITY AS CONDITIONS OF ATTENTION

WE have failed to consider in the last chapter two conditions of the attention that are ordinarily regarded as of the first importance. They are, in fact, the only conditions that are mentioned popularly. It seems well, therefore, to ask whether they are to be retained at all in the list, if a part shall be ascribed to them.

We may begin with interest, as it is the easier to dispose of, and seems to stand first in the frequency with which it is mentioned. In its simplest form we are always making the statement that we attend to an object because it is interesting to us. As a basis for our discussion let us ask what things are usually interesting.

In the first place, we find that we are interested in those things most closely related to our own past life. We are interested in the " local " items of our own town paper, while similar items when read in the paper which we pick up on the table of a friend seem ludicrous in their puerility. A student is interested in anything that is new to him, but at the same time is so closely related to the things which he has known before that he has no difficulty in connecting it with some previous bit of knowledge. And the closer the connection, and the more important to the person the things with which it is connected, the stronger is the interest. We say that a novel is interesting if it contains a sufficient admixture of human emotion, of love and hate, revenge and forbearance, to permit us to live again some phases of our own experience in a new setting, if we can feel with the characters and make them a part of our lives. A young boy who has not yet known what love is, is not interested in a love story ; nor is a girl ordinarily appealed to by stories of adventure.

The play of children again throws light upon their interests ; their games are in general a reproduction of the things in which they are interested. We can trace the effect of heredity and of the social environment upon the nature of the games. It is a matter of frequent remark among travellers that the play of the children of any race is merely an imitation of the activities of the adults of the same tribe. Play among savage boys is largely made up of mock representations of incidents of the chase and of warfare. Among civilized children these elements still hold a large place, but there is in addition a large increase in the number of games taken from mercantile and agricultural pursuits. Savage and civilised girls show the same differences, but the games of both are imitations of the duties of the home and of domestic labour generally.

In all of these cases we find that what is interesting is identical with the things which, as we have seen above, must be attended to from subjective reasons. They are the things that demand attention, because they are related to our previous experience, because our social environment compels it, or because of hereditary influences. Interest then is not dependent upon the object, but upon the nature of the man to whom the object is presented. As we develop, many things become interesting that previously were uninteresting. Interests grow with knowledge, and, in fact, are made by knowledge ; they are not fixed once and for all, even in the same individual. Of course it has been noticed almost daily that interests differ from individual to individual. What appeals strongly to one man will not call forth the least response from another. These differences can, of course, only be co-related with the different experiences and the different hereditary influences in the life of each. The objects which are interesting to all men alike are so, not because of a peculiarity of the things themselves or of any common characteristic of the things, but because of the common nature of man. That men have common interests is due to the common heredity—to the fact that men are born into a social environment in a large measure the same for all, and to the similar experiences to which they have been subjected. So we have seen that man is interested in the moving things because heredity has forced the race and the animal series as a whole to notice them. In the same way man must be interested in other men because heredity, social environment, and his individual experience have all combined to force that interest upon him. If the human race is to survive it must work in harmony, and if any individual is to survive he must co-operate with his fellows and consider their interests and desires at every step. The basis of such unity and consideration is an interest in everything that they do, and an understanding of their motives in the fullest sense. If the actions and feelings of others failed to attract our attention, and the expression of anger or of satisfaction upon a human face were no longer of interest, co-operation would become much more difficult than it is at present.

Interest then is but the objective way of looking at the conditions of the attention. It is merely ascribing to the objects processes and qualities that have their real origin in the man himself. Things are interesting because we attend to them, or because we are likely to attend to them ; we do not attend because they are interesting, to paraphrase Professor James's familiar saying about emotion.

While a thing that attracts the attention is interesting, not all the objects that attract the attention have the name applied to them. We do not think of those sounds as interesting to which we must attend merely because of their intensity—which force their way into consciousness whether permitted or not. In the same category fall all the things to which we attend from objective conditions. It seems that if there is anything in the nature of the object which accounts to us for its entrance, we are satisfied with ascribing that as the reason for the entrance, and do not mention the less apparent and more subjective term, interest. On the other hand, in the very complex case in which we attend from what we know as a sense of duty, we also do not think of saying that the object attended to is interesting, but think rather of the related considerations as accounting for its entrance. In other words, whenever there is any condition that may be named as the reason for the coming of the idea we do not say that it is interest which determines the attention, but when there is nothing that can be pointed to as the occasion for the attending we say that the object is interesting. It seems, then, that interest is applied to those conditions of the attention which are neither too subjective nor yet too objective, although an exact line of demarcation cannot be drawn. It is evident in any case that it is not in itself a separate condition of attention, but merely a name for one class of conditions, which by some curious development of popular consciousness has become referred to the object instead of the mind itself. [5]

There is another sense in which interest is used popularly, that is, as a word for a pleasant feeling that comes as we attend. We are said to be interested in anything that holds our attention, and this is pleasant. This fact and use raises the question of the relation of pleasure and pain to attention. It is frequently said that we attend to things because they are pleasant, and avoid attending to them if they are unpleasant. The argument tends to overlook two facts : that feeling comes after attention has taken place, and that attention is given to unpleasant as well as to pleasant objects. As to the first, it is evident that the pleasure or pain never comes until after the object has been attended to, and it is therefore very evident that it is not the pleasure or the pain in itself which produces the attending. We see the thing fully before it can give us a feeling tone of any kind, and by that time of course the attending is complete. The only fact that could be alleged then is that the pleasure would serve to hold the attention, once it had been drawn, while a painful impression would be at once banished from mind. But Külpe has pointed out in the second place that even this is not the case. We attend with equal readiness to unpleasant and to pleasant sensations. Tragedy holds us as long and as continuously as comedy. An accident in which human life is lost claims our attention as fully as the most entrancing landscape. It is evidently not pleasure alone that would be effective in determining the attention if we were to give feeling any place in the process.

That pleasure was ever considered to be a factor in the control is probably due to the fact that attending is itself a pleasant event. Things which are interesting please us, as we see from the ordinary connotation of the term interest; and if the interesting things are merely those which attract our attention, as we concluded in the last chapter, then it seems that we are driven to the inference that attention in itself is pleasant, without any reference to the feeling tone that may accompany the idea. If the feeling which is aroused by the idea attended to *per se* is unpleasant, it will lessen or destroy the pleasure of the total process; but in the majority of cases the attending seems pleasant. Pleasantness, then, in the popular regard has, like interest, passed over from being an acompaniment or product of the attention to be regarded as its condition, or one of its conditions.

Probably a large part of the opinion that pleasure and interest are conditions of the attention has arisen from the fact that there is in many cases a preliminary knowledge that a certain object is to come into the range of actual sensation. This preliminary knowledge takes the form of a centrally aroused sensation, either of a memory image or an imagination. It is attended to in that form, and this attention may give rise both to interest and pleasure.

The pleasure which is thus derived from the anticipatory process is a strong stimulus to seek to put oneself in a favourable place to receive the expected impression, and then, as we have seen in the last chapter, having had the idea before is a favourable condition for receiving it again. So that attending to a premonitory image is a real condition for receiving the corresponding external stimulation when it comes, particularly if the first be accompanied by pleasure; but the real condition of the attending throughout the process is to be found in the conditions of the first act of attention to the memory image, and this can be neither the interest nor the pleasure, for the idea—the attending—must have come before its entrance.

Another popular explanation of the conditions of attention which needs to be considered in this connection is that attention is the result of subjective activity, and that attention is effective when the self acts to produce a change in the mental field—in the clearness or intensity of the ideas. The evidence usually adduced for this view is that when we attend we feel ourselves active, we feel that we are in some way directly responsible for the change which is going on, we feel that we are struggling for greater clearness in some direction, or to retain a process already present. In recent years this phase of the attention process has been subjected to very close analysis by several writers, and the conclusion has been reached that it does not constitute an essential condition of the attention, but is merely a concomitant or sign of the attention. It is a feeling of the same kind as that which comes when one is lifting a heavy weight, or making other movements that involve much exertion. At that time it will be noticed that there are sensations of strain in all parts of the body, as well as from the muscles directly involved in the lifting. These sensations correspond to the contraction of the muscles which were mentioned in the chapter on motor concomitants. The contraction of the scalp muscles, the setting of the teeth, and the contraction of the other muscles of the body are all accompanied by strain sensations. These sensations are so widely diffused throughout the body, and the total complex comes to consciousness in one mass so often, and the separate elements appear in isolation so seldom, that an accurate analysis is extremely difficult, and the whole mass is regarded as a unit. From the regularity with which they accompany the movement they have been regarded as its real cause, and as something which has independent existence without any relation to the muscles or to any part of the physical organism. Careful analysis shows, however, as we have seen, that the feeling of activity is but a complex of sensations coming from the muscles, and that they only succeed or accompany the putting forth of energy—do not precede it—and so cannot cause the movement. There is nothing of an essentially new or distinct kind involved ; we are dealing with a new manifestation of the sensation that comes with each contraction of a muscle.

The same processes are involved in the attention. The feeling of activity is the same for both attention and voluntary action, just as we saw that there was the same overflow of nervous energy to the various muscles of the body in both, and consequently the same mass of strain sensations is present during attention as during physical effort. When attentive, sensations come from the contracted scalp muscles, from the muscles of the jaws, and from the voluntary muscles in the different parts of the body. In this instance, too, it is easily seen on careful observation that we begin to attend before the strains arise, or at the same time that they appear. Moreover, the most intense strain does not correspond to the period of greatest efficiency of attention. On the contrary, the strains are most pronounced when we are just beginning to attend, while we are warming up to the work, and are still not working to advantage ; they die away when the work alone is present in consciousness and we have reached the maximum of effectiveness. It is not when trying hardest that we obtain the best results, but when there is no need for effort, when the occupation of the moment seems to carry the attention, and nothing else is needed to reinforce it. It is when there is a sudden change in the direction of the attention, when there are two sets of conditions working to determine the attention from opposite sides, and the issue between them is in doubt, that the sense of effort is strongest. The rule is that when the conditions of the attention are most equivocal the sense of effort is greatest, and that there is no relation, except perhaps an inverse one, between efficiency of the attention and the accompanying feeling of activity. When the one set of conditions has obtained full control and the other is entirely excluded there comes a diminution, usually almost a complete disappearance, of the effort. While, therefore, this sense of activity is one of the most characteristic marks of attention, there is definite proof that the feeling of activity itself is not a condition, but an accompaniment of the attention process. It is a sign of the attention, or more truly of the struggle, that comes when several sets of conditions are striving for the mastery in consciousness, rather than a condition of the attention.

Against the position that the greatest strain was an accompaniment of attention under the greatest difficulties rather than of the most efficient attention, one who believed that the strain was a real sign of the activity of mind might argue that this was what one would expect if there was an active mind that was always striving to accomplish a certain result. If this result could be obtained easily there would be little necessity for effort, while when there was opposition much effort would be put forth, just as one puts forth more effort to accomplish the same result under unfavourable circumstances. We should also expect the least result under the same condition.

An argument of this kind, however, is at best but an analogy, and we do not know that any of the elements in the two cases are strictly analogous. Certainly one important factor in the analogy is lacking. That is that the forces which oppose are not external to the mind, as are the physical forces which oppose the bodily movement, but are just as much within as are the conditions which impel to the successful activity. When there is a struggle between the influences which would make one attend to work and those which impel to reading a novel, both are equally subjective. There are many factors of social and hereditary origin that impel toward the novel—our interest in man and human character, our love of adventure, of courage in a struggle, and of the heroic in general. On the other side there are other social and experiential factors—the feeling that one cannot afford to be regarded by his fellows as lacking in industry, the feeling that it is one's duty to work during certain hours enforced by the standard of work in the particular community and profession with which one's lot has been cast, the fear of consequences if the work is not completed, and so on throughout a long series. One set of influences is just as subjective as the other, and yet we have an apparent struggle, and the feeling of activity is present in large degree. Evidently then our analogy does not hold. We can hardly picture ourselves as fighting ourselves, and we cannot to-day take seriously the popular figure of speech that there are two selves, two attentions which are fighting each other, and that the strains are the signs of their conflict. All talk of such activity and opposition is purely figurative, and most of the metaphors are seen to be badly mixed when closely examined. There is no place for any activity of the kind in the process that actually takes place. The only thing left to do with the strain sensations is to regard them as a concomitant of the attention, arising through some overflow of motor energy which originates when two sets of conditions oppose each other.

The only effect which the contraction of these numerous muscles has upon the efficiency of the attention, is that it may slightly increase the adequacy of the attention beyond that which it would have had if the strain sensations were not present. It is found by a method which will be described in the next chapter that one can attend slightly better if he is exerting muscular force in some way—if he clenches his fist or presses upon a dynamometer. When the normal strain sensations are present, there is probably an effect of a very similar kind, but of slighter degree. This result is entirely analogous to the fact that it is possible to exert greater force with one hand when the other is also contracted. Both effects are probably due to an irradiation of nervous force from one nerve cell to another, which serves mutually to reinforce each. But you can no more regard the widespread contraction which follows the attention as the cause of the attention than you could call the contraction of the left hand the cause of the contraction of the right in the other instance.

Dr. W. MacDougall [3] records an experiment which probably affords the most satisfactory evidence we have that the back-stroke from muscle directly helps attention. He made use of an experiment similar to rivalry in the stereoscope. He varied the experiment by paralysing the ciliary muscle of one eye with atropine. Under these circumstances the field before the normal eye was seen much the greater part of the time, while with both eyes uninjured each was seen about the same length of time.

If now neither interest nor the activity process is of any real value in determining attention, and neither can be added to the factors which we have considered before, we are left with the view that we owe attention not to any one particular circumstance, but rather to the sum total of influences, external and internal, that are working upon us at any moment. These conditions include all of the actions of the individual, all of the impressions that have been made upon him in any way, and go back beyond the lifetime of the individual to the events that have affected his ancestors on the one side, and to the activities and relations of his fellows in the same society on the other. If any one of these events had been different we must believe that some aspect of the attention would have been changed in greater or less degree. The amount of change would depend upon the remoteness of the influence, upon its intensity at the time it was originally active, and upon the closeness of its relation to the other influences which have been at work at any time.

In any case the conditions of the attention cannot be dismissed with either of the popular formulæ that we attend because we are interested, for this statement is a tautology ; or that we attend because we try, for the "try" consciousness is but a sign of the working of certain factors which make for the attention, it is not in itself a real condition.

SUMMARY

1. Neither interest or "mental activity" can be regarded as conditions of attention.

2. Interest is either a general name for the subjective conditions of attention when ascribed to the object, or it is used to designate a mood which accompanies all attending.

3. "Mental activity" is really bodily activity—a mass of sensations that comes from the contraction of muscles in different parts of the body. The contractions result from motor innervations which accompany attention.

CHAPTER V

THE EFFECTS OF ATTENTION IN CONSCIOUSNESS

THERE are several facts in connection with the attention and its results in consciousness that are of considerable interest in themselves, and throw light upon problems of practical value for teachers and others, as well as being very important for the theory of the attention which must be discussed in a later chapter. Of these we shall consider the number of objects to which attention may be given, the time that it is possible to attend, and the effect of the attention upon the rate of perception and movement.

The first question is one that has played a considerable part in the older history of psychology and philosophy. It has long been a dogma of common sense, and was an accepted principle of the old rational psychology, that man can attend to but one thing at a time, that no more than a single impression can occupy the centre of consciousness at any given instant. The dogma undoubtedly has a purely a priori origin, and was deduced from the principle that the mind was a simple indivisible substance, and therefore could contain but one idea at a time. Recently this statement has been subjected to experiment and found not to be in harmony with the facts of experience, or at least not to be true in the naïve way in which it was formulated.

The experiments consist in exposing a number of objects for an interval of one-hundredth to one-fifth of a second—a time much too short to permit the impressions to be counted during the exposure—and noting the number of objects that can be correctly recognised in the period. Two facts of importance for our discussion were obtained. It was shown that four or five impressions could be noticed at one time instead of one, as the rational psychologists had assumed, and also that the number of objects which could be recognised was almost entirely independent of their size or complexity. Goldscheider and Müller [¹⁵ᵃ] found, for example, that it was as easy to perceive a complex group of dots arranged in some regular order, as it was to perceive a single dot, that the complex which goes to make up a letter is as easily recognised as the simplest impression. Finally it was found that a short word was seen as easily as a single letter. In spite of the great difference in size, and the greater number of elements in the word, it is in its connection just as much a single object as the single dot, and in spite of the fact that it is itself made up of letters, which in isolation are themselves objects, the word is as much a simple object as is any letter. This result is confirmed by the work on time of recognition first carried out by Cattell and repeated by Erdmann and Dodge. They all found that it took less time to recognise a word than a single letter, provided the word was short, and that words of eight letters were recognised as quickly as the separate letters.

There is a very similar set of facts in connection with auditory impressions. It was found that if a monotonous series of clicks were given in such rapid succession that counting was impossible, eight single sounds could be perceived in a single act of the attention. But if the sounds were rhythmically united into groups, either by varying the intensity of the external impression or by subjectively accenting some of the tones, it was possible to receive forty impressions in a single act of consciousness. That is, nearly as many rhythmical units could be noticed as single clicks. The combination into rhythmical groups renders the group a unit of the same kind as the single object.

These two groups of facts seem to show that what we

F

call the object, the simple existing thing, is not so much determined by its physical characteristics as by the use to which it is put and the attitude of mind at the time they are perceived. A thing may just as well be large as small, complex as simple. It is equally unitary at the moment of perception, no matter how many different elements go to make it up. It is as easy to recognise a landscape as any single grain of sand that contributes to some simple feature of the view. If aspects or attributes, sensations, or things, to speak metaphysically, psychologically, and popularly at once, have been used together, or have frequently come into consciousness at one time, they come to be regarded as a single object, they become isolated from everything else, and when they come to mind again they are treated as a unit. What determines the number and kind of elements that shall compose any object when there are several different combinations which can be made, is always the set of conditions that happens to be dominant in mind at that particular time. If the circumstances of the moment make the letter more important it will hold the chief place, will constitute the unit of perception at that time ; if on the other hand the word is adapted to the mental setting of the moment, then it becomes the object of the moment and the letters are not seen separately. The same statement holds of the landscape and its elements, for the picture and its details, for the locomotive and the minute oil-hole upon some insignificant part. What determines which shall be regarded as the object is in every case the mental attitude, not the physical mass which is offered to consciousness.

This line of argument brings us into conflict with the facts from which we started our argument, or at least with the bald statement that was made that it was possible to see four or five or eight single impressions at the same instant. From the present standpoint it would mean that there could be dominant in mind, without interfering with each other, four or five different mental settings, and that each was instrumental in bringing to mind some one of the objects, a conclusion which is plainly impossible if we are to abide by the results of our discussion of the conditions of the attention, and if accepted would alter our idea of the nature of attention itself. We are left then with the alternatives of regarding the process that results in the perception of the numerous objects either as the result of a series of successive attentions, or as the perception of a single object made up of a number of different parts, with which we have formed the habit of associating the numeral because of frequent counting. [27]

A study of the details of the experiments should permit us to decide between the two possible explanations. At the moment of perception there is either a group of homogeneous objects, a number of dots of the same kind, or there is a grouping of dissimilar things that can be thrown together as belonging to the same class, a number of letters that can be at least said to unite to form a mass of letters. In either case it would seem that the first perception is of a single object of many parts, but what is seen is the object, not the parts that go to make it up. The recognition of the parts takes place later as a result of analysis, and the analysis consists of nothing but a separate attention to each element.

That the counting should take place as the result of attention to the separate elements, and come after the first perception of the group as a unit, is made more probable from an examination of the time relations of perception in general. We know from experiments in reaction times that the process of recognition takes longer than the time necessary to give an impression of the objects to be seen. It must be true then that a part of the recognition process goes on after the impression has ceased to affect the retina. Recognition must be a result of the nervous processes of one kind and another which continue to run their course after the physical stimulus has disappeared. If these nervous processes can continue long enough to be recognised after the stimulus has ceased, there is no reason why they cannot also continue a sufficient time to permit a number of separate recognitions to go on. Introspection seems to bear out the same conclusion. The counting in many, if not in most cases, seems to go on after we have turned the eyes away from the screen, or after the objects are no longer exposed. It is the memory image or the after-image that is studied to obtain an idea of the number of objects, rather than the original impression. Everything seems to point to the conclusion that a separate act of the attention is required for the recognition or the counting of each separate dot, rather than that the whole process goes on in a single act of the attention. This, of course, excludes those simpler cases in which the grouping is familiar, and the word for the number comes up by immediate association as soon as the group enters mind.

What constitutes an object in the light of this discussion is not any definite amount or kind of external stimulus, but a collection of stimuli to which circumstances have compelled us to attend as a whole. A letter, a word, a group of dots in some particular arrangement, have been many times isolated and united by the attention, and so have acquired meaning as a unit, and it is that which makes them an object. The process of counting the objects consists in nothing else than in first receiving the large group as a whole, and then in going through the same process for each element whether it be large or small. The experiments which we have described prove not so much that we can attend to more than one object, defining object as we have, but that four or five things may fall upon the retina together, be recognised as a whole, and persist while we attend to and count each separately.

Hylan [²²] has confirmed this opinion experimentally since the above was written. He measured the duration of the memory after-image in a number of individuals, and measured the number of objects that could be perceived upon a single exposure. The results show that those individuals who had a longer persistence of the memory after-image were the ones who could see the greater number of objects with the brief exposure.

The fact that objects of greater complexity can be seen as easily as those of less complexity is the foundation for the word-method of teaching reading that has found so much favour in recent years. If the adult can perceive a word as easily and as quickly as a letter, it seems a waste of time for the child to spend his energy at first with the letters. It is a great saving of time and drudgery to make the word the unit from the first, and postpone the analysis into its elements until the words are acquired.

Corresponding to the problem of the number of objects to which attention may be given, is the question of the length of time that it is possible to attend to a single impression without flagging. That there are limits is a fact of daily observation. One cannot keep the attention directed to any line of work, however interesting or varied, without tiring and being compelled after a time to turn to something else. The length of time that one can apply oneself to these stronger impressions will of course vary with the individual, with his condition, and with the nature of the task. Its widest limits are marked by the length of the waking period of the day, and the time that can elapse before nourishment is required. There is no means of answering the question in this form. The truer test is how long one can attend to a single monotonous stimulation without losing it. When the student is engaged in studying even a single proposition the attention is constantly changing its direction and bringing out now one thing, now another. For stimuli of ordinary intensity there has been no investigation. It would probably offer a great many introspective difficulties, even if it were possible ever to reach a satisfactory result.

Much work has been done, however, on the limits of attention to very weak stimuli, with results that are interesting both in themselves and because of the light which they throw upon the general theory of attention. The first observations of the phenomenon were made by Urbant-schisch, a German specialist in diseases of the ear. While testing one of his patients for accuracy of hearing, he found that with no change in any of the physical relations of the sound, there seemed to come an alternate dying away and reappearance of the sounds, and that this alternation took place at fairly regular intervals. Similar experiments were set on foot in other senses, and it was found that there was a constant alternation in slight sensations from all sense organs. There was a constant reappearance and disappearance of the sensation no matter how strongly the attention was kept upon the stimulus. Many elaborate experiments were made upon the phenomena by Lange and others at Leipzig and by Münsterberg, and all with very much the same results. The period of the fluctuation varies from 3 to 25 seconds with different persons and under different conditions, but is very much the same for the same person under one set of conditions. It is slightly different for the different senses, but not very markedly.

These experiments can all be repeated with great ease by any one. If you will hold a watch at such a distance from the head that its ticking is just audible, it will be noted that for several seconds the sounds will be heard and that they will then disappear for a second or so. This appearance and disappearance will alternate with considerable regularity. For sight it is most satisfactory to use a rotating disc of sufficient rapidity to mix colours thoroughly. If on a white disc of this kind you will paste a bit of black paper that will give a just noticeable gray ring when revolved, it will be seen that the ring comes and goes in very much the same way as the ticking of the watch, and at about the same rate. A still simpler method that will often prove successful is to make a dot upon a bit of paper and move away from the paper to a distance so great that the dot will be barely visible. It will then be noticed that the image of the dot comes and goes as did the gray ring.

Any faint sensation will show the same alternations. A very light constant pressure, a weak electric current, or any other weak stimulus that suggests itself, may be used to advantage.

The same rhythmic alternation shows itself when, under any circumstances, two nearly equal stimuli of different qualities which will not combine are applied at the same time to the same sense organ. One good instance of this has already been noted in an earlier chapter in connection with the experiments of Dr. Breese on retinal rivalry. The alternations between the colours presented to either eye go on at much the same rate, and are undoubtedly due to the same conditions as the coming and going of the faint stimulus. Dr. Breese found also that there would be a similar fluctuation if by means of mirrors two colours were thrown upon the same retinal area at the same time. Lange also found that if a prism were drawn in ambiguous perspective so that it might be interpreted to be either concave or convex, it would be found that the two interpretations would succeed each other at regular intervals as soon as both became equally familiar. The rate of fluctuation, again, is not so very different from that of the same individual for the minimal stimuli or for retinal rivalry. Memory images undergo the same change. If you will think intently of some simple stimulus, it will be seen that it does not remain permanently before the mind, but comes and goes rhythmically in a way similar in every respect to the changes shown by the weak sensation.

Of much greater interest than the facts themselves are the interpretations that the different investigators have put upon them. These theories fall into three distinct classes : the theory (1) that the fluctuations are due to fatigue of the muscular mechanism of the sense organ or of the central nervous system, (2) that we have to do with a rhythmic activity of some special mental function like the attention or apperception, and (3) that there is a transfer in some way of the rhythms of circulation or respiration to the activity of the central nervous system. There are different subdivisions of each theory, and in some cases there has been an attempt to combine several theories in one.

1. There are three forms of the fatigue theory. The oldest of these makes the fluctuation depend upon the fatigue and recovery of the muscle of accommodation in the eye, and of the *tensor tympani* in the ear. This was first proposed by Münsterberg, and was later supported by Heinrich. The second form of the theory is that it is the nerve itself that is fatigued, and the third is that the fatigue has its seat in the sensory cells of the cortex. This is the explanation offered by Professor Titchener. The first two forms of the theory may be disposed of very quickly. Experiments by Pace have shown that the fluctuations continue even after the muscle of accommodation has been deadened by homatropine. Dr. Slaughter experimented on a man who had had cataracts and had had the lenses removed, and found that the fluctuations still continued as in the normal person. In neither of these cases could there have been fatigue of the muscle of accommodation, and in the last case there was no chance for fatigue of convergence to play a part, as only one eye was used. Eye movements of sufficient size and regularity to affect the results would easily be observed. Moreover Münsterberg himself has shown that the fluctuations go on unchanged except in rate during voluntary eye movements. Thus it seems improbable that involuntary movements would have a different effect. And if eye movements were held to account for the change there would be no reason for stimuli of greater intensity not showing the same phenomena. The muscles of the ear, as we have seen, probably play no part in the accommodation process, and we should therefore hardly expect fatigue to play any part in explaining the fluctuation in the auditory stimulus, even if Urbantschisch had not already shown, before Münsterberg wrote, that a patient without the tympanum could still notice the fluc-

tuations. On the skin the muscles play so small a part in the perception that it would not be possible to explain the fluctuations by them. The theory of fatigue of the sensory apparatus then seems to be absolutely untenable.

The theory of Urbantschisch that the fluctuation is the result of recurrent fatigue of the sensory nerve is not in harmony with the results of modern nerve-muscle physiology. There is no evidence that a nerve fibre is ever fatigued, or at least the fatigue comes on so slowly that it is of no value in explaining the phenomenon in question. A discussion of the part to be assigned to fatigue of the central cells can best be understood if taken in connection with a later theory.

2. The theory that the fluctuations are the result of the periodic functioning of the attention, of apperception, or of some other mental function, is in effect but a restatement of the facts in terms of a more unknown process, and in no sense an explanation. The observations which Lange made in connection with his theory, and which in part led him to formulate it, are of some value for the general explanation. These are in general the fact that a figure in ambiguous perspective seems to change its outline in connection with a regular alternation of the accompanying ideas in mind. Just before the convex pyramid becomes concave there is a change in the dominant idea from a support or weight to a receptacle of some kind, or if the object drawn in ambiguous perspective is a flight of stairs the ideas would change from thinking of walking upon them to an idea of some kind of shelter from the rain. His theory was that there was a periodic change in the ideas, and that this periodicity resulted in the corresponding change in the interpretation of the drawing. Later he came to speak of it as due to a periodic functioning of apperception. This is of course nothing more than a verbal expression for the fact that there is a rhythm in the perception. As we have seen, nothing is known of a force which could be subject to a change of this kind. The

facts are equally well explained on the assumption that there is a periodic fatigue and recovery of the nerve cells which reinforces one interpretation or the other. When the cells that have made for the interpretation of the figure as convex are fatigued, their activity is cancelled by the action of the cells that turn the interpretation to make the figure concave. These two sets of cells, as first one, then the other, is fatigued and recovers, are sufficient to decide between the two interpretations equally favoured by the objective conditions. At the same time, however, there is undoubtedly a corresponding fatigue in the cells which are actually involved in the sensation or perception. From this simple physiological point of view the theory of Lange and the theory of Professor Titchener become practically identical.

Eckener suggested the theory that there are two kinds of fluctuations of the attention, one objective, the other subjective ; but later authorities seem not to accept the distinction as valid. Dr. Hylan recently revived the theory and attempted to prove that the objective fluctuations were due to the fatigue of the mechanism of accommodation, the other to some central change. His only ground for the assumption is that during the time that the minimal stimulus cannot be perceived, it is still possible to imagine the corresponding sensation. This he thinks shows that the central cells are capable of receiving the impression when the stimulus is imperceptible. A very slight examination shows the flimsy character of the argument. We must of course assume that the central cells would respond to an impression of moderate intensity during their period of least sensitiveness, and it is apparent from daily experience that it is possible for the central stimuli from association to excite the cells more strongly than the minimal excitation from the external world. In that case a memory image would occur during the time that the cells were too exhausted for an external stimulus of such small intensity to be perceived at all.

But there is still needed to complete the explanation some factor that will account for the regularity of the fluctuation. It does not seem probable that a cell would of itself grow fatigued and recover with such constancy. The suggestion of Exner, Roy and Sherrington, and Patrizi, confirmed by the experiments of Dr. Slaughter, fill this gap. These distinguished physiologists suggested independently that attention waves are probably connected with Traube-Hering waves. Dr. Slaughter found as the result of a number of experiments that the alternations were correlated with changes in circulation and respiration. The most frequent rate of fluctuation he found to run parallel with a rhythmic increase and decrease of the volume of the finger. This change in volume is produced by the contraction and relaxation of the muscles in the walls of the arteries. It is controlled again by the rhythmic action of a centre in the medulla, as was shown conclusively by the discoverers, Traube and Hering. These Traube-Hering waves run through a complete cycle in from 6 to 15 seconds, but in a time of mental strain, as during the period of concentration required to mark the fluctuations, their rate is kept pretty constantly at the shorter period. This corresponds very closely to the time given by most investigators as the average length of the attention wave. Mr. Taylor rendered the explanation even more probable by showing that the waves change their rate when the organism is affected by various kinds of stimuli, in very much the same way that the respiration and pulse rates do. So, if while watching the gray rings on a disc the subject is stimulated by an electric current, there will be either an increase or a decrease in the period of fluctuation depending upon the intensity of the stimulus. Muscular exertion, strong odours, and even mental excitement, have the same effect. Dr. Breese, in the work mentioned above on retinal rivalry, found that the rate of change in the alternation was influenced by the intensity of the illumination of the fields and by the contraction of muscles in different parts of the body, but he did not offer any explanation for the phenomenon. Further confirmation of this theory is offered by Mr. Galloway's results that the length of the Traube-Hering waves is always increased by sensory stimulation in subjects whose attention waves are also lengthened. He also finds that in three individuals the average length of attention and vaso-motor waves is almost identical. [14] All these results serve to make more plausible the theory that the fluctuations are closely connected with the vaso-motor rhythm.

Lehmann had already shown that the waves were closely related to the changes in respiration. In an investigation of the relation he found that the great majority of changes in the perception, whether towards appearance or disappearance, took place in a particular phase of the respiratory process—at the beginning of inspiration. There was, however, no relation between the length of the two rhythms. Mr. Taylor confirmed Lehmann's results in this regard, and Dr. Slaughter discovered one subject whose attention waves were of the same length as the respiratory cycle. It would seem then that the breathing rhythm takes the place of the Traube-Hering wave in some individuals, and that in the others it has an influence in determining the place of change by prolonging the time of perceptibility during the active part of the respiratory process after the effect of the longer wave has disappeared.

Both Dr. Slaughter and Mr. Taylor found indications of a still longer wave also correlated with a longer circulatory rhythm of unknown origin. In one person this became the predominant element, and determined the length of the attention wave as a whole ; in most persons, however, it showed itself only in a rhythmical increase and decrease of the primary wave, the mental correlate of the Traube-Hering wave. The length of this wave is approximately 25 seconds, and is probably identical with the longest of the waves mentioned in the literature of the earlier period of investigation. Dr. Bonser has confirmed the relation between the Traube-Hering and the attention waves. [²]

If we can feel assured of the fact of a close relation in time between these physiological rhythms and the attention waves, there is yet to be faced the problem of the explanation of the facts and of bringing them into harmony with the well-established parts of the other theories. Probably it is simplest to think of the physiological rhythms as merely marking off the temporal relations of the fluctuations, while the variations themselves are due to fatigue of the cells involved in the sensation, either as the correlate of the sensation itself or of the reinforcing influence. We might think of the cases of attention to a minimal stimulus as due entirely to some reinforcing influence from the cells of the medulla, that when the reinforcement was strongest it was possible to perceive more accurately than when it was weakest ; but when we consider the cases of retinal rivalry, and of the alteration in the interpretation of a figure drawn in ambiguous perspective, it is evident that this will not suffice. There is no reason to assume that one set of nerve cells, whether those correlated with the sensation itself or with related ideas, will be subject to the reinforcement and not the other ; and there is no reason why one should be weak while the other is strong, and vice versa. If, however, it is a fatigue process, the first set of cells involved would become fatigued during the first period, and would be overcome in their influence by the fresh cells that were in every respect as ready to be thrown into excitation as the first. That the substitution should come in the same rhythm as the physiological process would be due merely to the fact that the sudden decrease in the reinforcing process would still further increase the effect of fatigue. The fatigue plus the decrease in the reinforcement are together sufficient to give the rested cells an advantage. Here the physiological rhythm would be the influence that gives regularity to the fluctuation. It is but one element in the total complex of determining factors.

We can bring the apparently simpler case under the same head if we think of the minimal stimulus as one of the opposed members of the pair, and all of the other stimuli that are possible objects of the attention as the opposing member. The fresh cells that should replace those fatigued during the attending to the gray ring, would be those that were appealed to by any objective or subjective stimulus, not some particular one. This, too, would then be a case of alternate fatigue and recovery in cortical cells, and the physiological rhythm would be but the agent in determining the rate of change.

There are again two ways in which it is possible to think of the activity of the vaso-motor centre as influencing the central nerve cells. The first suggestion would be that there was an increase in the activity of the cells when the cerebral blood-vessels were in one state of relaxation or contraction, and a decrease in the activity when the blood vessels were in the opposite phase. There are several objections to this view from a consideration of the general physiological principles known to be involved. In the first place, it is regarded as doubtful if the nerve cell would be so quickly affected by change in the blood about it. Probably at the lowest stage of blood supply there is a sufficient amount to permit the cell to be completely nourished, and any increase would be in excess of the demands. A fuller discussion of the objections to a theory of this kind must be given in a later chapter in connection with the circulatory theory of attention in general. We shall be satisfied here with the statement that there are grave doubts as to the validity of the theory in terms of blood supply, and proceed to discuss the other explanation.

The second explanation is in terms of the spread of nervous activity from the cells in the vaso-motor centre in the medulla to the central nerve cells as a whole. The picture of the spread of activity must be developed in detail later, but we may look upon it for the present as of very much the same kind as the spread of energy from one motor cell to another. It is found in general that if two groups of muscles are excited both will respond more vigorously than if either alone is excited. A greater pressure can be exerted upon a dynamometer, even if held in one hand, if the other hand is contracted at the same time with the one which holds the instrument. There is similar reinforcement in case any other muscle is contracted. More closely related to the phenomenon in question is the effect that the vaso - motor rhythm exerts upon the heart rate. It is found that the rapidity of the pulse increases and decreases at regular intervals in time with the Traube-Hering waves. This effect can only be explained in terms of an overflow from the vaso-motor centre upon the centre that controls the heart rate — the vagus centre. The respiratory impulse spreads to the heart centre in the same way, and also to the vaso-motor centre. To assume that there is a similar overflow to the cells of the cortex is but to extend the explanation in degree, not to change the principle.

A complete theory of the attention waves then would involve three of those given above. A fatigue of the cortical cells that are the accompaniments of the sensations themselves, a fatigue of the reinforcing cortical cells which correspond to the ideas which Lange found to precede the change in the fluctuations in the interpretation of figures drawn in ambiguous perspective, and finally the physiological rhythms which originate in the circulatory and respiratory centres in the medulla. No one alone is sufficient, but all taken together seem to furnish an explanation for nearly all the points which the experiments cover.

Recently Hammer and Ferree have suggested that the visual attention wave is to be explained in terms of retinal adaptation coupled with eye movement : that the retina becomes exhausted during steady fixation, and the impression is brought back by slight eye movements. The weak points in the suggestions are : (1) that the attention waves are found where the object fixated is too small to be constantly fixated, if we accept the results of McAllister that the eye is continually making movements of several angular minutes ; (2) that there is no reason why eye movements should occur with the regularity that attention waves show.

Hammer also asserts that with sounds of constant intensity the auditory waves are not present. This, however, is contradictory to the results of other investigators with equal control of sound intensity, as Dunlap, Seashore, and Jackson, and observers in my own laboratory.

Heinrich and a pupil have brought forward additional proof of the Münsterberg peripheral fatigue theory. For sounds Heinrich finds that noises fluctuate, tones do not. This he would explain on the assumption referred to in Chapter II, that the *tensor-tympani* accommodates for noises, not for pure tones. Ostmann, however, found that intense sounds alone produce changes in the muscle, and the lower limit of response is far higher than would be necessary to justify Heinrich's theory. Visual fluctuations seem, according to Heinrich's results, to correspond to changes in the lens.

All the explanations of these later observers are inconsistent in ways that the authors have not considered with results previously obtained. While, then, one must admit that the question is still open to dispute, there seems no reason to assume that these fluctuations are not central, as the earlier experimenters demonstrated them to be.

There are two other effects of attention upon the temporal aspects of consciousness which need to be considered briefly. In the first place, attention seems to hasten the entrance into mind of the idea attended to. The classical experiments in this connection were performed by Wundt, and were later repeated by Professor Angell and Dr. Pierce. In outline these consisted in comparing the time at which a single impression entered consciousness from one sense with the entrance of some one of a series of impressions received through another sense. Usually the concrete experiment has been to decide where a moving pointer stands upon a dial when a sound is heard. It is found that by attending to the sound it is possible to hasten its entrance by from ·020 to ·060 seconds, while attention to the dial and pointer delays the entrance of the sound, and hastens the entrance of the visual impression. The results were also modified by the rate at which the different sounds succeed each other, by the number of impressions that were given at once, and by the senses that are used in the comparison. All of these circumstances may be thought to have an effect through their influence in determining the ease and accuracy with which we can attend to the stimuli.

The influence was one of those which played a part in the personal equation of the astronomer in the old method of taking the transit of a star by the eye-and-ear-method. The astronomer watched for the passage of the star across the wire of his telescope, and at the same time tried to determine the relation of the observation to the strokes of a bell that marked the seconds. Each observer developed a peculiar habit of attending during the process, one chiefly to the visual impression, the other mainly to the sounds of the bell, and each obtained correspondingly different results. The differences were great enough to lead to confusion in the observation, and finally brought about the abandonment of the method and the substitution of a registration method which makes the personal error more constant, and more nearly alike for all observers.

The small difference that is shown always to be present by the experimental method corresponds very closely to the fact that we all notice very frequently in daily life that a sensation not attended to comes to mind very slowly. So frequently when working we will rouse ourselves to remember that the clock has struck some time ago. In a case of this kind the sound has often been kept from consciousness for several minutes by the fact that the attention was already engrossed by some other matter. All

G

the physical and physiological conditions for the entrance
to consciousness, other than those involved in attention,
have been completed, as is shown by the persistence of the
impression below the threshold for such a long period and
its final entrance into mind.

Another effect of the attention that deserves mention
is its influence upon the rapidity of movements. It has
been found that the reaction time is considerably shortened
when the attention is complete, as compared with a period
of relaxed attention. Professor Cattell found that there
was a difference of from two to three hundredths of a second
between the length of a simple reaction when the attention
was voluntarily relaxed and when voluntarily strained
upon the stimulus to which the reaction was to be made.
In the same way any stimulus that distracts the attention
has a very marked influence upon the time of the reaction.
An irrelevant noise at the moment that the reaction was
to be made might increase the time of the reaction by eight
hundredths of a second.

Another experiment of similar import has reference to
the preparation of the attention. It is found that unless
the attention is aroused by a suitable signal, given about
two seconds before the stimulus that is to call out the reaction, that the movement does not reach its maximum
quickness. The signal gives the highest degree of adaptation of the attention, and so is but a sub-head under the
preceding. It is also significant that the period by which
the signal must precede the stimulus is nearly half of the
length of an attention wave, so that part of the adaptation may consist in the time it takes for the attention to
rise to its highest point.

SUMMARY

1. The number of separate objects that can be attended to is four or five for vision, five to eight for audition. But probably this result is to be interpreted to mean that the result of a single glance persists long enough for four or five acts of attention to take place.

2. The duration of a single act of attention is from 3 to 24 seconds ; most usually 5 to 8 seconds.

3. These fluctuations of the attention are to be explained in part by the fatigue of cortical cells ; in part, so far as the length is concerned, by the overflow of the rhythms of the respiratory and vaso-motor centres of the medulla upon the cortical cells.

4. Attention increases the quickness of entrance of a sensation to consciousness, and shortens the reaction time.

CHAPTER VI

THE METHODS OF MEASURING ATTENTION

IN recent years many attempts have been made to find ways of comparing the mental capacities of individuals. The ultimate end of the attempts has usually been practical in its character. Education and psychiatry, as well as many more immediately practical fields, would be much benefited were it possible accurately to measure the attainments and capacities of individuals in advance of actual trials, or even to draw a sharp line between the normal and the abnormal. Obviously, if one could by a series of tests decide in the psychological laboratory what children were capable of profiting by different kinds of training, select men for the various employments of life, and say for legal purposes what men should be confined in asylums, psychology would become a practically important science. While the advance that has been made is not yet remarkable enough to justify the assertion that we are near the goal, it may be worth while to consider the results so far as they concern attention. For attention, as one of the central mental processes, has shared to a considerable extent in the lists of tests.

There are two great difficulties in the way of selecting tests for attention. The first is that it is almost impossible to discover tests that shall give the basal capacity for attention, rather than some special facility that has been acquired through training. In the second place, it is almost impossible to find a test that shall not in part depend upon other capacities—upon the acuteness of the sense organ, upon

84

the retentiveness of memory, quickness of motor response, or some other extraneous capacity—that really accounts for the difference between individuals, which on the gross result of the test we should be inclined to attribute to the attention. There can be no certain method of differentiating the two processes involved.

Tests of attention may be divided into three groups. One sort of test would measure the adequacy of attention directly in terms of the amount of accomplishment in some task that involves attention in as high degree as possible. A second makes some secondary change in the course of the operation stand as a measure of attention. So, for example, the fluctuations of the minimal stimuli or stimulus differences, and the variability in the performance from moment to moment, have been used in this connection. The third general group would make the breaking strain, or the amount of stimulus that is necessary to distract attention, the gauge of the strength of attention. Each of these may again be divided into sub-classes, in so far as they are adapted now to the determination of the capacity for attention over long intervals, and now to brief acts of attending, or to pulses of attention.

1. The more important tests of the first class that have been used are the discrimination of two points on the skin, reaction times, memory span, the time, accuracy and number of observations necessary for copying figures, letters and geometrical patterns, counting dots, marking the letters of one kind in a page of a foreign language or printer's " pie," and filling out omissions in a discourse. Each of these tests is open in some degree to both of the objections that were mentioned above. Perhaps the most complete test that has been made of them is by Binet. [1]

Binet chose for his subjects eleven school children, who had been divided by their master into five bright and six dull. It was assumed that the intelligent children would have greater powers of attending than dull, and that the degree with which the results of the experiments harmonised with that assumption could be regarded as significant of the value of the test. If we run through each of the tests, partly with reference to his results and partly to a priori considerations, it will be seen that each is open to the objections mentioned above. The accuracy of discriminating two points upon the skin is open to both objections. It is known that the points just noticeable as two are at shorter distances after practice than before, and also that the accuracy varies from individual to individual, and in places very close together in the same individual, merely because of the distribution of the sensory nerve endings. As a measure of fatigue it has been found entirely unsatisfactory by recent workers, and it is highly probable that attention must be subject to fatigue in high degree. Binet found this " limen of twoness " [1] one of his most significant tests, but only, it must be confessed, in the earlier experiments of the series. With practice bright and dull pupils became very much alike. The differences disappeared at the third set of measurements. [2]

Very much the same assertions must be made of reaction times. As we have seen, in any given individual, reaction times are shorter when close attention is given, but apparently any individual is capable of attending to so practical a process as the reaction in sufficient degree to give his maximum rate of response. Then, too, natural motor quickness undoubtedly cuts across the influence of attention, and it is difficult to say that any difference may not be due to that rather than to attention. Reaction times, again, are subject to training very markedly, and while perhaps few individuals are specifically trained in them, it is not yet demonstrated that training in neighbouring fields might not have sufficient influence to destroy the significance of the result. The theoretical refutation is not necessary, as both Binet and Whipple [3] have found in practice that simple reaction times are not significant. The more complicated forms of reaction times, choice and association times, are more significant in showing mental differences, but the processes involved get farther and farther away from attention as they become more complicated. They involve, it is true, related processes, but the thing measured would not be identical with what was measured in the other tests.

The memory span again depends in part upon attention, but it also depends in part upon native retentiveness, and one could not say what was due to one, what to the other, in any given result. The copying test in its various forms is in part dependent upon memory, and is still further influenced by special training in attending to one thing rather than to another. The artist copies much more quickly than the layman because he has been trained to *see* as well as because he has been trained to *do*. The method of counting dots was significant at first for Binet, but was found to be very closely related to training. As a result the unintelligent did as well as the intelligent after a very brief period of practice. Chance training in this test then could obscure any defect of attention that might be present. The Ebinghaus method of filling in omissions in connected discourse has proved successful as a measure of fatigue and of intelligence in general, but it is too little dependent upon attention in any strict sense to be considered in any detail here. The detection of the omissions could be regarded as a function of attention; the process of supplementation, however, would involve more general, if related, processes of understanding what was intended and association processes in supplying the omitted words.

Perhaps the most satisfactory method of all that come under this head, is the marking of the " a's " on a page of print. It has been used frequently with satisfactory results, and is open to few theoretical objections. There is more dependence upon the quickness and certainty of noticing the sensory elements relatively to the extraneous motor and other processes ; it is dependent on an activity that is relatively rarely subjected to special training, and such general training, from reading, e.g., as is beneficial, is practically universal and equally common to all. The only extraneous element that is important is motor quickness, and this plays a much smaller part relatively here than do the disturbing and variable factors in the other tests.

This list does not, of course, exhaust the possible tests. Any operation that can be subjected to measurement is certain to involve attention in some degree, and so might be regarded as a measure. Any of the usual Weber's law experiments might be used, as might any of the other memory experiments. The tests that have been mentioned are those that have been used most frequently.

2. Of the second group Wiersma, Heymans, and the author have made use of the attention wave as a measure of fatigue, in a way that should also show variations in the capacity for attention. The ratio of the period of visibility to the period of invisibility was taken as a measure of perceptive capacity, and it was found that this varied with the state of rest or fatigue of the subject and his general mental condition. It would probably be an accurate indication of the general adequacy of attention, apart from any special training. This is particularly probable in view of the fact proved by Marbe, confirmed by Wiersma, that the ratio increased with increase in the intensity of external stimulus. The disadvantage of the method is that you cannot compare one individual with another with any degree of certainty. The ratio of the periods would vary so much with the acuteness of sense organs that any influence of attention would be lost in the other variation. Perhaps a truer test would be the amount of distracting stimulus that would bring about a decrease in the ratio of visibility to the total time. It will be remembered from the discussion of attention waves in an earlier chapter, that the time of visibility was first increased and then diminished by any extraneous stimulus. Moderate stimuli ordinarily increase the period ; stronger stimuli decrease it. The strength

of the exciting stimulus that could be endured without producing a decrease in the period of visibility might serve as a measure of the capacity of the individual to attend against distraction which is at least one form of effectiveness in attention, if not the same capacity that has been measured by the methods discussed above.

Another method, related to the preceding in so far as it uses a variation in the continuous accomplishment as the measure of attention, has been suggested by Oehrn. [4] It is that we use the mean variation, the average departure from the average accomplishment, as a measure of the degree of attending. If we make any series of measurements under the same objective conditions, it will be found that no two are exactly alike, and in one series the variations from the average will be large, in another small. Since the objective conditions are alike, the variation must be in the subjective factors, most important of which is attention. The mean variation would then indicate variation in degree of attention, and since that is assumed to be variation from a maximum, it follows that the mean variation indicates the degree of attention during the series. The results of any experiment whatever, properly interpreted, would furnish a measure of attention. There are probably other factors involved in the variation than attention, and it is by no means certain that the greatest variation would come with least attention, but it is a measure that is promising for further testing.

3. The third form of test was first suggested by Kraepelin, [5] although independently by Külpe, and was tested by the latter, Münsterberg, and Miss Hamlin, having already been experimented upon by Bertels, at the suggestion of Kraepelin. The method was suggested to Kraepelin by the fact that what most clearly marked off the insane from the sane was the ease of distractibility. They cannot long be held to any one thing. Effective attention, on the contrary, is marked by ability to attend in spite of difficulties. Kraepelin suggested then that if one could

measure the amount of stimulus necessary to distract from a task of any kind, we would know how much attention was being given to the operation. The suggestion was seconded by Külpe, and practically tested by himself, Münsterberg, Miss Hamlin, Mr. Moyer, and Miss Birch. All used as the primary task comparison of two liminal stimuli, and as distracting stimulus mental computation, counting the strokes of a metronome, or identifying odours. In each of the investigations the primary operation required but an instant of concentrated attention, and as a consequence it was found to be performed in some interval of the distracting process. The only exception was in some experiments of Miss Birch, where the attention demanded by the recognition of odours was sufficiently absorbing to prevent noticing one or the other of the two stimuli to be compared. In the other experiments the distraction served rather to increase the attention given momentarily to the comparison, and the experiments failed of their purpose. Miss Sharp [6] applied the method to experiments that should produce continuous distraction, and with satisfactory results. It was found that if one attempted to read aloud, and at the same time write " a " or the alphabet, there was a considerable loss of time as compared with the time required for reading alone, and that the more complicated operations delayed the reading more than the simple. In each of the actual investigations that have been carried out there has been failure to comply strictly with the conditions that Kraepelin set. In no one of them were the subjects working with full attention to one task alone, to be distracted in part by some extraneous stimulus that should draw him against his will. In each, on the contrary, there is merely an attempt to attend to two things at the same time, each of which is known in advance by the subject. It is a problem in the distribution of attention rather than in distraction, and it is known that attention can be distributed successively only, not simultaneously. Probably, however, as Stern [7] has pointed out, it would be very difficult to realise Kraepelin's conditions that the object attended to should be the only thing the observer was prepared for, and the distracting stimulus should always come unexpectedly and unwillingly. At best, the distracting stimulus could be given but rarely under those circumstances, if the observer is not to suspect it is really a part of the experiment and become prepared for it as one part of the regular task.

And even were all of these difficulties overcome, it would be no easy matter to measure the amount of distraction that could be attributed to the stimulus. This would not depend altogether upon the physical intensity, but must vary from individual to individual with the amount of interest that the process could excite. Probably, after long practice, it would be possible to arrange stimuli in the order of their distracting effect for one individual, but the series must be worked out anew for each individual, and this before the experiments on measuring attention could be begun. When the preliminaries were out of the way, there would already have been determined one set of values for attention, and the distraction method would be needed to answer but one small part of the problem. The value of the distraction would depend upon the way the stimulus attracted attention. One must therefore measure attention before the distraction values can be determined. It would probably be almost as satisfactory to make the test by the first direct method and very much quicker.

Each of the three methods is still in a tentative, experimental stage. There is no one of them that does not require extended use before it can be asserted that it is applicable, or if applicable how satisfactory it may prove. Before much can be accomplished it will probably be necessary to work out a long series of comparisons between different methods, so that results obtained by one method may be comparable with those obtained in others. Attention, in fact, is a word that covers so many different processes that no single test will probably ever be devised that shall measure all the part processes satisfactorily. Now we mean capacity for attending in general without reference to any single content, which may not exist at all. Again, we may mean capacity for long continued attention under difficulties, and we may mean ability for accurate observation in some one field, or even a determination of the field in which the individual as he is at any one time can attend most easily and effectively. Tests of any one of these capacities might be called tests of attention, and yet a test for one would throw very little light upon any other. One cannot say that any one is more valuable than any other, to say nothing of asserting that one measures attention and the other does not. The tests that have been developed do not distinguish between these different phases, and have not been adapted one to one phase, another to another.

If we may be permitted to suggest tests on a priori grounds, with the full consciousness that any suggestion must be tried time and time again before one can be at all certain of its value, some such distribution as the following may prevent our coming to an entirely negative conclusion. Ability to attend against odds might be measured roughly by one of the distraction methods, or perhaps more easily by the method of recording attention waves and noting when the period of visibility was diminished by an extraneous stimulus. The capacity for attention due to training would require a test of ability to notice some element of a complex that was perceivable with difficulty, and the test would needs be different for each province of perception to be measured. The most general of these tests is apparently marking some one letter or letters, preferably on a page of some unfamiliar language. Natural acquired interest could be tested by presenting a large assortment of objects, and requesting the subject to select those that were first noticed. A very similar test in a related field is to ask the individual to describe what is seen in an ink blot, or to draw the first figure that comes to mind by Royce's method. Capacity for attention in general as inherited, and not in any way due to training, probably could not be analysed from the complex. The nearest approximation could perhaps be given by averaging a number of tests in which the individuals had been as little trained as possible. A thorough test in all of these respects would, of course, give a measure not alone of attention, but of general intelligence and capacity as well, a conclusion that harmonises with the far-reaching relations of attention discovered on the theoretical side.

SUMMARY

Measures of attention may be divided into three groups : direct, by means of accomplishments in some operation or other ; indirect, by fluctuations of attention or by the mean variation in a set of measurements ; and by the amount of stimulus necessary for distraction.

No one of the methods is altogether satisfactory, and no two measure the same capacity.

Taken together they aid in giving a knowledge of the capacity of an individual, but they all need further investigation and comparison one with another before they can be regarded as satisfactory.

CHAPTER VII

ATTENTION AND IDEAS

ATTENTION is effective not only in determining what sensations shall come into consciousness, but it also has an effect in controlling the course of sensations once in mind upon their return to consciousness. We have to deal not merely with the sensorial attention, but also with intellectual attention, to use the somewhat objectionable terms of the older psychology. By intellectual in this connection, however, we mean to indicate no higher or more important form of mental processes, but merely to designate those which come to mind without external stimulation, but in accordance with purely mental laws. They include the fundamental processes of memory and imagination, and in fact all processes other than perception.

That attention does play a considerable part in controlling the course of these processes is evident from the simplest observations of our daily life. We very often catch ourselves studying the field of thought in much the same way that we study a landscape, or the field of sensation. There is the same apparent running the mental eye over some scene that was real years ago, the same series of strain sensations, the same successive coming into clear consciousness of one feature after another that is so familiar in the so-called sensorial attention. All these facts, then, point to an identity with, or at least some relation to, the phases of attention that we have already considered, and suggest that it may be possible to bring the centrally excited ideas into close connection with the simple perceptions.

We must, in beginning the work, undertake an examination of the nature of the raw material of the ideas, and attempt to determine the conditions which govern their entrance. While we could in a large measure take for granted the action of the external objects upon the nervous system, and start with the sensation as already in mind, it is not so easy to assume an immediate knowledge of the way in which impressions once vanished return to consciousness. There is a greater difference between the popular and the scientific conception of the matter, and also, be it confessed, a greater variety of opinion among scientists.

The treatment of centrally aroused ideas is rendered easier by the present day assumption that memory images and the original sensation are of precisely the same character. The memory of the face of a friend seen years ago is of precisely the same kind as the visual impression of the face. Our mental image of the old homestead is not different in outline or colouring from the perception of our childhood, and what variations there are in details are only sufficient to prevent confusion between memories and perceptions. In fact, recent work by Professor Külpe [2] proves that centrally excited sensations are very easily confused with peripherally excited at slight degrees of intensity. Trained psychologists, in many instances, could not decide correctly whether to call faint sensations from the eye or skin real impressions or imaginations. A decision could be made only on the basis of secondary characteristics, such as the stability of the impression or the after-image which is left. We seem to be justified in calling the elements of both memory image and perception, sensations, as Külpe has suggested.

It would render our statement much stronger if we could affirm positively that the same cortical cells were involved in memory as in perception. A decision in regard to this point would seem to depend largely upon an interpretation of pathological cases. If we could find patients suffering from loss of memories of a certain kind, and still capable of perceptions from the same sense organ, we would probably have to grant that there were separate memory centres ; if, on the other hand, memory and perception disappeared together in every instance, we could assume that memory was merely the re-excitation of the parts of the cortex originally excited in perception. Unfortunately, however, there is so little agreement as to the meaning of observed phenomena, that we cannot say that either opinion is generally held. The patients are usually very little skilled in introspection, and so are often incapable of deciding whether they remember the object in terms of the same sense which is affected in perception or not. It is perfectly possible that a man who has lost his visual sensations through injury of the visual area of the cortex could remember the objects once seen by means of the words they had previously suggested, or from the tactual sensations which had been received from them, and still be incapable of seeing them. Unless accustomed to studying his mental imagery, he would not notice the change in the material of his ideas, and might very easily assert that he could picture the object to himself as well as ever.

In the light of so much uncertainty in the pathological evidence, it would seem that we are justified in looking to the facts of normal life in deciding the question. One consideration appears so be decisive. That is the close connection which must exist between the area which receives the sensation and all other sensory areas, including even the memory centre, if we assume that it exists. We never have a sensory impression that is not connected with very many returned sensations. This we shall see in detail in the next chapter, and may take for granted now on the basis of a few simple facts in perception. When you feel an object in the dark you do not merely feel it, but also have a mass of impressions from vision which are called up, and which make the impression what it is. You see with the mind's eye before you feel assured of the real nature of the impression. When you hear a dog bark at a distance, you again have a picture of the dog at the time the impression is received. And so, in general, any impression that is received does not come in alone, but has connected with it a mass of remembered impressions which give it a great part of the form and content, which change it from a mere sensation to an object. You cannot, then, separate the sensation of peripheral origin from the centrally aroused sensation, and it is very difficult to decide how much is mere sensation and how much is memory image in any given case. And similarly you cannot cut the memory image off from the sensation. If there is a different area at the basis of the memory, it must at least be excited simultaneously with the sensory area, or there would be no possibility of its re-excitation at the time of recall. But if both the memory area and the sensory area are in activity when the sensation is received, who can say which is responsible for the sensation ? Both centres must be involved in perceiving as well as in remembering, and this indissolubility in function constitutes unity in the only meaning that can be given to the term. The close connection between the memory image and the perception compels us to assume a constancy of interaction between the corresponding cortical areas that, in practice at least, makes them indistinguishable.

If, then, centrally and peripherally aroused sensations are of the same nature, and are due to the excitation of the same cortical cells, the only important difference would lie in the way in which they are brought to consciousness. We may, in fact, think of remembering as merely a second excitation of the nervous elements originally involved in the sensation.

The second activity can be said to be an expression of the general biological law that any tissue will do more easily later whatever has once been performed. The only difficulty which remains, then, is to determine the conditions which lead to the renewed activity.

Assuming as our starting-point that we are dealing with a process of exactly the same kind as in the preceding chapters, our first problem is to consider the way in which the raw material of memory comes to consciousness, the laws of entrance of the centrally excited sensation, and the ways in which its entrance may be influenced by the attention. The centrally excited sensations, like the peripheral, have their primary origin in the senses, come in from the external world ; but their return demands a new set of conditions distinct from those that lead to the entrance of the original sensations. The laws which determine the entrance of the stored impressions, and which correspond to the laws of the physical world for the original sensations, are known as the laws of association. Just as the external world offers an immense number of impressions to the mind from which certain elements are selected by the attention, so association may be said to offer the mind numbers of re-entering impressions from which the attention must select. In each case the raw material is offered by mechanical laws, and from the raw material selection is made before the impression really enters mind. But before we can understand the effect of the attention, we must turn to a study of the way in which these impressions are brought back.

The primary fact upon which all explanations of the re-entrance of ideas is based, is that when a connection has once been made between sensory processes it tends to persist throughout the lifetime of the individual. Just as we saw above that each impression upon a sensory cell seems to modify the cell in such a way that there is a tendency for the cell to act in the same way again, so when two cells have been active together, or in immediate succession, there is left a tendency for one cell to become active again whenever the other is excited to activity. There are, of course, some complications which must be considered, but this is the fundamental fact, and all others are modifications of it. On the mental side, where we can observe the process directly, we find that any sensation is constantly calling up some older impression for which there is no occasion in the external world, but which has been received at the same time as the first sensation at some earlier time in the life of the individual. The sensation of pressure received from a billiard ball at once suggests the visual impression of a white glistening object ; the sight of a candle flame at once awakens in the mind of the child who has had his fingers burnt, the sensation of pain from the burn ; the roar of the sea reinstates the image of the dashing waves and so on *ad infinitum*. These are all instances in which the excitation of one sensation implies the return of a number of other impressions which have been connected with it at some previous time when the element now first and the element it excites were both in mind as parts of a single whole. We may regard this as the simplest form of recall.

The second form, less different from the first than one would suppose at first thought, is that in which the exciting impression disappears as its successor enters. We find an analogous case in sensations which are excited by a stimulus of such short duration that the sensation does not arise until the stimulus which produced it has ceased to act. If, for example, the eye be stimulated by an electric spark, which persists only a few hundred thousandths of a second, the spark will first be seen a tenth of a second or so after the stimulus has disappeared. In the same way the centrally aroused sensations which are called up by association may only appear when the exciting process is no longer conscious. We have an instance of the phenomenon each time we think over any series of words as we expect to speak them, or whenever we recall a number of events in the order in which they occurred. The Associationist school of psychologists opposed successive association to simultaneous as an entirely different process. It is probable, however, that the causes for the succession, if analysed, would not be found to be other than the causes for the simultaneous return which were discussed above. The second element comes back because of a connection established at the time of the previous presence in consciousness, but it does not enter consciousness until the earlier process has disappeared. Probably very few of the concrete thought processes are composed exclusively of either form of association; in much greater measure they combine both.

Most often the starting-point is an idea composed of a group of centrally aroused sensations due to simultaneous excitation of a group of cortical cells. This would probably in every case be in large part the result of association by contiguity in terms of the older classification, although there might be some part played by the immediate excitation of the separate cells by an external stimulus. Starting from this given mass of central elements, all change comes from the fact that some of the elements disappear and are replaced by others through a second series of associations by contiguity. The parts of the original idea which remain serve as the excitants for the new elements which arise. The nature of the process is exactly like that by which the elements of the first idea were excited, and no new process comes in. These successive associations are thus really in their mechanism but a series of simultaneous associations in which the elements that make up the different ideas are constantly changing, but with some elements that persist from idea to idea. There is thus a constant flux of the ideas, but there is always a part of each idea that persists over into the next and serves to start the mechanism of revival. There is never an entire stoppage in the course of the ideas, never an absolute break in the series, but the second idea is joined to the one that precedes by an identical element in each. In its simplest terms, then, all association and all reappearance of ideas that have once been experienced is to be explained by the fact that sensations once united in mind tend to return together when any part of the group returns. The only modification of this principle which needs to be made is that there is a continual dying out and renewal of the sensations that are present, but the renewal, the entrance of the new impression, takes place always in terms of the same general law. So, for instance, when one building reminds us of another, there is first a vanishing of parts of the one, and then the remaining part, the feature that is common to both buildings, brings into mind the other elements of the new building, as in dissolving views part of one of the pictures gradually fades over into and is replaced by another.

The effects of attention upon this process must be considered in exactly the same way that they have been in connection with the entrance of the sensations which come directly from the sense organs. The laws of association have exactly the same relation to the intellectual attention that the laws of sensation and of the physical universe have to the sensorial attention. Both furnish the raw material upon which the attention acts, the crude first product that must be worked over again before there is any consciousness. Association alone no more explains the presence of a thought than sensation alone explains a perception. The later stages are those of greatest importance, although, of course, neither could be present without the other.

As in the case of sensorial attention we may divide the conditions of attention into two great groups, the subjective and objective conditions, so we have two sets of conditions of the coming to consciousness of the remembered impressions. Corresponding to the first, which in perception were to be found mainly in the nature of the external stimulus, in the sensation itself, we have on the central side the nature and strength of the tendency to associate. Corresponding to the subjective factors in perception we have also subjective conditions of association or of return, which are to be found in the more general conditions of consciousness just as were the subjective conditions of the attention in the earlier chapter. We might as readily divide the two sets of conditions into laws of association and laws of attention, but it seems more in accordance with the earlier precedent to use the terms we have.

In a general way we may formulate the objective conditions in the statement that the stronger the associatory tie the more likely is the corresponding mental element to enter consciousness. The concrete factors which determine the strength of association were very well formulated by James Mill, and may be taken over almost bodily from his discussion. They can be classed under the various attributes of the sensation, intensity, duration, and extent, in very much the same way that we classified the objective conditions of the sensorial attention. These conditions are as purely mechanical and as simple in their action as are the conditions that bring the external stimulus into contact with the sense organ and through that to consciousness.

Under the first head, intensity, we can only say that two impressions tend to become more closely connected the more intense one or both of them may have been at the time of ·their original entrance. The mutual irradiation of one upon the other, which may be regarded as joining them, is stronger the more intense the sensations themselves. A very bright flash of lightning, a very loud clap of thunder, will be more likely to be recalled by some contemporaneous event than a very weak one. A severe pain, a strong pressure, or a very intense odour will be more closely connected with other sensations which came at the same time than would a weaker sensation of the same kind. The size of the object on the skin and the retina has an exactly analogous effect to intensity, as was the case for the external impression.

But in addition there are several subjective factors that serve to strengthen the connection between the two events associated. What is at the time of its activity a decidedly subjective condition becomes in its later effects on the same level and of the same kind as the purely objective intensity of the sensations which are joined. Most important of these is attention. If both of the events are attended to carefully at the time of their original entrance there will be a greater tendency for one to recall the other than if either or both has for any reason received but slight attention. The more interesting two events are at the time the more closely will they become welded together. There are daily instances of this fact in the class-room. Two interesting statements always tend to recall each other, whereas if one or both seem commonplace or unimportant at the time there will be no close association between them. It is a familiar experience that any statement that has been accompanied by a story will be remembered, even if everything else of the hour's work be forgotten. Another influence of very similar character is the· emotional attitude toward the experience. Objects that have called out an emotional mood, whether pleasant or unpleasant at the time, gain greatly in their effectiveness for association. Any other impression received at the time, no matter how indistinct it may have been, inevitably recalls the event that excited the emotion, even after a considerable number of years. The witnesses of a tragedy find it for days continually recurring to them. Every tree or stone that bears the slightest resemblance to those that were seen at the time brings back with a rush the whole harrowing scene, and every event of the daily life seems to furnish some resemblance to the scene which is sufficient to recall the complete event. In the same way if there has been a striking personal victory achieved in any line it is constantly recalled even by events that seem to be only remotely connected with it. In both cases we have the highly subjective processes that control the emotions, becoming of the same effect as the objective conditions in their control of the associatory processes.

The temporal conditions of association are just as important, although not quite so simple in their method of action. There are two ways in which associatory processes are affected by time. They are more closely connected the more recent the time of their appearance together, and also the more frequently the elements in question have been united. The first of these laws needs to be little more than stated to have its validity accepted. It is a familiar fact that what we have learned to-day is much more easily recalled than what we learned a week ago even if the conditions are exactly the same both in the external world and in the mind of the individual in question. Professor Ebbinghaus has made an experimental determination of the way in which the closeness of this connection decreases with the time, and found by a method to be described in Chapter IX that there is a very constant rule that governs the dying out of the connection between impressions once associated. The loss of the association is most rapid soon after the association is formed, and decreases in rapidity, so that after the first day the decrease in the strength of association in a week is not much greater than on the first day in a single hour. In mathematical terms it is asserted that forgetting is a function of the logarithm of the time.

Another law, sometimes called the law of primacy, is that the first association is the strongest. Associations formed in early childhood seem to persist more strongly than those which have been formed at a later date. This tendency for the connections of a relatively early period to be preferred to the associations received late in life, in spite of the temporal remoteness of the period, depends in all probability upon the greater plasticity of the nerve cells in youth and the consequent greater strength of the connections which may be formed, together with the fact that associations become more effective with age, if of equal strength with recent associations.

The third law under this head is equally a fact of everyday remark. Repetition is the one means ordinarily relied upon to produce and strengthen associations. From the experiences of the lowest animals up to the most important operations of mankind, frequency of repetition is counted upon to strengthen associations and to facilitate recall. It is probable that this principle plays some part in the explanation of the strong associations formed in early childhood. The associations are frequently repeated because they are relatively so few, and it may be this frequent repetition in part that produces the increased liability to recall in later years. However, the progress of the same tendency in old age, where the impressions of middle life always die out before the events of childhood, would point to the change in the nature of nerve cells as accounting, at least, for the greater part of the effect.

In all these cases of the objective conditioning of the association, we may say that the whole process depends upon the degree in which the elements in question were interwoven at the time of their original entrance. There is probably an increased closeness of connection between cell and cell, which makes for a greater likelihood of recall for one when the other comes into consciousness. The effect of the conditions mentioned up to this point is as definite and unvarying, so far as one can see, as the conditions which cause any external disturbance, light wave, mechanical pressure, or chemical change on the tongue to enter consciousness at any moment. If there were no other factors to be considered it would be a simple computation to determine what idea should come to mind at any time. There would be no variety, and the number of ideas would be extremely limited. At most we could but live over our recent and striking ideas in the same order in which they had previously entered, and our mental life would be much less rich than that which we actually experience.

The variety and completeness of our consciousness is due to the operation of the subjective conditions, just as all forms of control of what shall enter consciousness for the first time depends upon the subjective conditions. The subjective conditions work upon the materials which the objective conditions offer in very much the same way that the subjective conditions of the attention work upon the material offered to the senses. Every thought process is the resultant of both subjective and objective conditions, and can be explained by neither alone. It was a neglect of the subjective conditions and the insistence upon the objective side of the problem that has led the English Associational School into disrepute. The explanations that they gave were true as far as they went, but their incompleteness vitiated the conclusions as soon as they laid claim to universality. There are two points in the associative train where the subjective factors make themselves felt. The first corresponds almost exactly to the effect of the attention in the field of vision or upon the entrance of any sensation. When a remembered object appears in consciousness it is acted upon by the attention in exactly the same way as a perception from the external world. The only difference is that whereas in the latter case the attention determines what impressions shall enter, in this case the attention determines what parts shall remain. The parts which are attended to become clearer and are retained in consciousness, while the others die out and disappear. This is of particular importance in the course of ideas, because it is the portion of any image retained that serves as a starting-point for the next image, and consequently as the part attended to varies, the course of thought will change.

The conditions which are effective in determining what shall be retained are the same as those which we have already discussed in connection with the sensorial attention. The ideas that have been in consciousness just before are the immediate conditions, but there are to be added the general purpose or set of the mind at the time, and the more general effects of training, social environment, and heredity, as they have crystallised in what we call the character of the individual. Each is effective in exactly the same way and in approximately the same degree as we found it to be in the sensorial attention in Chapter IV. In part each acts directly upon the retention of the particular element, in part only indirectly through the influence of those factors, in determining the purpose of the mind at the moment. In this, as in all other aspects, there is very little difference between the subjective conditions here and the subjective conditions of attention in general.

The second way in which the subjective conditions affect the course of ideas is in choosing between the different possible associates which might attach to this particular retained element. Not only must we regard the strength of the connections as due to the intensity of the sensations at the time of the original entrance of the different elements involved and the time of that entrance, but we must consider all of the contents of the mind at the time and much of the preceding mental life of the individual.

The easiest way to show that there are these subjective elements which determine the course of associations is to see what results would follow if these elements were not considered. If we were to consider only the objective conditions there would be no chance but that a given element *A* should excite some second element *B* without any reference to the circumstances under which it entered mind. We could not have " *a* " calling up now "*b*" as we recited the alphabet and now " *man* " as we were speaking in a general conversation, but it would suggest either one or the other, according to the circumstances under which the two sounds had last entered consciousness. In such an instance the many times that the letter had been associated with " *b*," and the early age at which the connection had been begun, would for ever forbid its use as an article, or the entrance of any other connection. In the same way the first strong connection of one impression with another would tend to persist for ever and preclude the association of that impression with any other under any circumstances or at any time.   It could only be broken by some very powerful new impression, and then would be lost for ever.   It is at once evident that no such relations hold between our ideas.   It is only in some form of mental derangement that we find hard and fast connections that are never broken or varied.   In a well-balanced, normal man such cases never occur.   What we really do find as we study mental processes is that the associations into which one element or sensation enters constantly change from moment to moment.   *A* evokes now *B*, and now *C*; "*a*" is the article in one sentence of the word "*man*" and at the next with the word "*plant*," and it is not possible to prophesy from the past history of the connections from one moment to the next what the direction of the association shall be.

It is evident then that a very large and very important part of the problem of association is yet to be discussed. All the variable elements which make and break what would otherwise be rigidly fixed connections have not yet been considered.   For it is no more thinkable that the variation which we find should be a matter of chance, than that there is no variation present.   These conditions are to be found in very much the same series of circumstances that we saw before to make up the subjective conditions of the attention.   For them we must look to the present state of that particular consciousness and to its past history.

We may again begin our enumeration of the different conditions with those that stand nearest the particular connection in question and go backward to the more remote and general.   The first of these factors is to be found in the context of the moment, the general purpose of the thinking at the time.   That in reciting a verse of poetry one word rather than another shall follow any particular word is determined by the meaning that the verse has, your intention in reciting it, and other related circumstances of the kind.   No one can believe for an instant that the strongest associate of a word that occurs twice in the same line will vary between the time of the first and the second recital. What does change is the thought that the word is to express, the mental situation of which the word is the outcome. In the same way any train of mental images is not a mere aimless wandering from picture to picture or from point to point in the experience, but is strictly subordinate to the general aim, to the general line of thought at the moment. You do not find, for instance, that the physicist working with coils of wire in the galvanometer recalls the garden hose, however close the recent connection between coils and hose may have been. The line of thought will continue toward a solution of the particular physical problem that he has been working upon. That problem constitutes the purpose which for the moment dominates his mind and excludes all associations that are not in harmony with it and which do not tend toward its solution. In every mind at any time there is some general tendency due to the conditions of the moment in the surroundings, to the ideas that were in mind just before, or to even more remote conditions, which decides between the different possible associates and selects those that are in harmony with the tendencies.

Dr. Watt [5] has very completely demonstrated experimentally the influence of purpose in the control of associations since the above was written. He asked men to give the first word that came into mind after a printed word was shown when first one, then another task had been set. At one time, for example, they were asked to name the class, and at another to give an instance under the class which the word shown designated. It was found that the word suggested always, and automatically, corresponded to the purpose dominant through the task that had been set. Not only the course of association, but the average time required to make response, and the character of the sensory image, varied with each purpose. These facts, with the observations of the experimenters, are convincing proof that the purpose is fully as important as the direct connection in determining the course of ideas.

The experience that set the problem for solution constitutes the conditions of the attention on the second level of generality and remoteness. These conditions are to be found partly in the larger whole of the science in which the particular individual is engaged and in his knowledge of that science. In part, again, they are to be found in the general principles of the science, in the earlier trains of thought, in the events of the preceding days, and farther back in all of his previous experiences that have had a bearing upon the question in hand. If you ask why the physicist is interested in solving a problem of magnetic activity, you must consider the previous advances of knowledge in relation to that subject so far as they are known to him, the related facts in the science that depend upon a solution of this problem, and the different theories that will be rendered more probable or destroyed by the facts that may be established. If you would know why any particular scientist is working with a particular problem at a particular time, you must know the other related problems upon which he has been previously engaged, the difficulties that have confronted him in them, and a thousand details of his past life and work that the scientist himself could not tell you at the time. They are the essentials of his workaday life for a long period back.

Still more remote in time we find the entire training and experience of the individual. To continue our illustration, if we would know completely why our imaginary physicist is devoting himself to the solution of this particular problem, and why the associations are such as we see them to be, we must go back to those experiences of his early life that led him to become interested in that science and finally to become its devotee. Some chance remark, some presentation of a phase of the subject that was at the time in harmony with another experience that was absorbing his attention, may have furnished the first incentive to the study that has largely engrossed his later life. Every element that led to the choice of his profession, and every circumstance that has strengthened that purpose, may be considered among the conditions that are now effective in determining the course of his associations. In general, every circumstance that we found to be effective in controlling the attention would also be effective here in governing the course and strength of the associations.

Here, too, we are driven back to the hereditary and social factors, and find in them an explanation for so much of the associatory process as is not supplied by immediate experience. The hereditary influences have been covered over in this case, too, by the results of later experiences, but it is hard to think that heredity does not exert some influence, which although its immediate effect upon the particular association may be almost negligible, yet indirectly through determining the nature of the earlier experience at critical points has had in the total a decided part. The social forces can be more easily illustrated. Any one who has seen how the ideas of a people, political, religious, and ethical, will persist unchanged in a particular community, how the course of their associations will be the same under the same circumstances for generation after generation, while the neighbouring race will think entirely differently under the same circumstances, is prepared for the conclusion that the society in which a man is born exerts a great pressure in directing the train of his thought. More immediately it is undoubtedly social pressure that impels one to keep one line of thought constantly and persistently in mind in spite of the greater present pleasure to be derived from another series or from letting the ideas come " at will." It is the ideal of future accomplishments, of social approval, or of social blame that makes an unpleasant series of impressions dominate a pleasant one, that overcomes the present temporary tendency of the course of ideas by a more permanent controlling force.

As the result of our investigation of the course of ideas we find that they too are subject to the control of the same factors which we found to be active in the control of sensorial attention. The ideas in mind, the general attitude of the hour, the past experience of the individual, and the social and hereditary influences to which he has been subjected constitute in both cases the factors which finally determine the nature of the process. Here, as in the preceding instance, however, we cannot regard either the subjective or the objective conditions as alone effective in determining any mental process. In association, as in attention, the outcome in any case is the result of the action of both sets of influences. When two subjective tendencies are pretty evenly balanced, the objective elements will decide ; if the objective are of nearly equal strength, the balance will be turned by the subjective conditions. In any given case both will be effective, but each in a different degree. There are some states of mind, such as reverie and dreams, where the objective seem largely to predominate, but even in them the subjective factors play their part. The course of the dream, and of the ideas in a " brown study," depends upon the past experience, the mood of the moment, and the other more remote influences that have played upon the individual. It is only by an abstraction from the real concrete experience that one could say that the laws of association are really the determining causes even in an extreme case like this. That would omit the more important for the less important. On the other hand, it would be just as far from the truth to mention only the subjective factors ; but it is not necessary to devote so much attention to this side of the question, because so far no one has sinned by excess in that direction. A complete explanation of association demands that both sets of factors be taken into account ; to omit either is to fail in the solution of the problem. If either is to be omitted, it is probable that the objective conditions could be dispensed with more easily than the subjective. Association, like attention, is not the outcome of any one set of conditions, but is an expression of the totality of mind at the time the association takes place.

SUMMARY

1. Attention plays very much the same part in controlling the centrally excited processes as the peripherally excited.

2. We may regard all centrally excited processes, imagination, etc., as the outcome of two sets of conditions, association or objective, and attention or subjective conditions.

3. The closeness of association depends upon the intensity of the two sensations when they first entered consciousness, upon the attention that was given them at the time, and upon their frequency and recency.

4. The subjective conditions which decide between the possible associations are practically identical with the subjective conditions of attention, the mood of the moment, the general training of the individual, his social environment, and heredity.

CHAPTER VIII

IN this chapter we seem from the title to be harking back to a subject that has already been treated, or at least to one that logically precedes the last chapter. It certainly seems, in the light of the ordinary opinion, that perception would be a simpler problem than association, and that sensations must get into the mind before they are associated. While this is true of sensations, ideas or objects are not recognised so immediately, and are much more complex than they seem at first glance. In reality all perception involves association. Objects are largely built up in consciousness, they do not merely walk in through the senses in their completeness. We have omitted all consideration of the entrance of objects from this aspect, and have allowed it to appear that as soon as an object was attended to every condition for its entrance had been completely satisfied. This is by no means the case. The group of sensations which constitutes the object for us is only partly given in peripheral sensation; for the most part the idea or object is merely suggested by the elements that come in through the senses, the remainder is supplied by centrally excited sensations, by material already in mind.

Take any single concrete perception and determine by analysis how much comes from the senses immediately, and what comes indirectly through association. It will be found that by far the greater part is made up by the latter, while the immediate sensory elements contribute but an extremely small part. The sensations that you receive from any article of furniture form only patches of colour upon the retina, but the object that you see is hard, smooth, has solidity and strength. Each of these qualities comes not through the senses, but from association. The smoothness is a tactual element that arises by association with the visual impression, and could not come at once from the eye. The immediate occasion for its appearance is the lustre or sheen of the surface, and this, again, is due to nothing else than the fact that the source of light is rudely reflected upon the surface. Reflection can take place only if the surface be smooth, and therefore serves to call up the sensation that we have previously received when the fingers are passed over a polished surface. The texture suggests the hardness, while the solidity of the object is a complex association in part made up of movements, of tactual impressions, and of the knowledge that the object would show another similar surface if it were turned in either direction. The whole complex is called out by an equally complicated set of sensations made up of the shadows upon the surface of the object, the double images that it casts upon the two retinas, and of eye movements. The whole process is very much involved, and while we cannot go into the details, it is probably safe to assume that the whole perception is made up of a complicated series of associations recalled from past experience.

Much more evident and natural for most of us is the association that leads from the other senses to sight. As we run our fingers over the surface of the table in the dark we are usually not so much conscious of what we feel as of the way the table would look were there light. The changes in the sensations of pressure and movement call up at once by association the visual picture that we would receive of the outline and of the nature of the unevennesses on its surface if we were studying it with the eye. So, too, the sound of hammering upon the building across the

street brings to mind the uplifted hammer, the nail half
driven and the beam and board which it is to hold together.
Visual impressions received in past experience return to
cluster about the sound that is entering and give it
meaning, transform it from a mere sensation into the perception that makes the experience a real event in our
consciousness.

A more complicated instance of the same general principle is offered by the interpretation that we put upon the
facial expression of our friends and acquaintances. We
can at once decide whether a companion is provoked,
amused, well disposed, or ill disposed toward us at the
moment, but very few people could tell at once exactly
what the difference in the features is that leads to the interpretation. A slight contraction of a muscle in the
forehead or about the mouth, and we feel a change in the
mood of the friend, and modify our later remarks in terms
of that feeling. But it would be extremely difficult, even
if we were studying the face at the time, to pick out the
particular change in the features that leads one to the
conclusion. What we get in perception is not a series of
muscular contractions, but a total impression of a friend
angry, or a friend delighted, of a mood serious, or a mood
playful, and we adapt our action and our conversation
to the perception as a whole. The specific sensations upon
which the perception is based are entirely lost in the interpretation that we give them. The interpretation is of
course due to associations on the basis of numerous experiences with people in general, and with this person in particular, which now come in to supply the perception from
many memories of the remarks or actions that have followed
the various expressions at different times in the past.

Another instance of very delicate decisions on very
slight sensational basis is offered by our reading from the
eye of another the direction and distance of the object at
which he is looking. We can tell at a glance and with
great accuracy what the object is that is attracting his

attention. The far-away look in the eye is very characteristic, and in conversing with a person is as effective in
stopping one's remarks as a request. Delicate estimations
of the distance of the object looked at are possible to a
very surprising degree. The data for these estimations
are always extremely slight. It is only the relative amount
of white sclerotic and conjunctiva that shows on either
side of the dark iris, as the eyes are converged or turned
to one side or the other. The changes in these distances
are very small, and it would be very difficult to notice them
even if that were the object of the moment. But again
the estimation is never made in that way. One is seldom
if ever conscious of studying the area of white exposed
on the outside or inside of the eyes. As soon as the position of the eyes is noticed, we have the impression that
the person is looking at an object at a certain distance.
We think nothing of the position of the eyes and usually
almost as little of the eyes themselves. What does come
into mind is that there is some interesting object at a
certain distance from the person observed and this alone.

Another excellent illustration of the participation of
other mental processes than sensations in the perception
is given by the familiar process of reading. Experiments
by Erdmann and Dodge, by Huey and others, have shown
that a very small proportion of the matter read from the
printed page is really seen in the individual letters. Nearly
all is supplied by association under definite subjective
and objective laws. Erdmann and Dodge proved that
the eyes in reading do not move constantly and smoothly
over the line, but go by a series of short movements with
rests between. Reading takes place only when the eyes
are at rest. It is quite easy to determine from the length
of the line and the number of rests the number of letters
which are read at a single glance. It was found that this
was considerably greater than the number that could fall
at one time upon the area of the retina sensitive enough to
permit them to be read. The other letters must, it is

evident, be supplied by association from the material gathered in the earlier experiences. Reading has peculiar advantages for the investigation of processes involved in perception, because the conditions that control the associations can be more readily made out there than elsewhere, and the experimental results are more clear cut and easier of interpretation than in most of the other domains of perception. For that reason we shall draw largely upon it for illustrative material in discussing the nature and control of the processes involved in perception.

In none of these cases do we ordinarily analyse the total impression into its elements or distinguish between the sensations that come at once from the senses and those which are centrally excited through association. The object seen is taken as a whole, and it is very difficult to tell where the immediate contribution of the senses ceases and the work of association begins. The whole is what we know as the percept or the object, and we never think of questioning how it is made up. In fact, it is very doubtful, in spite of much careful investigation, as to how much of any perception can be called immediate sensation, and how much is due to association at second and third hand. Certainly very much more than one ordinarily suspects of what is said to have been seen has not been seen at all, but has been supplied by association. It was this supplementing of the sensations by centrally excited sensations that led Helmholtz to speak of many processes of the kind as unconscious inference. He pictured the process as unconsciously deducing the real nature of the object from the incomplete sensation that was obtained. A similar interpretation of the relation leads Binet to assert that all perception is judgment. Both of these terms serve merely to point out the similarities of the perception process to the more complicated mental processes, and in so far we may accept them. But neither really gives us an idea of the details of the process, and if all perception follows this pattern, as we seem justified in assuming on the basis of the illustrations, it is not of much advantage merely to note the similarity and emphasise it in a classification. Moreover, as we shall see in the next chapter, judgment and inference can be reduced to processes not so very different from perception. Whatever the advantages for general philosophy of recognising the higher in the lower, it is more in harmony with the axiom of science to bring the simpler under the head of the more complicated.

Clearly, if perception depends to so large an extent upon association of old impressions with the newly entering ones, we have a problem to solve very similar to that which we have already treated in association. We must, that is, decide what the conditions are that lead us to make the associations at the right time, that always bring us to see the same thing under the same circumstances, and consequently make the world the same for everybody. For it would seem at first sight that if the perception is thus dependent upon association or other purely mental processes there could be no agreement as to what was seen under the same conditions, but as each man's mind is different, so even if the same object were offered to the senses each man who looked would receive a different perception.

The factors that are at work here are almost identical with those which were found to be active in the control and production of associations. We have to do again with an association under the influence of attention and the more general subjective conditions derived from the experience of the individual and the race, which we have already found to play so large a part in the control of attention and association. The simplest determinant is the association in its physical form depending upon the intensity, recency, and frequency of the original connection. Of these the frequency of the previous connection is probably the most important. There are some instances in which apparently this mechanical connection is the only determinant, or, at least, the element that finally wins in the struggle. Reading under unfavourable conditions furnishes many illustrations. If single words are shown for a very brief time, or in a weak light, the associatory influences are given full sway and can be studied for themselves. The effect of the central conditions of mental environment and context are reduced to a minimum by the fact that the words are given singly, and so the simpler conditions of recall run their course unhindered. The most marked results here are the tendencies of the more frequently connected letters to recall each other when one is seen. In English it is found that " t " will very often bring up " h " when it is seen alone in the midst of a number of blurred letters, or of letters indistinctly seen. Similarly " n " is succeeded by " g " or " t," and " l " by " y," on account of the many times these combinations occur in English, when the first letter is near the end of the word, or the letter that follows is indistinctly seen and not enough of the word be read to preclude the possibility of the connection. In some cases a word will be built up by association to fit a combination that has been made in this way. Sometimes, indeed, we find that the element supplied by association will conquer against a component actually given in senses, and again the letter supplied through association will alternate with the actual sensation; first one and then the other will gain the chief place.

Miss Hempstead [3] obtained instances of the same phenomenon in some experiments on the perception of geometrical figures in a faint light. It was found that there was always a tendency to extend lines whenever the extension would unite parts of the figure that were disconnected. Whenever there were two or more points from which lines radiated which were themselves disconnected, a line was usually supplied that should connect them. This is probably because in ordinary drawings two centres of radiation of this kind are connected, and when the two points were seen they called up by association a line that should join them. The instance is not so simple as in the case of the letters in the word, but still the more important element of the perception is undoubtedly the mere association of element to element. Another instance in still a different connection is furnished by the simple conjuring trick of Hermann and others, in which a ball or other object is made to vanish when thrown into the air. The trick consists in going through the movements of throwing and so skilfully concealing the object at the moment it should leave the hand that the mind supplies the actual flight through the air. The movements call up their most usual associates, and all the other conditions are so favourable to the interpretation that the movement through the air is taken for real. Many other conjuring tricks have a similar explanation, but further elaboration would probably not make the principle clearer.

The same law is at work in every perception, but in most the association is in harmony with the sensations that would be received if the examination were more careful, and it is therefore impossible to prove that it is not the sensation which comes into consciousness rather than the association. Only when the processes that ordinarily give rise to what we call true perceptions give false results is our attention attracted to them. Perhaps the clearest examples of the process from the range of normal perception are to be found in the instances where impressions from one sense call up sensations from another, owing to the frequency with which they have appeared together. The visual impression that comes up when we hear a dog bark at night, the tactual qualities that we ascribe to a surface as we hear a metal rod drawn across it, and the idea that we get of the nature of a surface as we run a pen or a cane over it, are all evidences of the immediate effect of the simple mechanical associations in perception. There are undoubted influences of the process to be seen within the same sense as when we fill up the area in the field of vision corresponding to the blind spot with the colour of the surrounding field, or extend the colour of the visual field to the area beyond the range of vision. There is probably no case of perception in which these objectively conditioned associations do not play a part.

The subjective conditions are just as important in determining the course of association in perception as in the association of ideas. In discussing them here we must go over almost the same ground that we have covered in enumerating the conditions of the attention and the subjective conditions of association. But the repetition may be pardonable in view of the fact that new illustrations may be used, and that each exposition may make clear some point left dark in the others. Certain of the conditions are best illustrated by processes in one of the manifestations of subjective control, others by those in another field. Illustrations from all mutually supplement each other, and it is to be hoped that the gain will outweigh the disadvantages of the threefold repetition.

The first condition here, as before, is to be found in the mental content at the moment of entrance, in the setting, mental or physical, at the moment the sensation enters. In reading we can find many instances of this. The associations between the letters of the isolated words are largely determined by the word that has been already recognised from its outline and the very few letters which are read accurately. What word shall be made out from these impressions is again largely determined by the context, if the word is given in a sentence, or by the mental content, if the word stands alone. Experiments by Professor Münsterberg, repeated by the author, demonstrated that if an associated word were called just before the word were shown it facilitated the reading of the word and prevented the noticing of misprints. The word of related meaning at once made more certain the association of the word as a whole with the impressions received, and strengthened the effect of the word in controlling the associations between the separate letters. When the words are given in a context, as in reading ordinary matter, there is a very much stronger directing force at work in the general meaning of the article that is being read and in the trend of the discussion that has already been received from the earlier sentences. The large gaps between the words and letters which are actually read are supplied by association in terms of the knowledge of what is to be said, as was shown by the results of Erdmann and Dodge. They found that the more familiar the subject-matter and the language, the more rapid was the reading and the fewer the words actually seen. In terms of our problem, the more definite the control by knowledge, the greater the amount that could safely be trusted to the associative factors, and the less that need be seen. This is evident again in the fact that in reading a work that is very familiar it is possible to gather the meaning of the pages by noting merely the more striking words, and inferring from them what is printed on the pages. The more adequate the control of the subjective factors the less need there is for the objective. Dr. Bagley found the same general principle to hold for the perception of the spoken word. It was much easier to recognise the spoken word in the sentence than if it stood alone, and much more difficult to recognise mispronunciations and omissions. As the context became more definite, more was left to association under its control and less attention was paid to the actual sensations received.

The same principles hold in general perception. The patch .of white in a stage scene would be recognised indifferently as a rock or as a sail according as the surroundings were representative of the meadow or of the sea. The mental setting is just as important. The change in the interpretation of the figure drawn in ambiguous perspective was seen in a preceding chapter to be due in part to the changing of the other ideas in mind at the time. Much of the interpretation is undoubtedly due to the associated impressions that are aroused by the lines actually drawn, and the nature of the association is determined by the other ideas in mind.

Better instances are to be found in illusions. When Sir Walter Scott mistook the hanging garments for Byron just after hearing of Lord Byron's death, and while his mind was yet full of that sad event, we have a case of the control of associations by the mental content. The sensations from the garment, instead of suggesting merely the texture of the cloth and the purpose of the apparel, took an unusual turn and called out the familiar outline of the poet's figure. The reason for the unusual course of the associations was to be found in the fact that the mental setting dominated the objective setting and called out the corresponding connections. In the same way we can account for the great variety of forms that the luminous mask takes on for the different persons in attendance on the spiritualistic seance by the widely different expectations of the different observers. The puzzle picture varies its form as the outlines call out one after another of the various groups of impressions that have been connected with the contours that are seen upon the paper. As you look first, you see nothing but the landscape that the picture, as a whole, suggests, and look as closely as you will there is no departure from the usual outline of the verdure. When a friend suggests that there is a face in the tree at a given place, and you look again with that idea in mind, the face is seen at once, and once seen is never missed again. The difference in the two cases is to be found in the direction that is given to the course of association by the different mental contents. So, everywhere, the mental content at the moment and the general trend of the mind at the time exert a powerful influence in determining the nature of the perception.

Behind these conditions stand the past training, the general ways of life of the individual in question. This is well illustrated by an incident related to the author by a well-known school inspector. He was experimenting with school children of Sault Ste. Marie, Mich., on the recognition of different outline drawings, among them a vague sole-

shaped contour. Nearly all the boys recognised it at
once as a paddle, on account, doubtless, of the almost universal familiarity with boats and boating in that community.
The school children of Lynn or Brockport would have recognised it just as quickly and unequivocally as a sole.
And so each tradesman or professional man is ready to
see in any object of vague outline some instrument of his
daily use. An ink blot or the embers in the fireplace
reflect back the mind and the profession of the man who
looks into them. The associates which are called up by
the vague outlines are determined in their course by the
past experience and by the daily task and the momentary
thought of the man who observes them. Another excellent
illustration of the same fact is given by the difference
between a landscape painting and a photograph, or by
the difference between two paintings of the same scene
by different artists. Even assuming the same point of
view, it will be seen that one man will emphasise one aspect
of the view and the other, another. The sensations are
the same for both, but the associations and the elements
that control them mirror the past life of the two artists.
The perception is not dependent merely upon rock and
hill and meadow, but upon the previous life of the man
who sees and paints it.

Still farther back we have the constant pressure of
heredity and social environment. Both of these act again
mainly indirectly to determine the form that the training
shall take, the choice of the profession, and affect the perception itself only indirectly. It may be that heredity
directly controls the course of the first associations, and
so the nature of the perceptions in some degree, but that
is a proposition which admits of no direct proof. Still,
as we can see that the early movements show the influence
of heredity, it seems very probable that sensory associations
also should show some effect of the same influence. Social
pressure undoubtedly also expresses itself in the nature
of the perception, although again the only evidence for it

is to be found in the fact that the different races and communities give different interpretations of the same objective impressions.

The whole problem of perception then is in very small degree a problem of sensation, and in very large degree a matter of association and of the control which is exerted by many subjective factors. We see an extremely small part of what comes into our mind. An object is made up in very slight degree of impressions immediately received from the sense organ, and in very large measure by the returned elements of old sensations and impressions. Perception is not the immediate consequence of environment and sense organ, but is rather an expression of the entire past life of the individual in the fullest sense of that term.

If perception is so closely related to association, if we supply so large a proportion of the object in the external world and sensation so small a part, the question naturally arises as to why there is such universal agreement as to the things that are seen, why the world is so nearly alike for us all. The answer is to be found in the common nature of human minds and in the identity of the subjective conditions that are at work at all times in determining and controlling the mental processes. Mankind as a whole, and members of the same community in particular, have a common past as well as a common present. Men of the same nation have, as a rule, seen the same things under the same conditions, their training has been very much alike; and through the widespread systems of communication of the modern world, through books and newspapers, by post and telegraph, the experience of any man in any country becomes promptly the experience of every man throughout the civilised world. This fact, that all men come into a common tradition, have in large measure the same experiences and heredity, is the most important factor in making the perception of any object the same for all who observe it. The mental setting into which the sensations are received is alike for all men as well as the sensations that are received. It is as much the identity of subjective conditions as of the impressions that makes agreement in observation possible. But given this community of ideas, a true perception of the external world is just as possible as if all depended upon the identity of physical conditions at the moment of perception.

More than this, however, man's interpretation of the physical world assumes a constancy of natural laws. The associations developed yesterday will only serve to-day in place of sensations if the series of events in the external world is the same now as then. It is only safe to assume that the white patch in the landscape is a rock if you can be assured that sailing wheeled vehicles have not come into vogue over-night, and that light is always reflected in one way from the surface of the sea and in another from the grass of the meadow, and that the laws of reflection cannot change at random. If there were any such irregularity in the physical forces, if a cause had one effect at one time, and another at another, it would not be possible to use associations to determine from some slight sensational clue what the entire connection must be. As it is, we may regard all perception as based upon the fact of the relative constancy of external connections. As a rule a given sensation would be accompanied or followed by certain others, and it would prove much less satisfactory to stop to make a complete test each time than to trust that the connections once experienced will remain permanent. Exceptions are so rare, and the time saved by the process so great, that there is immense gain over what would seem to be the more accurate method and the one which is usually supposed to constitute the process of perception.

When by any chance the idea which the sensations suggest is found on closer examination not to be in harmony with the sensations received under conditions that have been found to be more favourable to accurate observation, we have an illusion. This occurs only when there is some lack of harmony between the objective and the subjective setting, and the factors that control the course of the associations are not suited to the circumstances of the physical world. Either there is some unusual relation of objects or events on the physical side, or the subjective conditions are not only very strong, but those which are dominant are for some reason not the ones that would ordinarily be called out by the circumstances in question. When the lack of harmony is more pronounced, and the sensory element becomes very much smaller in amount than usual, we have an hallucination. In either case there is only the operation of the normal laws of perception, but they act in some unusual way. The result is not that which the mass of people would obtain under the same conditions, or which we would obtain under normal conditions. Both processes serve to emphasise the earlier results of this chapter, that perception is not a bodily walking over of objects into our consciousness, but that it is, like memory, the result of a mental construction. While it obeys a law, its law is not merely physical, but involves psychological laws as well. The unusual manifestations in illusion are not mysterious, but are the result of the operation in an unusual way of laws which ordinarily operate with such great regularity that we have never even suspected their existence.

SUMMARY

1. Perception is not as it seems, the mere entrance of a group of sensations, but an arousal of old experiences by a few newly entering sensations.

2. Attention both determines what sensations shall enter and what associations they shall arouse.

3. Again the conditions of perception may be divided into subjective and objective. The subjective, as in the earlier discussions, are to be found in the past history of the individual, the objective both in the environment of the moment and in the mechanical conditions of association.

CHAPTER IX

ATTENTION IN MEMORY

TO complete our survey of the facts of attention, and the place that it holds in mind, it still remains to discuss the effects which it exerts in the more complicated mental activities. We must see what it contributes to the so-called higher processes. That it will play a part even in these processes is evident from its importance in the simpler ones that go to make them up. Attention could not play so considerable a rôle in the entrance of sensations into mind, and in their combination after entrance, without also being a significant factor in every other mental state, however complicated, for it is a generally accepted fact that all other mental states are but combinations of sensations in some form or other. In fact, in the words of Professor Titchener, we might regard the elementary states so far discussed, if we include in them the fact that attention is accompanied by motor phenomena, as the structural elements of mind. All the others are merely combinations of these for different functional purposes. All of the processes of cognition and action then would be but compounds of the simple elements, which because they had different functions, accomplished different purposes, had been marked off with separate names, but which really in themselves contained nothing new, and even demanded no new general principles of explanation. All that is necessary now is to study the manner of combination of the elements already discussed in the more usually mentioned higher mental processes.

To avoid dragging the discussion out to an inordinate length
we may confine ourselves to the three which are most
often mentioned, and which for the teacher are probably
the most important, or at least are those most talked about
in connection with pedagogical questions. These are
memory, will, and reason.   They are moreover the functions
that are of most interest to the popular reader, and a discussion of them will probably suffice to indicate the part
that would be assigned to the others.

Perhaps memory, of all these so-called higher processes,
is the one that is of most general interest.   It is the function that one most often attempts to train or to strengthen,
and which seems of most practical value.   We may do well
then to begin our discussion with it, as it is also the simplest
and the most closely related to the elementary processes
already discussed.

As follows from the principles set forth in the earlier chapter on association, attention would affect memory at two
points, at the time the impression is first received and at
the time of its later recall.   Both effects are important,
but in an entirely different way.   It is the *conditio sine qua
non* of all later recall that the impression be attended to
at the time that it first enters consciousness.   The events
which pass entirely unnoticed are never recalled.   Furthermore, in very large degree the likelihood of recall varies
with the degree of the attention.   Statements or events
that are closely attended to are more easily remembered
than those which are only given passing notice.   Every
teacher has observed how the statements that attract the
attention are retained.   The stories that are told, and
the facts that are illustrated by them, particularly the
stories, are sure to be recalled in the class discussions and
in the examination paper, while more important matters
that received greater emphasis in the lecture and are in-
herently more important seem to have vanished utterly.
Retention then runs parallel to the degree of attention
at the time the impression is received.   The nature of

this action was dwelt upon at considerable length in connection with the problem of centrally excited sensations, and needs no further discussion here, as memory is but one phase of the general problem of centrally excited sensations.

These statements hold in general for the relation of attention to learning and retention. Fortunately, however, we need not restrict our statements to these general terms. Within the last decade a large amount of experimental work has been done upon the memory process that enables us to state accurately and in much greater detail the laws of learning and the influence of attention upon these memory processes. The two cannot easily be dissociated in a discussion of this character, and it is hoped that the resulting laws of memory will be to the reader interesting enough in themselves, and the influence of attention be regarded as sufficiently striking to justify what may at first sight seem a digression into a related but nevertheless distinct field.

To understand the results at all it will first be necessary to sketch briefly the methods that have been used in the investigations. The material most used for the experiments is the nonsense syllable. Its use has the advantage of doing away with any possible influence of earlier formed associations that would make words and phrases of varying value for memory and serve to introduce numerous confusing factors. The nonsense syllables are arranged by making all possible combinations of vowels and consonants that give a consonant at the beginning and at the end, and then striking from the list all that make words in the language in which the investigation is undertaken. These constitute with the German vowels somewhere in the neighbourhood of two thousand. From the list, series are prepared by lot. These series are pasted upon a drum that revolves behind an opening in a screen and shows the syllables one by one at regular intervals, or some other apparatus is used that will show them with constant exposure and interval. The syllables are ordinarily spoken as they are shown.

There are several procedures for using the syllables in the investigation of memory laws, but all are alike in that they make the number of repetitions a measure of the ease of learning. Ordinarily the number of repetitions required before the series can be said once through without mistake is made the measure of the ease of forming associations. For the degree of retention under different conditions or for different individuals there are three recognised measures. The first method, employed by Ebbinghaus [4] in his earlier invesgation was to relearn the same series after the lapse of several hours or days, and to use the number of repetitions necessary to relearn to the point where one repetition could be made without mistake as the measure of retention. A second method, used by Müller and Schumann, was known as the method of successes. As the name implies, the amount of retention was measured by the ratio of times that a syllable could be given correctly when the preceding syllable was supplied. Still a third measure that has been suggested by Ebbinghaus, although not very frequently used, is the method of promptings. This makes the number of times a syllable must be suggested the measure of the degree of retention. A subsidiary indication of the amount of retention, and one that is usually taken advantage of in connection with the method of successes, is the length of time required to make the association with the syllable suggested. Each method has its advantages, and each probably measures a slightly different phase of the memory process.

The results obtained by these methods have to do immediately and directly with the associatory processes. They have served to demonstrate or to confirm most of the facts of association that were mentioned in the earlier chapter, but in addition there are a number of facts in connection with memory proper that have developed in the course of the different investigations, and these are

almost all connected with attention either positively or
negatively. As there is no way of separating sharply the
effects of attention from the effects of association proper,
and no way of making clear the influence of attention
without giving a statement of the fundamental processes, it
is necessary to enumerate the more important results and indicate the way in which they have been affected by attention.

The fundamental fact which makes the measurements
applicable directly is that each repetition is of equal value
in the formation of the association, it makes no difference
where they may occur in the series. The fiftieth repetition
increases the strength of the association just as much as
did the first or the second. It follows from this that the
number of repetitions may be used as a measure of the learning without correction of any kind. This, of course, always
on the assumption that attention was equally strong at
each repetition, or that sufficient trials are made to average
out the deviations from a standard degree of attention.

Another fact that is of some interest in itself as well
as for the methods of experimentation is that the number
of repetitions necessary for learning grows very rapidly
as the number of syllables in a series is increased. Ebbinghaus, again the pioneer in the work, found that the adult
could learn from six to eight syllables with a single repetition ; when the number of syllables in the series is increased
to twelve, from fourteen to sixteen repetitions are needed
for a single correct repetition ; for sixteen, thirty or more
were necessary ; for thirty-six, fifty-five. Ebbinghaus [5]
suggests that the phenomenon is an expression of the narrow-
ness of consciousness. This statement carries with it the
implication that a series to be remembered as a whole
must be grasped as a unit. The number of successive
impressions that can be thus attended to is limited, and
as the maximum is more and more nearly approached,
greater difficulty is experienced in holding the mass of
material in consciousness, and the greater the number of
repetitions necessary to unite them. This fact is very

suggestive of the problem of the range of attention. It may, by analogy, be said to be an extension of the fact that the field of attention is narrow, from the simultaneous to the successive realm.

A third phenomenon that seems thoroughly demonstrated is but slightly connected with attention, although the general principle is one that is important indirectly in explaining the influence of remote experiential factors upon attention. This is that memory takes place with greater ease when the repetitions are divided among several days than when they are all accumulated in a single day. So Ebbinghaus showed that a series of syllables repeated sixty-eight times in immediate succession required seven repetitions the following day to reinstate it. If, on the other hand, it was repeated seventeen and one half times on one day, twelve times on the second, and eight and a half on the third, but five repetitions were necessary on the fourth to bring it back. Thirty-eight repetitions extended over three days are more effective in forming associations than sixty-eight when they are confined to a single day. Jost carried the experiments very much farther, and found that the same principle held to the end, that the more you divide the repetitions the greater the amount of saving. The most economical application of twenty-four repetitions was to make two repetitions on each of twelve days, rather than to repeat more frequently on fewer days. It would seem at first sight that the explanation of the results was that one could attend better for the first repetitions, or that one became fatigued by the earlier repetitions. But this cannot be the entire explanation, for Jost [⁷] noted that the principle still held, if the smaller number of repetitions was preceded by a number of repetitions of some other series that was equal in number to, or slightly exceeded the number made in a single day in divided learning. In spite of the extra fatigue the divided repetitions were much more effective than an equal number made in immediate succession.

Greater attention during the short series may play some small part without reference to the fatigue, but it is probable that the explanation of the phenomenon is to be found in the fact that older associations are more effective than the more recent of the same strength. Jost demonstrated that if two series, one old and the other new, give an equal number of successes when tested by the method of successes, the old can be brought to the degree of effectiveness necessary to give one correct repetition much more quickly — with fewer repetitions—than the new. Apparently then an association which is so far latent that there is little or no trace of it in determining the course of recall—that seldom supplies the older second syllable when the first is suggested—is as easily brought back to full efficiency by new repetitions as more recent connections that are superficially much stronger. It is consoling to know that information that never shows itself in consciousness is nevertheless capable of being reinstated when occasion demands with very little effort, compared with the pains of the original acquisition. As an explanation of the advantages of divided learning this fact would involve the assumption that the repetitions of the one day actually increase in strength during the time that elapses before the next repetitions are made. The fact again furnishes some justification for the undemonstrable assertion of the older psychologies that nothing is ever completely lost from memory. In connection with our study of the conditions of attention it explains how the more remote experiences may still exert a control upon the course of perception and thought without themselves being conscious at the instant.

A law of memory that betrays a more direct influence of attention than those previously mentioned was first suggested by Miss Lottie Steffens. [12] This is that it is much easier to learn a selection by rote if the entire selection is read through as a whole than if it is read and learned part by part, as one is naturally inclined to do. The influence of attention here is negative rather than positive, the law would hold more completely did not attention act in the opposite direction. Miss Steffens found that the law held absolutely, and that the saving was greater the longer the selection to be learned. But she worked with an instrument that compelled the repetitions to be made at a regular and pre-determined rate. Pentschew, [11] however, performed some of his experiments without mechanical aids, and determined that then while fewer repetitions were required to learn the material as a whole, yet the reading was so much slower under those circumstances that the learning really required more time. That reading tends to become slow is evidently due to the fact that the reader is unable to attend to the matter to be read after it had become familiar from the first few repetitions, and before any particular accomplishment was apparent. When in poetry, for example, stanzas are learned separately, one can see at each moment that something has been accomplished and there is constant incentive to attend. Under those circumstances, the loss through bad method of associating is more than compensated for by increased attention. Ebert and Meumann [3] succeeded in combining the advantages of both methods. They would have the whole poem read through twice each twenty-four hours until learned. Attention could be held to the relatively new material offered each time, and there were none of the needless repetitions of the usual method. The defects of the ordinary method are undoubtedly due to two factors. (1) There are two associations formed between the last word of each stanza, one with the beginning of the stanza as it is repeated the next time, the other with the beginning of the next, and these two associations tend to interfere with each other and partly destroy each other. (2) Certain parts of the selection are repeated more often than is necessary in order to make the weaker strong enough. The earlier learned stanzas are repeated each time a new one is learned in order to connect them with it. The strength of the chain is the strength of the weakest link, and some are forged more strongly than is necessary, while others are still too weak to hold.

Still another of these recently recognised laws in which attention plays its part is that the rate of repetition has a very marked influence upon the ease of learning. Ebbinghaus obtained results that would seem to indicate that the relation was a direct one; that learning took place in less time and with fewer repetitions if the rate were fast than slow, and that the validity of the law was not limited above or below. Moreover, the gain in ease of learning was not counterbalanced by any lack of retention. Fully as much of the material was retained twenty-four hours later when the learning had been at the rapid rate as when the series had been learned by the slower. Ogden,[10] however, repeated the experiments of Ebbinghaus at great length, and determined that there was an upper as well as a lower limit to the most favourable rate of repetition, and that the most rapid rate was less favourable than the moderate even when tested by the time required alone. Ogden, however, is of the opinion that the time alone is not an accurate measure of the energy used in learning, but that the number of repetitions should also be taken into consideration. He suggests, therefore, that the product of the time into the number of repetitions is a true indication of the amount of work that is done. On this basis the most favourable rate is given by the repetition of two syllables per second. There are, of course, considerable individual variations. One of logical memory will learn more easily with a relatively slow rate, while a pure rote remembering is favoured by a considerably higher rate. For all, however, the most favourable rate was one that permitted attention to be adjusted most easily, and with least distraction from an attempt to adjust the repetitions to an unfamiliar or unusual rate, and which also left no time for attention to extraneous material.

The most favourable rate then is determined very largely

by the conditions that make for most complete attention, although it is not unlikely that the rhythm may influence association more directly. This harmonises with the familiar experience that often more is accomplished when one must work rapidly to prepare a lesson, than when one has plenty of time. When working more leisurely much time is wasted thinking of irrelevant matters, while under pressure attention is concentrated upon the matter in hand. There is always gain in rapid work until the attempt to hurry produces a flurried condition. Then waste of effort appears.

A law of memory that is very suggestive of attention is that things which have at any time formed parts of a common whole tend to be remembered together, and also to be remembered more easily than isolated things. Here, again, we come back to matters that have to do with the nature of an " object," which was discussed incidentally in connection with the " range of attention." As there the number of objects that could be attended to was independent of the complexity of the objects, so here the ease of remembering depends not upon the nature of the units, but upon the number of units. Ease and quickness of learning is the same whether the series be composed of one-syllable or two-syllable words, whether of single words or of phrases. If the material to be learned is the ordinary prose, the unit is the idea, and it makes no difference whether it is expressed in a word or a sentence, so far as ease of memory is concerned.

The uniting of separate elements into larger wholes is what makes rhythm so great an aid to memorising. All investigators agree that nonsense syllables are learned very much more easily if repeated in suitable rhythms, and in practice all learning is by rhythmic units. One reason for the favourable influence has been demonstrated by Müller and Schumann [9] and Müller and Pilzecker [8] in the very close connection that subsists between the elements of the rhythmic unit. The connection between the elements of a trochaic rhythm is very much stronger than between either element and the next succeeding unit, or the next preceding. If a series of nonsense syllables has been learned in a trochaic rhythm, and single syllables are presented with the request to mention the first syllable that comes to mind, it appeared that in nearly every case the other element of the metric unit presented itself, even if the syllable presented were the last in the unit, so that the course of the association must run backward. Müller demonstrated the same fact even more conclusively by arranging two series, the one composed of five trochaic feet selected from a series that had been learned twenty-four hours earlier, the other composed of five pairs of contiguous syllables that did not belong to the same foot in other series learned twenty-four hours before. He learned the first series in an average of one and seven-tenths repetitions, while five repetitions were necessary for the series made up of contiguous syllables belonging to different metric units. This influence of rhythm in facilitating learning is in part at least due to the fact that the two elements in the foot are attended to together and tend to become parts of a single whole. The number of things to be learned is thus very nearly divided by two.

The advantage for learning that ordinary sense material possesses over nonsense is in part an expression of the same general principle, in part it is due to the greater ease of attending to matter that makes sense. Whatever has meaning tends to belong to a logical whole, and the units are all. grouped in lesser wholes which can be attended to at once, and tend to become for memory single ideas rather than separate disconnected things. That one can remember from eight to fourteen times as many ideas in poetry as nonsense syllables is by no means strange when one thinks of the links of rhythm, rhyme, and logical connection that serve to make the apparently distinct words parts of larger and larger groups.

That all parts of a series of nonsense syllables that has

been committed to memory have really been welded into a whole was demonstrated in the earlier experiments of Ebbinghaus by a highly ingenious method. After several series of syllables had been learned in the usual way, new series were formed by selecting from them each alternate syllable, or every third syllable, and so on, to series composed of every eighth syllable in different earlier series. It was found that there was some slight connection between syllables thus separated by from one to seven intervening syllables. The association overleaps the contiguous syllables and extends in a degree dependent upon nearness to all the other members of the series and binds all the elements into a unit. As a result the series made up of non-contiguous syllables from series already learned could be learned more easily than series of entirely new syllables, and the greater saving in time occurred when the component elements had been nearer each other in the original series. The association also runs backward as well as forward. Syllables once learned in a given order can be learned more easily in the reverse order than they could have been learned originally. The larger unity of the whole series which we have used to explain the greater ease of learning in rhythm, in ordinary sense material and elsewhere, is not a matter of supposition, but can be demonstrated to have real existence. Things attended to together, or in immediate succession, become united into a single whole.

The influence of age on memory is probably very largely dependent upon the influence of attention. Contrary to popular opinion, capacity for remembering increases with age. One learns most easily and remembers most completely when maturity has been reached. There is a gradual increase in memory through the earlier years until about eighteen, and then no change until the beginning of senile decay. All investigations seem to agree on this effect of age, no matter what method is used for the test. It has been suggested that the only change is in the capacity for attention, and that the capacity for bare learning or associating remains constant or decreases slightly. While there is no certain method of discriminating between attention and memory in this connection, it is probable that increase in knowledge is effective both in increasing interest in widely divergent fields, and so makes attention more certain and more strong, and that it prepares more associative bonds to receive the new material, and so makes association possible in more directions, and thus indirectly aids in remembering. In addition, firmness in holding oneself to the task increases with years, and in part explains the increased memory. In spite of all of these suggestions, however, it is by no means certain that the best time for forming the physiological connections at the basis of remembering may not be in early maturity rather than in childhood.

Apart from the improvement with age, it is probable that all increase in memory is due to factors closely related to attention. It is probable that memory increases with practice only in fields that are closely related to those in which the original practice was had. One obtains a better memory for psychological facts as one reads more in this field, but the results obtained do not improve memory for any other science except in so far as the two sets of facts overlap. As one knows more of a subject interest in the subject increases, and it is more easily understood. Moreover, new facts are no longer entirely new, but they can at once be assigned to some familiar head and classified with others already known. The work of remembering has been already partly done, and the completion of the process is much simpler than would be learning from the beginning. The previously acquired experiences help the elements to be learned into associative bonds in very much the same way that they help in the entrance of sensations as elements. And while, as was said above, the influence of training cannot be said to extend beyond the related field, there is so much in common between all kinds of knowledege, no matter how far removed they seem, that it is impossible to say with any certainty where the indirect benefit of any bit of information will cease to make itself felt.

Apart from the training that depends upon acquirement of facts, there is apparently a more general effect that depends upon getting accustomed to the apparatus and the particular methods of learning that are used. Ebert and Meumann subjected the 'question to an extended experimental investigation, and discovered that the facility for learning nonsense syllables constantly increased with practice for considerable periods of time. Moreover, facility acquired shows itself in learning other than nonsense material. It is plausible to assume that much of this, if not all, comes from the greater ease in fixing attention after practice under the relatively new experimental conditions. The authors quoted believe, however, that their results indicate that some general training may result from exercise in a limited field, and in a measure justify the old doctrine of formal discipline.

If attention is thus at work in determining ease and certainty of learning at every point, it is equally a factor in deciding what and how much shall be retained. As has been seen incidentally so far, those things that are attended to closely and so are learned easily are also retained well, even better in fact on the average than the things that are attended to less completely and so require more pains in the learning. We may go even farther, and assert that anything that is attended to well and easily, meaningful prose or poetry, for example, will be retained for much longer times or more completely than material that has no appeal through earlier training or mood.

We owe to Ebbinghaus [5] an investigation of this phenomenon also. His results show that with Byron's " Don Juan " there was a retention of fifty per cent after twenty-four hours as compared with thirty-four per cent for nonsense material. He asserts, too, that the influence of poetry once learned seems never entirely to disappear.

Stanzas of " Don Juan " learned once showed a saving of seven per cent after a lapse of twenty-two years as compared with stanzas that had never been learned. Stanzas that had been learned at four different times showed a saving of twenty per cent after the lapse of seventeen years. In each case there was nothing of the poem remembered in the ordinary sense, no parts of it could be recalled at will, but the connections once formed in the nervous system had left behind some traces that could be more or less easily brought to complete effectiveness when new repetitions were made.

An interesting and practically important negative influence of attention upon retention has been demonstrated by Müller and Pilzecker. [8] They found that retention was much impaired if attention were turned at once to something else after a series had been learned, while if one rested, thought of nothing in particular, for a few moments after the task had been finished, the relearning was very much easier. If after a series of nonsense syllables had been learned, the learner turned at once to mental computations, to learning other series or to performing any other work whatsoever, but twenty-four per cent of the series could be recalled six minutes later, while if nothing was done in the interval, fifty-six per cent could be recalled. Or for relearning an average of eight repetitions was required to reinstate the series, while after the same interval spent in rest, but four and nine-tenths repetitions were necessary. The rest should last approximately six minutes, as shown by the fact that after six minutes forty-eight per cent of correct answers were given, while if work were first begun after seventeen seconds only twenty-eight per cent correct answers were made. It appears from these facts that an important part of the process of fixing the associations runs its course after the repetitions have been finished. An indication as to what this process is, is furnished by the fact of the memory after-image that was mentioned in an earlier chapter, or what Müller has called the perseverance tendency of associations or ideas, a tendency to remain in consciousness for a period after the stimulus has ceased. This period of inertia of nerve cells seems highly favourable to the fixing of associations, and, if interrupted by vigorous attention to anything else, is correspondingly diminished. Quiet contemplation gives the connections time to set and become permanent.

If every feature of learning and of retention is thus shot through by attention to so great a degree that it is difficult to say at any time whether, in the explanation of any phenomenon, the bare capacity for forming associations is more important than adequacy of attending it is also equally true that recollection is very largely influenced by attention. Particularly is it true that if the fact recalled is to be suited to the problem in hand, selection from among the associations must be made by the wider group of conditions that we know in connection with attention rather than by the bare physiological connections dependent upon intensity, frequency, and recency of occurrence.

The effect of attention upon the return of the impression is again almost exactly the same, in fact, is identical with the effect in controlling the direction of association. What is recalled at any moment depends upon the idea that was in mind just before, and upon the mental attitude of that time—the general setting that gives the particular association its direction. As attention has a large part in determining what shall have been in mind at the preceding moment, and as it is also largely effective in turning the course of the associations, it is evident that recall as a whole is in large part a function of attention. What any event shall suggest to you depends not only upon what other events you have experienced before, but also upon your capacity to see in the present event some similarity to the preceding experience that would be useful in this emergency. And that, again, depends upon the attitude you can take toward the present circumstance. This ability to take the proper attitude toward the set of events at the right time is also, again, dependent upon your general knowledge, upon having an organised system of facts into which the new element may be fitted, upon being able to attend to it properly, and so observe the features which are essential. A large part of what we ordinarily call a good memory consists in nothing else than this ability to think of the right fact at the right time. The invention of the steam-engine was assured when a possible use for its energy was suggested by the force that the steam from the spout of the tea-kettle exerted. Many men knew of the value of force in general, and many men had observed that a straw would be bent by the steam from the spout, but no man before had also analysed the characteristic of force, and had the suggestion of the adaptation to a practical end, at the same time. All other elements were present in the mental content except the right conditions of the attention to bring about that analysis and to direct the train of associations into that particular path. This hung upon the presence of just the right knowledge and just the right attitude toward the problem at that time. Being in possession of the fact is not sufficient, there must also be sufficient acuteness to apply the knowledge at the proper time, and this is largely a problem of the attention. Even in the schoolroom inability to answer questions is not so much lack of proper knowledge as inability to see in the question the proper cue to the answer and lack of the proper related knowledge that will direct the train of associations to the particular fact desired. All this, of course, depends upon earlier experiences, upon knowledge in general, as has been pointed out so often before in this volume ; it is not lack of the particular bit of knowledge in question, but of the more indefinite and widely distributed general knowledge, that shall make the particular effective at this time and in this connection.

Recognition, the third phase of memory in the traditional treatment, is rather less dependent upon attention than

L

the two preceding, but nevertheless is by no means un-influenced by it. As has been so frequently asserted, recognition of the time and place of occurrence of an earlier event is essential if recall itself is to have any value. If one could not distinguish between an original experience and a returning idea, or if the old were known merely as old without knowledge of its date and the circumstances that attended its earlier appearance, memories would be rather a source of confusion than an aid in the mental life. Recognition proper is always a mark added to the returning impression that stamps the time and place of its earlier experiencing, very much as the inscription on the coin marks the year and country of its issue. Both marks are largely indifferent to the quality or character of the thing marked, but are of value only for purposes of classification. What the mark of recognition is has not altogether been agreed upon. It has been suggested by different men that it is an old or habitual mode of reaction to the entering mental process; that it is a mood or feeling of pleasure that comes with an old experience just because it is old, but which is not further analysable; that it is the addition to the returning impression of some distinctive other idea that has already been assigned a definite place in our experience, or the reception of the new into a familiar general class by the addition of a word or other generalising symbol. Probably each of these statements will apply to certain cases of recognition, but no one will satisfactorily cover all. The more self-conscious processes are due to the calling up of associated images or events, the inter-mediate stage is not infrequently a reference to a familiar standard or word, while the most reflex and immediate pro-cess may involve easy and ready response in an appropriate way. Most of these processes too are accompanied by a pleasant mood, although that is probably a resultant of some one or several of the processes mentioned above rather than itself primary.

However recognition comes about, we may be certain

that how we recognise an object depends upon the way we are attending at the moment. Every idea is capable of being recognised in several different ways. A book is at one time a source of information, at another a paper weight, and again in an emergency a fuel. Which of these divergent things it shall be at any moment depends upon the mood one is in and the external circumstances of the moment. If we consider recognition of objects rather than of ideas, we find that attention of a given kind will render one liable to illusions of either a positive or negative character. Things will be recognised as belonging to a given class when they are of an entirely different character, or other objects for which we are not at the moment prepared will be entirely denied recognition, although as familiar as can be in the usual mood. In a strange city, or in a foreign land, a familiar face will be denied recognition, while the association or mood of recognition will leap out too soon to meet an individual when some one in particular is expected.

Very much the same statements are to be made of the recognitory process as it attaches to ideas. Some returning ideas are recognised too easily and falsely, others are refused credence momentarily, because we are not prepared for them, or are too intently expecting something else. Every one remembers in his own experience recognising pseudo-facts suggested by an opponent in debate and accepted because they fitted in with other facts, only to find to his chagrin on reference that the recognition was false. Again ideas will be denied recognition if they do not harmonise with present conditions, even if they have been experienced comparatively recently. Cases of this kind suggest that attention and similar processes are at the basis of most of the faults of recognition, and indicate that it is probably equally important in the normal process as well.

Wherever we turn in the consideration of the memory problem, then, we find that we cannot account for memory even superficially unless we consider its connection with attention. Whether it be learning or retention, recall or recognition, the key to the effectiveness of the process and even to its nature is to be found in attention. A good memory is not something that can be acquired in isolation, but depends upon adequate attention, wide interests, broad knowledge, and manifold experiences.

SUMMARY

1. Memory is influenced by attention in each of its three processes.

2. Retention is dependent on the degree of attention that was given at the moment of learning. In the experiments upon memory, most of the methods that are favourable to retention are favourable to attention.

3. Recall is always directed by attention. If the mind is attentive in the right way, the correct bit of information is recalled, if not, the recall will be in error.

4. Recognition is influenced by attention both in its quickness and correctness. When one is attentive, recognition is quick; when attentive to the object that appears, recognition is accurate; when expecting something that does not appear, recognition is likely to be false.

5. All training of memory is through training of attention.

CHAPTER X

ATTENTION AND WILL, OR ACTION

ANOTHER function that cannot easily be dissociated from the attention is that which results in action—what is ordinarily known as will. One phase of the subject has already been discussed and has been found to be practically identical with the problem of the attention. This is what is ordinarily known as internal will, the ability to choose what is to enter consciousness and to direct the course of ideas. But the control of the entrance of ideas we have seen to be dependent upon the attention, to be conditioned by a series of circumstances rooted in heredity, in the social and physical environment, and not to be the exhibition of any new or peculiar process. The control of the course of thought is also a function of the same influences, and can, as we have seen, be ascribed to attention with equal right. There remains to consider the so-called external will, or the manifestations of will in the control of bodily movements. The close connection of the internal will and attention would at least suggest that there was a close connection also between the attention and the external phase of the will problem, or would at least be sufficient to suggest that we consider the relation between the two.

There is one general principle in connection with all forms of action which is sufficient to raise the general presumption that attention is a highly important condition for the voluntary processes. This is that every movement must be preceded by a sensation, that without the sensation there can be no movement, and that every movement is determined both in its intensity and in its direction by some sensory process. On the physiological side, this means that every movement is the result of the stimulation of some sensory nerve, that there can be no stimulation of the motor nerve in its normal connections except through a sensory impression or stimulus of some kind or other. So far does this go, that if the sensory nerves from any part of the body are destroyed there is a loss of control of the corresponding muscles. Under those circumstances it is only by guiding the movements of the member by vision that any movement, or at least any accurate movement, is possible. One case of tabes is cited, in which a woman who suffered from general anæsthesia of the arms could hold her child only so long as she looked at it—when she closed her eyes or looked away it at once slipped from her grasp. If it is so completely impossible to isolate movement from sensation, then evidently all the conditions which control the course of ideas would *ipso facto* exert a very great influence upon movement also. As attention is in almost complete control of the entrance of sensations and of the course of ideas, we naturally expect it to play a large part in the direction of the bodily movements as well.

The concrete facts of our experience bear out the theoretical conclusion. Everywhere we find that attention to the movement to be made or to the result to be attained by the movement is the conscious experience that precedes action. As we saw before in discussing the motor concomitants of attention, if any one object in the field of vision catches the attention, there is at once a turning of the eye in such a way as to bring the object upon the centre of the retina, upon the point of clearest vision. There is no intermediate link. Attention to the object and movement seem united as parts of a single process. It is only after considerable practice that it is possible to observe the object with the side of the retina—to look out of the side of the eye without turning the eye to permit the impression to be received upon the most sensitive portion of the retina. And even when this is accomplished, it is by dividing the attention between the object to be seen with the periphery and some other directly in front. The half attention to the impression upon the fovea keeps the eye fixed in the desired position.

Exactly the same statement holds of the other voluntary movements. If you will study the mechanism of any action you will see that to keep firmly in mind the movement that you desire to make, or the object to be attained by the movement, is the one prerequisite for initiating the movement, or for controlling it when once it has started. Picture your hand in a certain place, and it will immediately proceed to move towards that place, unless, as in the case of holding the eye at rest while attending to an object at one side, you also attend in part to the present position of the hand. Fix your attention upon an object upon the table closely and completely, and you will usually find yourself fingering that object before many moments have passed. Of course you will answer that looking, even with picturing your hand moving towards the object, does not necessarily involve handling, and this must be granted. Look more closely, however, and you will see that even the refraining is due to the attention. There is always a tendency to move with attention, and when the tendency does not become realised it is because the attention is turned later to something else, or is at the time divided between two objects in different positions. Usually the restraining attention consists in attending to the hand in its present position.

Much clearer are the instances that come from games. " Keep your eye on the ball " in golf is a familiar statement of the fact that the movement of the arms is controlled immediately by attention to some object in the field of vision. There is little or no thought of the movements to be made or of anything else except the place upon which the blow is to be delivered. Again, it is a familiar experience that if the mind wanders to any other idea than that of the proper place, if you think how far the ball is likely to go, or of the position of the arms at any point of the movement, or of any other extraneous matter, the wandering of the attention will be recorded in the inaccuracy of the stroke. The stroke is determined not by one, but by many attentions, and the blow is a resultant of the different tendencies. The novice at bicycle riding will for the same reason run into every obstacle that he sees. The tree, the bystander, the stone in his path, are the objects which attract his attention, and so are the objects towards which he directs his course. It is only as he learns to direct his attention to the part of the path where no difficulties lie that his way becomes smooth. Similarly, in guiding a team around the corner, the beginner must think which rein to pull, must attend to the position and movement of the hand at each moment; but with increased practice, although the movement is still directly under the influence of attention, it is only necessary to attend to the direction to be taken. The movement is made without any idea of the separate elements involved. The more highly developed the movement, the less attention need be given to details, the more general is the cue that will serve to initiate the entire process.

This general result is really but an extension of the fact mentioned in an earlier chapter, that every act of attention tends to pass over into movements which are usually unconscious, but which in what we call voluntary action are fully known at the time of their occurrence. Another instance that will illustrate the close relation between these unconscious movements and the ordinary movements of everyday life is found in the control of the organs of speech. If you will record the movements of the larynx by a suitable mechanism while repeating some verses aloud, and then will take a record while you merely think through the words without any vocal expression, it will be found that the two tracings agree at every point except that the movements made when the words are merely thought are slighter than when expression is given to them. This tendency to follow the course of thought by movement may go so far that there is an unconscious expression even in perfectly normal persons. Lehmann and Hansen [4] obtained indications of this kind in some experiments in which they attempted to investigate the results of the Society for Psychical Research that seemed to show communication between mind and mind at a distance with no known physical intervention. One man was placed at a distance from the other and was asked to think of letters or figures, while the other was to record anything that he might be thinking of at the time. The result showed that frequently the second person would write down symbols that more or less closely resembled those which the first man had in mind. Close examination showed that the first man actually whispered the words that he thought, and these whispers were transmitted farther than was to be expected, because the walls of the room were so placed as to form a rude lens that had one of the men at one focus, the other at another. Apparently, then, all thinking in words is accompanied by an actual expression, or at least by actual movements of the vocal organs. Under conditions of unusual interest these movements give rise unconsciously to audible tones, and when the inhibitions are removed the ordinary speech follows at once upon the idea of the words. The only difference between thinking in words and talking is in the degree of movement of the organs of speech, and the difference is made by restraining the natural tendency in thinking, not by the addition of something new when we think aloud. The conditions of ordinary speech, then, are to be found altogether in the subjective conditions that bring the ideas of the words into consciousness. These, as we have seen in the earlier chapters, are to be found in the earlier experiences of the individual, in short, in the attention.

But we must consider the effect of attention not merely in the fully developed consciousness, but in the development of action as well. If we find that all action is preceded by and dependent upon ideas, the natural query comes, how did this particular movement come to be connected with this definite idea ? In the early stages of accomplishment we will many things that we are not able to perform. The ideas are apparently present in full completeness, but no movement follows, or at least the movement that would lead to the end desired does not follow. In the course of time and after numerous struggles the proper movement is acquired, and after that desire leads at once to satisfaction. If we ask the general question how was this brought about, we recognise two classes of connections with reference to the time of origin. Some are already present in some degree of perfection before birth, others are acquired in the lifetime of the individual. Some of the pre-natal connections are present fully formed at birth, others develop with increasing development of the nervous system, but without any learning on the part of the individual. These are both known as reflex, or instinctive actions, and must evidently be explained on evolutionary grounds.

If we reject all theories that imply the inheritance of acquired characters as modern biology is inclined to, the explanation of the instinctive and reflex actions would depend entirely upon the survival of those organisms in which the movements that are suited to the environment in which they find themselves make their appeareance owing to changes in the structure, and the elimination of all others not adapted to react in a suitable way. It is a process of trial and error, in which the trying is represented by chance changes in the germ plasm, success implies increased liability to survive and consequent increase in numbers over those species less fit, and failure involves increased liability to death from environmental agencies or starvation. In all this attenton can play little real part, for acquired habits that attention favours would die with the body and not be transmitted. It is only in so far as the capacities for attention are among the physiological characteristics transmitted that it would play any part, and then it would not constitute a fundamental principle of explanation, but would be one of the many effects of the changing nervous organism.

Adaptation within the life of the individual may be made to follow the same general scheme, but here the influence of attending is everywhere apparent. Here, again, there is little or no conscious foreshadowing of the result to be attained, but from among the movements that chance to come from organic causes there is selection of those which best suit the purpose of the moment or the situation. A certain number of responses are predetermined at birth by the racial acquirements of instinct, but in man and the higher animals a vastly greater number of movements are possible from the side of the nervous connections than are fixed or predetermined. The process of learning seems to depend entirely upon selecting from the movements that are possible at birth those which are either important for the individual or are more important than the movements given at birth in full perfection. Some instincts are retained and acquire new strength from use, others are checked and destroyed, still others are modified to suit the new conditions of the individual. To the instincts are added new movements selected from the indefinite random movements of childhood, become definite by selection and fixed by habit.

Evidently in an animal of fairly high development, the movements acquired by a process of selection are even more important than the movements inherited, and an understanding of the method of selection is highly desirable. That animals learn by this method of chance trial was made clear by Thorndike [5] in some experiments on dogs, cats, and chicks [3a, 4a]. The experiments were performed by placing the animals in cages, with fastenings of different degrees of complexity, and determining the methods they used to free themselves under the stimulus of hunger. The method used in every instance was to bite and scratch about at random until by a lucky chance some movement successfully opened the door. After the first success, shorter and shorter times were required until the connection became so close between the stimulus provided by sight of the catch and the movement of escape that the appropriate response was executed at once, and learning was complete. These experiments have been frequently repeated on animals of all grades, and it has been found that the method of learning holds from below the vertebrates to apes. This seems for animals the only possible method of acquiring a new movement. Both scientists and animal trainers seem to be agreed that an animal cannot be taught a movement by being put through it by the hand of the trainer. The impulse to action must originate within the animal in an idea or stimulus, if it is to be permanently learned, if any trace of the action is to be left in the organism as a basis for later action. So far, too, experiments seem to demonstrate no certain evidence of imitation in animals. They do not seem to perform a movement more quickly or easily from seeing another do it. At most, seeing the movement made by another attracts attention to the movement when they themselves make it by chance, and so indirectly hastens its acquirement, but even this aid in animals has not been demonstrated to be important.

Bair investigated the same problem in man where the mental processes could be studied directly, and found a similar law to hold. Bair chose as the movement to be learned the contraction of the retrahens of the ear, the muscle behind the ear whose contraction draws it back. Few men, and none of those investigated, have control of this muscle, although the nervous connections are ready to permit its contraction. It stood to the men investigated in approximately the same relations as the muscles of the body as a whole to the child at birth. Bair first attempted to teach the men experimented upon to use the muscle by contracting it for them by means of the electric current. The method met with very slight success. It seemed to do no more than indicate to them the general region in which the contractions were to be made, but brought with it no power of repeating the movement. There was still the same feeling as at first, that one had the same relation to the movement as to turning a door-knob on the other side of the room. It was perfectly possible to will it to move, but no movement followed. The first successful movement came by chance in connection with the production of known movements of scalp or jaw. Part of the innervation spread to the ear muscle, and that contracted with the other muscles that were already under voluntary control. When the movement to be acquired had once been performed with the others it was more and more likely to become an element of the complex whenever the others were made, whenever the idea of the total was held firmly in mind.

The next stage was to isolate the new movement from the complex in which it had developed. This was entirely a result of attention. By keeping attention fixed definitely and continuously upon the desired element to the exclusion of all other parts of the conjoined movements it was finally possible to hold that idea alone in mind, and with that the other movements fell away. After the ear movements had been isolated from the first complex, both ears still moved together with the single impulse; it was not possible to contract one alone. By the same process of neglecting one and attending to the other, it became possible to move either alone at will.

An interesting by-result of the experiment was an illustration of the statement that it is the idea alone that produces the action. In one set of experiments the men were asked to hold the ear relaxed against the current, to prevent its contraction. The result was just the reverse of that intended. After some control of the movement had been obtained, the idea of not making the movement resulted in contracting the ear and holding it contracted during the entire period that the experiment lasted, acted, in fact, in just the same way as did the idea of moving. The specific idea, not the general intention, brought about the contraction. These results and other observations seem to be conclusive evidence that all learning is by selection of random movements. There is apparently no possibility of learning to make a movement on the basis of rational considerations. One might have complete knowledge of the anatomy of muscle and nerve and still be no nearer the performance of a movement than the most ignorant. Unless the muscle has at some time been moved in response to an idea, there is no possibility of making it contract, no matter how much one may know about its connections.

All of these laws are illustrated to the full in the learning of a child. At first all movements are bound together, and when any stimulus or idea presents itself, diffuse movements occur in widely separate parts of the body. The first vague reachings of the arms are accompanied by corresponding movements of extension in the legs as well. As one hand makes a grasping movement the other contracts, and at times the toes may be seen to make homologous contractions. From the mass are selected those elements that produce satisfactory results; all the others are neglected, and through neglect die away. At first the entire complex that results from a stimulus is often the exact opposite of the movement that is suited to the occasion. So for days all of the elements of the creeping process may be present, but the hands may be put too far forward, with the result that all movements are away from the desired object rather than toward it. It is only a question of time until the correct complex will appear by chance, and then the learning will be complete. That will then be permanently chosen and stamped in by repetition, because it brings a reward. Thus learning in the child is seldom the result of intention, rather the child selects the best from what comes out of its organism by chance. Fortunate it is that the responses of the organism are so varied and persistent that all of the valuable movements make their appearance sooner or later, and can be seized upon by attention and made permanent by repetition. Even in adult life the acquirement of a new movement is by much the same method. The more important difference is that we already have control of a series of movements that are similar to the one desired, and we need only to modify them to suit our immediate need. The modification, however, is one of chance trial and selection by attention of the correct variant. In learning a stroke at golf we adapt the swing of an axe or similar swing in a way to make it useful in the new connection. The adaptation is not immediate, and trial alone will enable one to hit upon the correct complex; when it comes attention is given, and habit confirms the acquirement.

Learning to move then is at every stage very largely a matter of attention. We select the complex of movements that is most suitable from the movements that chance to be made, and then from the complex we select the element that is important and neglect all else. The selection of both complex and element is the result of attending to the sensations that come from the movement or to the result that is attained. When, later, either the original stimulus, the idea of the sensation of movement or of the general result attained comes to consciousness the movement is reinstated.

When series of movements have thus been learned and frequently repeated in the same connection, they become so chained together that one idea will suffice for the reinstatement of the entire series. That idea is usually some relatively remote end, rather than something connected with an individual element. Thus in walking, the desire to arrive at a remote place leads to a very complicated set of movements with very little thought for the intervening details of the execution. In writing, the idea of a general sentiment serves to initiate a whole series of movements with little or no thought of the separate parts. But even in these more complicated cases the initial stage is an idea, and the idea is selected and determined by attention. Here the idea is often general and remote rather than particular and immediate.

The more complicated actions that are ordinarily denoted as volitional offer even more striking illustrations of the influence of attention. By volitional action we designate those highly developed actions in which decision must be made between two opposing courses before movement can begin. In these instances too the action is always foreshadowed in idea. The choice is primarily between ideas rather than between actions. The alternatives are presented in the ends to be attained, and decision is complete when one of the ends is held firmly in mind and the other banished. If the choice is between going to one's room to read or going for a stroll, the decision is made when one idea or the other holds the centre of consciousness. The two ideas are balanced in terms of the relative desirability of the two ends. But this means, in terms of our conditions of attention, that one appeals to one set of conditions the other to another, and whenever one set of conditions predominates, the corresponding idea will gain the mastery. With that mastery of the idea the movements that have been associated at once come into play. When the day is pleasant and duty not pressing, or the company unusually agreeable, the idea of the stroll wins, and we start for the walk. Are the conditions reversed the idea of study table predominates ; we return to our rooms and work begins forthwith.

When the problem to be decided upon carries with it the performance of acts at a remote time or place the essential conditions are similiar, except that the movements are delayed to await an appropriate immediate stimulus in another set of circumstances. The choice of a profession or other life work evidently is a process in which no movement necessarily follows at the moment, but the decision is none the less effective. It narrows the range of indecision for all later decisions in that group, and carries with it, directly, decisions on a number of subordinate questions. It is decided e.g. that if sufficient money is available one university will be attended, if not another will be chosen, or work be begun on the apprentice system, if that be permitted by the rules of the community in which the youth resides. Each act is prepared for immediately, but its performance awaits the presence of suitable occasion and conditions. The decision acts at once to control and influence later attention. On the other side it is itself the outcome of present attention influenced by still earlier conditions. The decision may even act in advance to make attention at the moment practically unnecessary, or may at least do away with the necessity for any idea to intervene between stimulus and response, and produce what might be called a voluntarily prepared reflex. When the stimulus that has been awaited presents itself, the action decided upon in advance is performed at once without any intervening idea, although the movement in question may not have been performed before in that connection, or not frequently enough to have made the response automatic. Cases of this kind apparently have made Woodworth question whether ideas are essential for movement[6]. Woodworth leaves the problem with the not very definite or satisfactory statement that the movement follows upon a disembodied thought, after he has given experimental results which indicate that there is often no idea discoverable just before the movement is made. Dr. Ach [1] worked under rather more definite conditions, and was able to assign the determining elements in the process with considerably greater certainty. He employed reaction experiments, in which the observer was asked to respond, now to one stimulus, now to another, according to directions given in advance for each group of experiments. In many instances it was observed that the movement followed the stimulus that had been agreed upon when there was no definite idea of the action in advance of the response, and when nothing intervened

M

between stimulus and response. Under these circumstances Ach found that the task that had been set for the experiments dominated consciousness, and prepared the way for the response. When the stimulus came it resulted at once in the action, just as if there had been earlier practice, or as if some idea of moving had intervened. The physiological side of the preparation alone is in evidence in these cases, but for action the lack of consciousness is a matter of indifference. Attention is to the stimulus, not to the idea, and nothing else is necessary for the action to be performed. The same anticipatory readiness for action is induced by the decision as in the delayed action that was considered above. When the occasion implied in the decision presents itself, the response is rendered automatic in advance of practice, provided, of course, that the action is already under control and can be made in response to some other cue. In both cases the process is almost identical with the influence of mood or purpose in the control of association, as brought out in Watt's experiments. As the mood or question favours the rise into consciousness of the object that corresponds to it over all impressions not thus favoured, or the task makes inevitable one of the possible associates, so the decision or task set by another prepares the way for the action decided upon when the predetermined stimulus appears, and that without the intervention of any idea or other intermediary. It is a matter of one or more of the conditions working directly upon action ; it is attention to the stimulus taking the place of attention to the sensation or idea. We are dealing with nothing that involves a new principle, it is but a slightly different application of an old principle.

If, then, all choice is, in the last analysis reducible to the selection of one idea from among other ideas, or to direct selection of a movement by factors that are almost identical with those that control attention, it would follow that the conditions of attention are the real determinants of action. The ends that we desire are those that appeal to us because of heredity, training, or momentary mood, or those that have been forced upon us or made valuable by social convention. These are the forces that really choose when opportunity is offered. In fact, most difficulties in decision come because different sets of conditions favour opposed courses of action. Ordinarily, instinct or mood is in conflict with the social influences. Choice is the outcome, consciously or unconsciously, of the struggle. The struggle is not often conscious, and decision is marked by no new mental process. The only sign of conflict resolved is the serene dominance of the one idea or set of ideas that serves to initiate the movement.

Will, then, if we are to give the ordinarily accepted facts that are designated by the word a place in our scheme, might be designated as the dominance of the social factors and the appreciation of remote goods against the immediate goods that have the guarantee of chance mood and instinct. One may be said to have a strong will in whom the influence of remote social influences is strong and the influence of temporary mood and hereditary impulse is relatively weak or well subordinated; while a man is of weak will in popular estimation if he is not capable of retaining permanently or even for long periods the influence of general social standards. This difference is undoubtedly innate and but slightly subject to the influence of environmental forces. Whether a strong man takes good or bad standards will depend very largely upon the society into which he has been born and the educational influences that work upon him. Will in this sense is exactly in line with the social forces that we have seen to be at work in sensory attention, in the control of thought and now of action. In one sense we may say that these forces are identical in all four fields, and so justify the use of the word will as the most general influence in the control of mind, and distinguish two effects, external and internal. But in this we must be careful to insist that will is no thing or force, but merely a convenient term to designate the fact that the early and general social influences hold attention, thought and action toward the things that are permanent rather than to those things that are transient.

It seems that the problem of voluntary action is largely, if not entirely, a problem of attention, and a complete understanding of attention with its nature and conditions will also imply an understanding of movements. Some forms are more, some less closely connected with the attentive consciousness, but all are in some measure, and at some stage dependent very largely upon the ideas, and must also, in so far, be subject to the control of attention. Furthermore, the more volitional the movement, the more fully conscious the action, the greater is the amount of control that attention will exert upon movement. In common language, the more the will is involved in the action, the more completely it is subordinated to the attention. This phase of the problem of the will also seems to resolve itself into a sub-form of the general problem of attention that we have been discussing before. The processes which are effective in the control of a man's ideas are *ipso facto* effective in the control of his movements. The course of one's actions is to be explained in terms of his inherited tendencies, from his social environment past and present, and from his experience reacting upon the stimuli which he is receiving at the time in question, just as is the course of his ideas and the decision between the various sensations that shall enter consciousness at any given instant. A man's action is an expression of himself in the widest sense of the term, including in that term every experience that has affected him from before birth to the present moment.

SUMMARY

1. Action in general is dependent upon sensation. Movements only take place after corresponding sensations have been in consciousness. It follows, then, since attention controls the entrance of sensations that it must also control action.

2. In the developed action of the adult attention to a sensation is the practically invariable antecedent to action.

3. In acquiring a movement for the first time attention is effective in three ways : (*a*) it selects from the chance movements those that are interesting for further repetition ; (*b*) it selects from the complex movements thus first acquired the essential part, and the elements not attended to drop out from the complex ; (*c*) when there is necessity for modifying a familiar movement there is first attention to some movement already known which causes that to be made, and then selection from the chance variations in that movement of the most desirable variant for the purpose in hand.

4. Choice is a result of attending to one of two possible sensations or ideas with its corresponding movement.

5. In general, will may be defined as attention applied to the control of movement.

CHAPTER XI

ATTENTION AND REASON

THE third of the more commonly mentioned "faculties" that we must examine for its relation to attention is reason. The part that attention plays in the reasoning process comes out very clearly from the similarity in the conditions which control the two processes. That the mental environment, the traditions of the race or tribe, and many other elements of experience, if not of heredity, play an important part in determining the nature of reason is to be seen from even a casual examination of the inferences which different people draw from the same data. The Irishman who said on seeing a locomotive : " Faith ! what a lot of horses there must be inside," was reasoning from his past experience with as much cogency as the engineer who could deduce the horse-power that would be produced by a given amount of coal. In actual practice human reason is not independent of individual experience, but is merely the expression, at a given instant, and with reference to a present event, of the history of the race and of the particular member of the race in whose consciousness the reasoning goes on.

What distinguishes reasoning from imagination and memory is not the way in which the process originates, or the nature of the mental process itself, but is our attitude toward the mental state or the use that we make of those states. The thing that we imagine, merely, and do not believe to exist in reality, has all the substantive mental characteristics of the thing that we reason must exist in a certain place under definite conditions. The event that we recall and the one that we argue must take place in the future may be pictured in exactly the same way, may have exactly the same ideational content. Again, we can trace out associations for the remembered, the imagined, and rationally demonstrated event by exactly the same laws—all connections that appear in any one can be traced to older connections reinstated under the influence of more general factors, whether the resulting process is what we call reason, memory, or imagination. We must turn to their accompaniments of one form or another for the factors that shall distinguish them.

There are two criteria that mark the groups off as distinct. One, recognition, has already been considered. It serves to distinguish memory from imagination and reason alike. When the mark of recognition attaches we say at once that the product of our associatory processes then present is something that has been experienced before. The other events are denied the reference to the past, although they may be in all other respects identical. Imagination and reason are new constructions that lack the tag of antiquity.

Imagination is marked off from reason and memory again by the fact that we believe the latter process to be true, while we doubt the former or believe it to be but partially and reservedly true. The fundamental questions, then, with reference to all the stages of the reasoning process are, what is belief? when do we believe? and when do we doubt? and what are the conditions of belief? Here, again, in the answer to our problems, we get back to the conditions of attention. We can best understand belief from a study of the cases in which it is first lacking, and later appears, for belief is so generally present in our ordinary conscious states that it is hard to find a point for analysis. As Bain says, the natural state is belief, and the departures from that to doubt or disbelief are the states that really need explanation; they alone are the unusual, if not the positive processes. If we examine some case in perception where there is doubt, we find that doubt comes whenever two interpretations of an event are striving for the mastery. So if one is examining an object from a distance, an ocean liner for example, one finds that he is in doubt as long as he makes first one interpretation, then another. When some one near by suggests that it is one well-known boat you agree until you remember that you had read that the boat had sailed from a distant port so recently that its arrival would be impossible ; to another interpretation that comes to your mind you find some other strong objection in the number or the colour of the funnels, or there is some element in your experience that refuses to harmonise with the assumption that the boat seen is the one in question. Just as long as there is alternation between two possible interpretations there is doubt ; whenever one conquers completely and entirely, there is belief.

The same processes operate to produce doubt when one is dealing with more abstract problems, and with things remembered or imagined rather than with the immediately seen. So when you hear of any distant event you judge of its truth by the degree to which it can be made to harmonise with what you already know. Whenever there are some groups of experience with which it will harmonise, and others with which it will not, you doubt. When the statement is seen to harmonise with one and not to be in conflict with others, you believe. Ordinarily the weighing is not conscious. The systems which interpret the statement are not consciously present. There is only the presence of one of the alternative explanations, then the other, and neither persists. When one interpretation wins, it is believed, but the belief may be stated positively, or negatively, as disbelief of the alternative. Ordinarily, disbelief is merely belief in something else along with the consciousness of the rivalry past or present, not a third form of consciousness added to doubt and belief. The one possible exception is found in the case in which there are many possible interpretations that exclude each other, and no one wins ; under these circumstances and these alone do we find disbelief that is not really belief in something else.

In each of these cases the conditions that make for belief or doubt are the same as the conditions which we have seen to account for the original entrance of a sensation ; for the interpretation of an object of perception in one way or another, and for the control of association. It seems that the activity of these conditions not merely determines the course of consciousness, but also by their action induces a feeling that is for us the mark of the truth or lack of truth of the process in question. Just as there may be a temporary dominance of one group of factors, to be followed at the next moment by another group, so we may have a permanent control of belief by one system that is intentionally or unintentionally in control of mind. Thus the artistic attitude toward a novel or a painting or a statue is one in which we permit ourselves to feel under the dominance of one system, although we know it does not result in the production of complete truth. The artist has been controlled in his production by a limited set of considerations, and we, for the moment, accept the same set of experiences, and we believe in a partial way as long as he follows completely the tacit assumptions he has made. Here we have judgment of truth in terms of an artificially limited experience, and the result is a belief that is partial, but with a suppressed background of knowledge that the statements are not true finally and ultimately. Similarly in dreaming, part of the brain is asleep, and consequently what association processes are present are controlled by a partial, one-sided experience. Nevertheless, as long as the parts of knowledge that judge are also the parts that control the course of associations, the results are believed. When, however, we wake, and the results of the activity of the partial consciousness are judged in the light of the whole, the product seems at once bizarre and unnatural.

In every case then we find that belief grows from harmony of a particular interpretation with the total experience active at the moment. Whether there is a positive belief feeling-complex that arises from the interaction of part on part when the idea enters, as there is in recognition, or whether belief is but the absence of the positive doubt process, is difficult to determine from observation, and is not a matter of agreement. If the belief-feeling exists it is the conscious concomitant of the action of many physiological processes, themselves unconscious, but due to earlier experiences, which control the course of thought and perception in the many ways that have been noted in the earlier portions of the work. They would correspond to the processes mentioned in the last chapter as preparing for action when the stimulus was presented, even when there was no evidence that preparation had taken place. In the opinion of the writer, it is probable that the latter alternative is the correct one, that belief is the absence of the particular marks of doubt. Where there is conflict between two interpretations, or between the one interpretation and the whole of knowledge, there is a positive sign or mark, but there is no positive mark of harmony. In that case Bain would be right in his assertion that the natural process is belief, and that every experience that comes to consciousness unopposed is believed.

That the nature of belief, like the course of attention, is dependent upon the amount and kind of knowledge at any moment, is evidenced by the way beliefs change with growth of knowledge in the race or the individual. Many things believed at any one stage of knowledge are rejected at the next. Belief seems to be just as much the inevitable accompaniment of the knowledge of the man, and of the part of his knowledge active at any moment, as is attention.

Belief, then, as a mood or mark that attaches to mental states, characterises the results of reasoning as distinguished from imagination, as the mood of recognition distinguishes memory processes from reasoning and imagination. But to describe the results of reasoning in terms of belief tells us little or nothing of the actual forces that lead to the result. We must turn then to a more detailed discussion of the way in which the processes of association and attention are effective in reaching conclusions that shall be believed. It will perhaps be best in this discussion to follow the nomenclature of formal logic, in spite of the fact that there can no longer be said to be any agreement as to what the words shall designate either in modern logic or in psychology. This difference of usage may justify any departures that we may ourselves make from the definitions of any particular school.

Following current usage, we may say that the first stage in the development of reasoning is seen in the process of judgment. By judgment many different facts have been indicated in logic and in everyday life. All, however, have some points of similarity—more, it must be confessed, in extension than in intention, for while the actual processes designated are all somewhat similar, the definitions that are given are widely divergent. On the strictly psychological side, and apart from all considerations of language, we may distinguish four different facts that have been designated judgment in most recent times. These are comparison, evaluation, the ascription of meaning, and the addition of belief.

If we begin with the historically first, we find that Brentano defines judgment as the process of testing the bare mental contents with reference to their truth or falsity. He insists that there is a first stage of perception in which there is neither belief nor disbelief, and that a judgment is passed as soon as the process is affirmed to be true or false. We shall have reason to conclude that this unbelieved stage has no real existence in mind, but that every process is accepted or rejected immediately upon its first entrance into consciousness. Furthermore, belief is an outcome or an incident of the process of entrance into consciousness, and nothing new and distinct. While, therefore, belief is essential to judging, it is not the characteristic phase.

The important contribution of Brentano to the theory of judgment lies rather in his insistence upon the singleness of the judgment process, than upon his actual contributions toward a decision as to what the single process might be.

More widespread is the use of the term judgment to designate comparison. Popularly we speak of judging weights when we decide which is heavier, and we speak of judging when we compare time and space relations as well. Psychologically Külpe and Marbe have given the use currency as a technical definition. Comparison falls easily under the description that has been given of attention in what precedes. It is a process that follows immediately upon attentive observation of two objects when the question in mind as we look is which is greater, better, brighter, or what not. The resulting process is always a word, or other symbol. All that can be noted in the process consciously is attention to the elements and the outcome of the entire process in a word. What is common, however, to all comparisons is the mood or question that precedes the decision and determines what it shall be. If the question in mind be which is larger, one judgment will be passed, if which is heavier, another, and if it is a question of colour or position, still other comparisons will be made. In no case does any demonstrable conscious process intervene between observing with the suitable question in mind and the outcome in decision. The conditions, process, and result, are practically identical with those in attention to a single object. The distinction is only that two objects are attended to instead of one, that the question involves relation instead of one single quality. When we recall, however, that whether an object be two or one depends very largely upon how we attend, and that what is at one moment one may become two or more at the next, the difference is not great enough to make the two classes entirely distinct. Moreover, the relations that we have in comparisons are not markedly enough different from form or number or even quality to prevent them from falling under the general head of aspects of the larger whole, that are distinguished by attention.

Judgments of evaluation are similar to the foregoing, save in the single particular that comparison is made between the presented object and some earlier developed standard or norm. In many cases the standard is not in consciousness at the moment the judgment is made, and the only evidence of the comparison is the relative way in which the judgment is expressed and the implied presence of the standard. But absence of the standard is not characteristic of the process of evaluation alone. In cases of delayed comparison or of comparison in memory, where one is comparing a colour seen yesterday with one shown now, it has been noticed repeatedly that the first or standard impression is not ordinarily in mind when the comparison results. Further-more, the cases in which the image is present are not those that give the most accurate results. All that is necessary is that the determination to judge be present when the second term is shown and the result appears immediately. Another phase of the memory experiments that is suggestive for the more general judgment of evaluation is that the standard often develops during the course of the investigation. Lehmann, for example, noted that his observers could remember as many shades of gray as there were common names in the vocabulary of the individual in question. When a set of numbers was learned in connection with the grays, the number of shades that could be accurately recognised increased from six to nine. The different shades were evaluated as before, but new standards had developed, and evaluation was corres-pondingly more accurate. Very much the same process goes on as we judge a painting. The standards have developed gradually, and are not necessarily conscious. Evaluation, then, falls very readily under the head of comparison. It is comparison with a standard slowly crystallised from numerous experiences that may be represented by an image, a word, or may not be represented at all ; in the latter more usual case the only conscious processes are the mood or attitude that serve as condition, and the outcome, the evaluation of the object. The mood is as important here as in comparison. An object may always be evaluated in more than one way, by reference to more than one standard. A book may be an excellent paper-weight and a very poor treatise on psychology. If your mood or purpose is of one kind, the judgment good is passed ; if of another, bad or unsatisfactory.

This takes us even a step nearer the simple perception process than before. As we look at a simple object with a question in mind, we at once interpret it in terms of earlier experiences, and the character of the interpretation varies with change in the group of experiences with which it is compared, and by the mood we happen to be in as we look. Moreover, the interpretation is always a process of reference to types that have grown up gradually in our observations, and the attempts we have made to harmonise our perceptions one with another. To use our old instance, the table that we see is no particular single perception, but is unlike any single experience, in that its angles are all right angles, and it has solidity, while neither the rectangular surface or solidity are represented on the retina or have been immediately given in any single retinal image. Every interpretation as we look is thus, to repeat the statement of an earlier chapter, a reference to a norm that has arisen to standardise experience. As the mood or purpose determines the norm to which the object to be evaluated is referred, so the mood determines the way the object shall be interpreted, the particular crystallisation to which it shall be referred. As an object is satisfactory at one moment and unsatisfactory at the next, so it is now a beautiful mountain and again an example of volcanic action. Evaluation is closely related to comparison on the one side, but is difficult to distinguish from a simple case of attending on the other.

Still more obviously related to the attention process is the fourth process that has been designated judgment, probably the most technical of them all : that judgment is the ascription of meaning to the given. If we may be permitted to assign to meaning, as used by the neo-Hegelian logicians, any analogue in the concrete conscious process at all, we should find it in the general schemata that we have seen to constitute the interpretation of the immediately given conscious experience. The meaning of a table is the standardised table that is seen in perception in place of the surfaces we must draw. The tendency to proceed from sensation or group of sensations to the typical experience is general, so general, in fact, that it is difficult to say whether there is ever present in consciousness a mere sensation or given except as embodied in meaning. If we accept the definition of Bradley and Bosanquet, that it is the attachment of meaning to the given, we would have the process of perception at every stage a process of judging, a process of passing from the individual to the general, from the particular present to the universal past. All perception is in this sense an evaluation, although the question of value may not be prominent at the moment of perception. Yet never is an impression received for itself alone, but always we have a testing by old developed standards. What we shall judge, what meanings shall attach, depends again, as in attention, upon present purpose and past knowledge. Whether we shall at any moment be concerned with a bit of coal as a weapon of defence or a fuel, whether as a fossil tree or a relatively pure form of carbon, depends upon what the appreciated need of the moment may be, and what we have previously learned of the substance, its origin, chemical composition, and uses. In every case the nature of the judgment is dependent upon the same conditions that we have seen to be active in attention. In this, too, judgments of the simple ordinary kind are practically identical with judgments of comparison and evaluation. The two latter are but sub-forms of the former. The problem or need of the moment differentiates them. There must always be at least two objects, or two aspects of a common object present in comparison and evaluation, instead of one as in the attachment of meaning and attention. In other respects the process is similiar in all three, and all are identical in essential elements with the processes involved in attending. If we summarise the three latter forms we may say that judgment consists in attending to a simple or complex content with a definite purpose in mind, and that as a result there starts into mind a meaningful standardised object that we accept as true, as real. Moreover, it must be insisted that there is no sign of the uninterpreted given or sensation in mind. The pure sensation of the psychologist has existence only as another interpretation or meaning which the psychologist gives or applies as his interpretation of the experience, an interpretation under a new purpose, and consequently of different character, although it may be equally true with the interpretation of the scientist or of everyday life.

All this leaves out of consideration the process that the formal logician has designated as judgment, time out of mind. The formal logician has insisted that judgment is always a combination of at least two elements in a single whole. This definition has developed from the fact that the formal logician is concerned with reasoning primarily as it is expressed in words rather than with the mental processes that lie behind. The connection of subject and predicate in the sentence was made the type of the logical connection, and all the judgments of thought were crowded into that same mould. That the attempt has not been satisfactory, altogether, is evidenced by the great uncertainty among those who accept the statement as to what the relation is between the two elements in question. The attempts of the more modern logicians to find in the proposition the analogue of the attachment of meaning in the sense considered above can hardly be said to be more satisfactory. Ordinarily, as in Bradley and Bosanquet, it is asserted that the given is represented in the subject, and that the meaning that is attached is represented by the predicate. We have seen, however, that the given is probably not represented in consciousness at all, but that the meaning alone comes to mind. It is hardly likely that we should find expressed what is really not in mind. It is probable that there is no one to one relation between thought and language in this connection, but that what is single in mind is represented in language at one time by two terms, and again that two meanings are represented in a single proposition. Ordinarily, it is true, the meaning in the predicate is alone prominent at the moment the judgment is passed, and that the subject represents something that was attended to at the moment just preceding. Sometimes, too, the subject seems never to have been essential to thought, but to have been added by force of habit in speech. It would take us too far into the technicalities of formal logic to attempt to reduce each of its forms of judgment to a psychological equivalent. Suffice it then to say that in the proposition, or in each term of the proposition, we have represented a judgment, a process of ascribing meaning to the entering sensation, a process of affixing some one of the ready-made predeveloped schemata to the stimulus that presents itself from the external world, or is brought in by some one preceding link in the chain of thought.

Inference, the next stage in complexity in the reasoning process, is no less influenced by attention than is judgment. If judgment may be defined practically as the appreciation of a situation, inference is the imagined remedy for the situation, the means of meeting the situation. In inference something is added in thought that will remove the obstacle that has been recognised. The suggested improvement develops on the basis of earlier experience. If we have made perception or attention the correlate of judgment, association would offer the correlate of inference. In the simpler forms of reasoning we first appreciate the difficulty, we then look for means of obviating it. When we have opened a window and find the catch is broken and it will not remain open, we look about for a substitute of any kind.

N

The first step in the practical bit of reasoning is to appreciate that the catch is broken ; the second is a mental suggestion of a makeshift that will replace it. When the image of the window supported by a brush or ruler enters mind, it is accepted as a proper solution of the difficulty, and we at once turn the head and eyes to look for the object in its familiar place. The inference is complete, the conclusion is reached in these simple concrete forms of reasoning, when the picture of the difficulty remedied rises to mind. Here, again, the solution of the difficulty, like the appreciation of the difficulty, arises under the influence of definite subjective conditions. The solution must have been experienced before in some similar situation, and ordinarily many solutions have been put in practice at different times. Which of the many different solutions shall come out depends upon the character of the momentary mood and the education, in the broad sense, that the thinker has enjoyed up to the moment in question. One who reasons well in an emergency is one who appreciates the situation fully, who has an ample array of knowledge at hand to bear upon the situation, and whose entire knowledge is active at the particular moment in choosing from among the possible solutions that are known.

When one is dealing with more remote problems, problems that may be called general rather than particular, the same rule holds. In fact, reasoning of a general character is really reasoning in concrete terms ; the only difference is that the associations and connections are regarded as true of all instances rather than of the specific image alone. But this is not a marked difference, because, as we have seen in discussing judgment, we never even in perception have a bare or true particular. As we look at the most concrete object, we always see not the bare concrete, but the concrete interpreted by and transformed into earlier and developed experience. We see the type in every case, not the bare image. So when we talk of man in general the same thing holds. We think in concrete terms and reason what man can do on the basis of what we know of man, but we know that the concrete imagery means, and will hold true for, all men, or the particular group of men to whom we intend the property in question to apply. So when we assert that man is mortal, we may have in mind the death of a particular individual, but in so far as it is guided by all our knowledge of the constitution of man we believe it to be true of all men, of those now alive as well as of the multitudes who are already dead. The degree of truth of the conclusion depends, not upon the number of specific instances, but upon the amount of knowledge the man possesses, and the amount that is active at the moment the assertion is made. The concrete, but typical, then becomes typical because of the masses of knowledge that stand behind it, and is true or approaches truth as the knowledge effective at the moment approaches all possible knowledge. The course of reasoning is controlled by what we have seen to be the conditions of attention in exactly the same way as is any association.

In this discussion we have apparently taken issue with the statement of formal logic, that in every bit of reasoning there are three terms or three propositions involved. We seem to have nothing left but the conclusion, both premises have disappeared. This treatment is not altogether revolutionary, for even Thomas Brown had pointed out that the major premise really added no truth to the conclusion, and was rarely if ever present in the actual thinking process. If there is no major premise, the minor would be without dependence, and so valueless. If we study the actual thinking process, it seems that we rarely have anything but the conclusion when the decision is made. The only occasions when the major and minor premises come into play are when we would test some conclusion that has already been attained. When one asks how we know that a statement we have made is true, we refer to some general statement that corresponds to the major premise and assert in the minor that this case of ours is an instance under the general type.

Ordinarily the forces and conditions that lead to the assertion are in part represented in the general statement, but in no case can we do more than point back to some statement that has been accepted by speaker and hearer as systematising and harmonising the experience of each. What has led to the conclusion is this experience as a dynamic force, and it is part of the same experience that has been tested and harmonised in the major premise. For example, when one has decided in pictorial form that a rod will support the window in the instance first mentioned, it would be perfectly possible to construct a whole series of syllogisms to prove the truth of the conclusion. One might assert that a falling object will be supported by any object whose crushing point is higher than the force exerted by the earth upon the body, with the minor premise that the rod in question possesses the sufficiently high breaking point. But the assertion does not necessarily grow out of the premise. One would never take the trouble even to assert the premise unless questioned, and then the truth of the major premise is already involved in, and consequently adds nothing to the truth of the conclusion. And one might construct syllogism after syllogism as to the relations to gravitation, the dimension of the rod, the substance of which it is composed, and so on, all of which are representations of different parts of the knowledge that leads us to the conclusion, the only representative in consciousness of the forces that are at work in giving rise to the inference.

For ourselves, the major premise when it appears in answer to our questioning of the truth of some inference we have made, seems to serve to give definiteness and certainty to the conclusion. If we can see that some association, in itself new, is but some one form of an old familiar truth, the belief that attaches to the latter seems to spread to the former. So, while the major premise may be said never to appear before the conclusion in definite form, it is of value, where definitely formulated, in giving a resting-place for belief, as well as in being a type or sign of the forces that are really effective in governing the train of association that leads to the conclusion.

At every stage then reason is closely related to attention. If judgment may be defined as the selecting of the essential phase of a given situation and its proper interpretation, both under the influence of the forces that condition attending, inference may likewise be said to be an association under the influence of a complete knowledge that leads to the discovery of a needful change in the situation.

We are forced to the conclusion that reasoning is not a process distinct from association, and the other more common trains of ideas, but is only a special application of those processes in some of their more unusual aspects. In ordinary speech reason means either thinking in words in a way that enables one to pass from some statement already given to some other statement that seems to depend upon the first, or it means to think abstractly, to carry trains of ideas in symbols that have a general meaning, rather than in the concrete experiences. But no one of these definitions of reason is complete. We certainly talk of reasoning when no words are used ; one infers one object or set of relations from others when only the ideas of the objects are present, and there are no words attached. Again, we very generally speak of reasoning when the terms involved are perfectly concrete and involve nothing more than the objects offered to sense, or at least come as near involving nothing beyond the mere given series of experiences as any perception can. We have then to regard reasoning, by a process of exclusion, as merely thinking in succession of different objects or relations of objects on the basis of connections that our experience shows to be possible and valid. This we have seen also to be the basis of perception and of all association of ideas. In short, then, any purposeful train of ideas, or any one which follows lines in harmony with our experience as a whole and not merely with partial aspects of our experience, may be called reasoning. This harmony with the sum total of our past life, as opposed to the particular and temporary groups of experiences, constitutes what are for us the general or universal connections, and consequently are for the individual the ultimate tests of truth in his thinking. Reasoning then is but perception or association under the influence of the attentive as opposed to the merely mechanical or physiological conditions of thinking. It is a train of ideas or the interpretation of a group of sensations in the light of all that the man has known or experienced, and of all that the race or community has known down to the present time. In that sense attention is the controlling influence in reason as it is in memory and in will. The conditions of attention are at the same time the conditions of reason. One involves the other and cannot be separated from it.

In the same way we might go through the other more specialised mental functions and show that the principles involved in attention are all implied in them. Imagination, for example, is assuredly only different from memory and reasoning in that the set of conditions which control the associations are recognised as partial, and chosen with reference to the mere needs of the moment rather than drawn in harmony with the mass of the life's experiences. Each of the other special functions of mind might be brought into harmony with the facts of attention in the same way, but those already treated are sufficient to show the importance of the part it plays in the mental processes in general, and the other applications can be easily made.

It may seem that we have magnified the part played by attention in all of these processes, and that one investigating the same processes with the purpose of showing the importance of association or of retentiveness would find that each of these processes was equally involved everywhere. This is of course true. No one of the complicated processes can be explained without considering all of the simple processes, but the part played by the other simple processes will stand out prominently from our discussion. The objection is but one way of stating the now familiar dogma, that mind is not made up of isolated parts, but is a closely inter-connected unity. One part cannot be explained without all others. No treatment of attention can be a treatment of attention merely. Any explanation of it must necessarily involve an explanation of all the other mental "faculties."

SUMMARY

1. Reasoning in all of its phases is a new use of the processes heretofore discussed, attention, and association under the influence of attention.

2. What distinguishes reasoning from the related processes of memory and imagination is belief. Belief, too, arises from an interaction of experience upon the concrete process, i.e. from the same factors that are active in the determination of attention.

3. Judgment, the first operation in reasoning, is a process of referring the given to a type or meaning under the influence of attention. Attention decides to what type the given shall be referred, how it shall be interpreted.

4. Inference is a process of improving or changing the given as interpreted in judgment. It is a process of association under the influence of experience as a whole.

CHAPTER XII

ATTENTION AND FEELING, OR EMOTION

THE problem of attention in its relation to feeling and affective states in general is much more complicated than the relation to the cognitive processes already discussed. We can be sure that attention influences the feelings at every point, but in the nature of the case the relation cannot be experimented upon easily nor can introspection be very accurate. Consequently there is much opinion on all phases of the subject, and comparatively little agreement. The most that can be done is to mention those statements that are generally agreed upon, and endeavour to solve conflicts by reference to the general theory we have been following throughout the discussion.

Superficially regarded, we see in everyday life that the relation between feeling and emotion on the one hand, and attention on the other, is a mutual one, and in general one of mutual opposition. When we are attentive, feelings and emotions are usually of less strength ; when we are emotionally much wrought up, attention is generally difficult and more ineffective than in the moments of calm contemplation. The connection is at least close enough to deserve discussion even if the facts that have accumulated are not sufficiently numerous to make the conclusion very definite. We must begin our discussion in this realm as opposed to sensation by asking what we are to mean by feeling and the affective states generally. In usage feeling is a word that covers an indefinite field. In its broad use it has served to designate a mass of vague states, sensations from skin,

vague intellectual processes, feelings of belief as opposed to
rational demonstrations, the activities of mind in religious
matters—in fact, it has been used as a catch-all to
hold all the as yet unanalysed mental processes. In
this sense feeling is everything that has not been given
a definite place in our knowledge of mental states.
It is the original mass from which cognition develops
by a process of attentive analysis. In this sense, then,
anything that can be clearly attended to for itself
ceases at once to be feeling, and becomes perception, or
some other cognitive process. The narrow and probably
more usual current use of the word is as the equivalent of
pleasantness-unpleasantness, as a definite process on the
same general level of explicitness as sensation. This would
designate the tone that accompanies the sensation, agreeable
or disagreeable, as feeling and would leave over the vague
processes for some other term. We should have to distinguish between two fairly definite conscious processes, the
one designated as sensation, the other as feeling. The best
instance of the distinction in a single process is between
pain as sensation and the unpleasantness that accompanies
it at any moment. As sensation, pain corresponds to the
direct excitation of a nerve-ending in the skin which always
gives rise to that one sense quality. Ordinarily the sensation is unpleasant as well but occasionally a slight excitation of the pain nerves in the tingle from cold air or the
cutting of salt spray is pleasant. The feeling then is the
tone that accompanies the sensation, whether of agreeable-
ness or disagreeableness, and this is regarded for purposes
of description as a relatively independent mental process.
The third current use of feeling, in a measure a compromise
between the wide and the narrow uses, is represented in
the theories of Wundt and Royce. Wundt distinguishes
two more opposed pairs of feeling, strain and relaxation,
excitation and depression. Royce has added another,
excitation and quiescence. Wundt verges still nearer the
general use in the statement that feelings have different

qualities for each sensation with which they are associated.

With so wide a divergence in the use of the term, it is evident that we must discuss our problem of the relation of feeling to attention with each use separately. If we hold to the first use of the term, that feeling designates the as yet unanalysed, it is evident that attention, the fundamentally analytic mental function, must ever work destructively upon feeling. Whatever we analyse ceases *ipso facto* to be feeling, and in a measure, everything that can be attended to for itself is analysed, set apart as definite content, and becomes a cognitive process rather than feeling. For the narrow second use, very much the same relation is ordinarily asserted to hold. As we attend, objects tend to lose their pleasantness or unpleasantness and become entirely indifferent. Attention, far from increasing the clearness or intensity of feeling, causes it to become vague and indefinite, without affective colouring. So if we ask ourselves when displeased exactly in what the displeasure consists, it will be found, it is usually asserted, that the displeasure disappears. Similarly with pleasure, if we concern ourselves too much with the query: are we really enjoying ourselves at a particular task or game, we find that the answer is nearly always negative, while enjoyment continues as long as we play the game for its own sake without reference to the outcome of pleasure or pain. This fact, if we accept it, would make a conscious hedonism self-destructive. If we live a life for the pleasure there is in it, the pleasure is never found. If, however, we work for particular ends without reference to their pleasureableness, we find that the striving in itself brings pleasure. The statement rests primarily upon introspection, and seems to be undisputed by those who have considered the subject. Meumann and Zoneff investigated the problem by means of what is known technically as the method of expression. Just as we saw that attention has widespread effects upon the vital process, so it has been known for some years that feeling and emotion are accompanied by many changes in the vital processes. We need not consider for themselves in detail the somewhat ambiguous results that have been obtained in this field. Suffice it to say that Meumann and Zoneff assumed that if one can determine the presence of feeling by means of the organic changes, one should also be able to decide whether the amount of feeling is changed by directing attention to it, and how. One would first take records when the individual was attending to the stimulus or was passive, and compare these with similar records when attention was directed to the feeling itself. The results of the experiments conducted were largely negative. In ordinary attention to the feeling, pulse and breathing were not different from those taken during attention to the stimulus. When an attempt was made to introspect the feeling, probably merely a heightened attention to the feeling, the organic reaction seemed to be lessened slightly. The results in themselves would not be sufficient to warrant the truth of the statement that attention to feeling destroyed it, but they tend in that direction. It is growing more probable too that the organic reactions depend as much upon the character of the stimulus as they do upon the feeling, and if that be true, we would expect attention to have little if any effect. Even if attending to the feeling destroyed the feeling, the organic reaction would run its course unchanged. As matters stand, the introspective evidence is universally favourable to the assertion that attention is antagonistic to the pleasantness-unpleasantness process as well as to the vague unanalysed processes of consciousness.

The third group of theories is not related to attention in quite the same unambiguous way. Of Wundt's three pairs, strain and relaxation would not be opposed to attending. Most attention involves strain, but attention either to strain or relaxation does not necessarily diminish them or change their character. Of depression and exaltation it is difficult to speak, but it is by no means certain that attention to these processes would either oppose or favour their presence. The same holds also of Royce's second pair, quiescence-excitation. Attention need not either destroy or increase one or the other. Attention then cannot be said to act in any definite way upon any of the three new pairs of feelings. However, it must be confessed that the addition of these new definite qualities to feeling has not met with universal acceptance, and it seems probable from the different way in which they respond to attention, and from other considerations, that they are not processes of the same general character as pleasure and pain, but come more nearly under the head of sensation or of emotion than of feeling in this restricted sense.

For the purpose of our discussion then we shall restrict feeling to the narrow use as the equivalent of the pleasantness-unpleasantness qualities, although several of the conclusions that we shall reach in this use will hold as well for certain of the other so-called feelings ordinarily grouped in the vague general use. Attention has not only this general destructive effect upon feeling, but also when directed to the sensation or stimulus it changes the quality or character of the feeling processes. Whether we shall be pleased or pained by any object depends entirely upon how we look upon it. It is now pleasant, now unpleasant, according to the setting in which it is placed and our attitude at the moment. What to the poor are real hardships are to the youth on a hunting trip a source of pleasure. A remark which from a friend gives keen pleasure as an exhibition of wit, will, when spoken by a rival or a man who irritates us, cause keen displeasure. The common saying that there is a bright side to every situation is but the embodiment of the fact that pleasure or displeasure waits upon attention in nearly every situation of daily life. Attention then exerts the opposite effect upon feeling from that exerted upon sensation. That means, of course, when attention is directed to the feeling process itself and alone. When directed upon sensation or stimulus, feeling is increased in intensity, and also the nature of the feeling, whether pleasant or unpleasant or indifferent, depends upon the way in which we attend to the sensation or external stimulus by which the sensation is originated. Inversely, apparently, states of pleasure and pain, when intense, seem to render attention difficult. When greatly pleased or greatly pained there seems to be no attention. It is a question, however, whether there is any decided influence until we reach the stage of emotion. Certainly when pleased or pained we can attend vigorously to the stimulus that excites the feeling, although perhaps, even in the stronger stage of pleasure and pain the rules for attending to all else are no longer effective. That we do not attend primarily either to the pleasant or to the unpleasant has already been seen in connection with interest, and will be found to be true when we consider the theories of attention.

If, then, these be the facts as to the relationship between attention and feeling, it is evident that there must be some deeper-lying connection that should appear in the theoretical discussions. We find, in fact, that several of the most important theories of feeling would relate it to a general activity that in some degree or other overlaps what is called attention. So Herbart made feeling the accompaniment of hindered or furthered progress in apperception. When an idea is furthered in its entrance into consciousness, we are pleased ; when its entrance is opposed, when there is mutual opposition between the elements of consciousness, we have pain or unpleasantness. In modern form we find this same general attitude in Stout and in Dewey and his school, in the statement that anything that furthers the course of mental or physical activity at the moment is pleasant, whatever checks that activity is unpleasant or painful. Each of these theories goes back to what may broadly be called apperception, and each we shall see to be in part dependent upon a process that is similar to attention, and is often synonymous with it. More directly connected with the attention doctrine is the theory of Wundt, that feeling is the subjective side of the apperception process, the way in which the process of apperception comes to consciousness. On this theory feeling arises as a by-product of the acceptance of the newly entering sensation by the mass of earlier experience. When the earlier experiences react upon the immediate environment, the total process of reaction gives rise to a feeling. Much evidence can be adduced to support some such general theory. Many of our æsthetic and less fundamental feelings seem to grow directly from earlier experience. Things pleasant to individuals of one training will not please, or will even be distasteful to others of a different education. Much of pleasure comes not directly, but indirectly, through association and the character of earlier experiences of all kinds.

There are three characteristic differences between sensation and feeling that seem to indicate that feeling depends upon the reception of the sensation into consciousness, upon the way it is brought in, rather than upon anything in the stimulus itself. The first of these is that feelings cannot be remembered for themselves immediately and directly. What happens apparently is that we recall the situation, and then are affected by the situation anew, according to the way we react now. Consequently we find that an idea when recalled has frequently undergone a change since its original entrance. Many things that pleased us in the doing cause chagrin in recall, and many social *faux pas* of our youth that caused intense discomfort at the moment are remembered now with keen pleasure. Our appreciation of the event changes with our experience and knowledge, and pleasure or unpleasantness corresponds to the nature of that reaction. That the reaction then is different in idea makes a change in feeling tone as compared with the original appreciation. It is the way we attend, and our possibilities of attention, that determine the character of the feeling. Similar inference may be drawn from the fact emphasised by Külpe and others that feelings excited by remembered or imagined events are equally strong or at times stronger than the original event. Very frequently we find that things indifferent in original experience are pleasant or unpleasant in recall, and it is a proverb that many events are more pleasant in anticipation than in realisation. This fact, again, harmonises well with the theory that feeling is a by-product of attending, for certainly one attends just as strongly and in the same way to the faint ideas as to the strong perceptions. If feeling corresponds to the reaction upon the entering experience, we should expect what we find that feelings connected with memory and imagination would be just as intense as those connected with sensation and perception. Again, the fact discussed above, that attention to a feeling nullifies it, would harmonise with the theory. For, if feeling is dependent upon the response to a stimulus, then attending to the feeling would put an end to the response to the stimulus, and with that the occasion for the feeling would at once cease. There would no longer be attention of the kind that gives rise to feeling. In addition to these more definite facts, the pervasiveness of feeling, the fact that it has no particular sense organ, and its completely subjective character, all are in harmony with the theory that feeling is the conscious process which accompanies and corresponds to attending. While this theory of Wundt and Külpe harmonises very well with the facts, and would explain feeling in general, there is nothing in it to differentiate pleasure and pain. For this we have one of two alternatives—to go to one of the forms of the furtherance-hinderance theory already mentioned—or to turn to some form of an evolutionary theory. The former is more satisfactory for the complicated active pursuits of life, the latter best explains the simple sense pleasure and displeasure. The evolutionary theory would make pain and pleasure the accompaniment of sense processes that have in any way been adapted to improve or benefit the race in the course of its development. Whether the theory be applied historically or immediately, whether it be evolutionary or physiological, makes little difference. In the one case, whatever on the whole has benefited, the race will be pleasant ; in the other, anything that now is an incentive to an enhanced activity of the organism or benefits it in any way will prove pleasant. The former view suffers fewer exceptions than the latter, for the saving clause, " in the long run," can be applied to remove almost all apparent exceptions. If this view be coupled with the theory of Wundt, that feeling corresponds to the reaction of experience as a whole upon the presented stimulus, which explains the occurrence of the feeling, while the character of the feeling will find its explanation in the evolutionary benefit and injury, we have a theory that would cover most cases.

Even on the evolutionary theory, however, feeling would not be an active, causal mental process, but rather an accompaniment of other forms of activity. What is essential for the organism and makes for its survival is the nature of the reaction by which it responds to the stimulus, not the feeling process that accompanies the excitation. It is probable from observations on man that feeling is a mere passive accompaniment of sensori-motor action rather than an essential active element that intervenes between sensation and response. It is in the more fundamental racial theory a conscious accompaniment of the response to stimulus that makes for the survival of the organism, pleasant if the stimulus be beneficial and the movement one of approach, unpleasant if the stimulus is dangerous in the light of the earlier history of the race and the response is one of withdrawal. In the theory that makes feeling in part the outgrowth of individual experience, it is again the accompaniment of a reaction, but in this case of the interaction between older experiences and a newly entering experience. It is now an incident in the action of the forces that serve to select one element rather than another for entrance to consciousness. And these two theories are not altogether different, since we have seen that racial factors act with those of individual origin in controlling the entrance of sensations, the course of ideas, and the resulting actions.

While it would be rash to pretend that any of the theories of feeling here considered are final, yet whichever one we accept, we find that the fundamental process has greater or less resemblance to the phenomena that we have seen earlier to be connected with attention. The roots of the theories of feeling are everywhere intertwined with the roots of the theories of attention. The relation of attention to the more complicated affective processes, the emotions and passions, is equally close and of much the same character. Emotions are theoretically either instinctive responses that break the bonds of voluntary control, or complex feeling processes mingled with instinctive reactions. In either case we find that they are riotings of processes ordinarily under the control of attention or related activities, and consequently the relation between them is one of mutual opposition. When emotions are at their maximum, earlier experience is not at work in the control of thought and action, but some stimulus, owing to its instinctive appeal, has become dominant in unusual degree. When all of the conditions of attention are active in normal strength, emotion is suppressed. The instinctive responses are subordinated to the voluntary control, and, as we have seen, feeling is lacking. On the other hand, during moments of strong emotion attention is ordinarily weakened. At least one is capable in very slight degree of attending to anything but the occasion of the emotion, although probably anything at all connected with the emotion itself is observed with more than usual clearness. Attention cannot be said to be weakened in general, but is warped and rendered one-sided. One might even say that attention *per se* is not necessarily diminished in strength, but that there is a characteristic change in the conditions that predominate in the two cases. In the emotional seizure, attention comes under the sway of instinctive conditions. Social and general educational forces lose their effect, and always, too, the particular set of instinctive conditions are those that are grouped around the storm centre.

o

As to the theoretical causal relation between emotion and attention, there is nothing new to add to what was said of feeling. If feeling be an important constituent part of emotion, what holds true of feeling will hold in lesser degree of emotion. If we accept some more active theory of emotion, and regard it as the awareness of instinctive responses, attention would play at most a permissive part. Probably, even here, however, the appreciation of the occurrence is not unimportant to the character of the emotion. If we attend in the right way, any event can be classified among the mechanical non-personal resultants of some world action, and emotion is at best a waste of energy. If we attend in another way, the most impersonal mechanical happening may take on a personal character and become occasion for violent emotion. Seldom do we find purely instinctive response uncoloured and unaffected by the acquired conditions of attending.

We may say in general summary of the relation of attention to the sentiments, that they are mutually opposed. To quote Külpe, attention is the organ of quiet contemplation and is the enemy of sentiment in all of its forms, while sentiment again, or the conditions that give rise to sentiment, are not conducive to sustained or unprejudiced attention. When we look more deeply, however, we find that the superficial opposition gives way to fundamental unity. Attention determines at once how we shall feel, if not whether we shall feel, and we find some reason to assume that feeling is but the by-play in consciousness of the forces that stand behind and determine attending.

SUMMARY

1. The relation between attention and feeling, or emotion, is one of fundamental opposition. Attention is not so effective when feeling or emotion is strong, and attention to a feeling destroys or weakens it.

2. Feelings seem very definitely dependent upon atten-

tion to sensation. The nature of the feeling differs with the conditions of attending, and the attitude toward the sensation.

3. Theories of feeling all go back to attention in some form or other. Feeling is said to be due to the reaction of earlier ideas on the entering idea ; to furtherance or checking of the course of mental activity ; or is asserted to be the way in which attention becomes conscious : in either case the dependence upon attention is evident.

CHAPTER XIII

ATTENTION AND THE SELF

ONE last general relation remains to be considered, the relation between attention and the self. Popularly the connection between the two is supposed to be very close. We talk on the one hand of forcing ourselves to attend, and we also talk of attending to the self. One makes attention depend upon the self, the other makes knowledge of the self, at least, depend upon attention. Many of the implications of the relation have been discussed in earlier chapters, particularly those that have treated will and reason and the relation of effort to attention. It seems desirable, however, to bring together in a single chapter the results that follow from our general point of view, and state them with particular reference to the historical problems that cluster about the self.

It must be evident from the preceding discussions that there is no possibility of retaining the older conception of the self as something apart from or independent of the mental stream. The present status of the problem, as very generally agreed upon, is that on the one hand nothing resembling the self of the older rational psychology can be discovered by examination of the mental stream, but it is equally generally agreed that there must be something to explain unity and persistent identity, and the fact that mental states are *known*; and that this cannot be found in the mental states themselves as discrete elements. We may begin our discussion with the assumption of these two facts.

It shall then be our task in this first part to subject the doctrines of the self to a rigid scrutiny in two ways. First, to examine the axioms or felt needs upon which the construction is based, secondly to decide how far the solution ordinarily attained really satisfies the demands. Of the reasons that have been given for assuming a distinct mind, three are most prominent : (1) For the known there must be a knower. (2) The mental states can receive unity only from a unitary substance, and that is not to be found in mental states. (3) In a series of discrete mental states such as Hume assumed to constitute mind there can be no continuity, no real identity. Of the first we may ask, Is it a real axiom ; of all, Are they satisfied by a self of the detached character ? The axiom that everything to be known must have a knower may be, and has been, questioned as to its validity. True, in a common sense dualistic way we know nothing of the objects about without being ourselves present. Our bodily presence is essential to knowledge. This, as Professor Fullerton has pointed out, is the only conceivable way in which an axiom of the kind could originate, the only other possible application of the axiom in question. One may ask, however, whether the relation holds of anything more than the physical, spatial relations of body and object. There is no evidence that the same relation would hold within consciousness. It does not follow that because you must be present to have an idea of a tree or other external object, there must be something else present in consciousness to know that image. The two are on an entirely different level. Moreover, if the analogy hold, any other than a naïve dualism would probably be stopped from accepting the axiom even with application restricted to the relation between an external world and the knowing mind. If the origin of the axiom of the knower be this relation of body to object, or of mental stream to object outside, it is very interesting to note that it has persisted after the interpretation that gave rise to it has been abandoned. Now that we find not infrequently that no distinction is made between the existence of an external object and its being known, no distinction between its existence in the mental stream and its real existence, we should expect that the self-evidence of the axiom might at least be weakened. On the contrary, some of the writers who feel most keenly the advantages of obliterating the old distinction between knower and known in the more objective relation seem most loath to give up the axiom derived from that in its application to what we might call the inner hypostatisation; they still argue for a knower to know the content of consciousness although they believe there is no necessity for a known and a knower relation between outside object and mental stream. Moreover, if we are to accept this view in its entirety, it would be immediately destructive of knowledge of self. We must either have an infinite regressus of knowers for each of the lower series, or we must assume that somewhere there is an element that is at once knower and known. If the knower and known can thus be united in one member of the series, there is no reason why we should not assume that they are united at once in the first stage of the process. If there is no need of the tenth or millionth member in the regressive series, there is no need of the second. Even granted the existence of a knower, it is by no means easy to see how it can know the mental states. It must either take the mental states over into itself as mirror pictures, and then the problem comes as to how the knowing goes on ; or it must leave them unchanged, that is to say unknown. The representatives of mental states are in no different relation to the self when thus absorbed than the elements to the stream itself, and these are not known according to our original axiom. Even the infinite regressus discussed above takes us no nearer the problem ; it merely postpones its consideration indefinitely. At no stage is there any explanation that could not be applied also and equally to make one distinct idea in the stream know the others.

The argument from the demand for unity in the conscious series seems to lose much force if we ask how unity is given by the self. It is all very well to say that mental states are unified in some way, that they are not mere discrete elements in the series of experience, but it is not so clear that unity of any kind could be given by a unitary something placed beside or above the stream. If they are to be unified they must be taken up in some way into the unitary subject. Mere propinquity with a unitary something cannot conceivably give unity, and of the unifying somewhat we have the same problems and the same difficulties that face us in solving our difficulty where first the problem arose.

Almost the same remarks apply to the argument that would have the self give continuity to the discrete stream, that would make it the basis of identity amid change. Neither continuity nor identity as an effective phase would be in any way explained by the presence in or above consciousness of a unitary substance. That might be present, and the other elements be discrete. Unless the elements of content work in some way upon the self, and it in some way upon them, there is no identity for them in any real sense. There is no conceivable way in which identity can be given them by any added something unless they become part of it or it part of them. In either case it loses its absolute identity as well as its unity.

If we regard the states again as receiving identity from being taken into the unitary substance, then apparently the principle of persistency must again come from some relation between the elements themselves or between the permanent existing substance and its contents. Mind, then, becomes itself changing, and it is just as difficult to conceive how changing interacting elements could take on the consciousness of identity with themselves in spite of change inside of or beside an unchanging somewhat ever identical with itself as it is to see how a series might always be identical with itself through mere continuity of the elements. If we summarise the three advantages that are asserted of the presence of the self above or beside content, we find that, examined closely, the advantages disappear. They are verbal rather than actual.   One can no more conceive a knower knowing the elements of knowledge than the mental states knowing themselves, and besides, some element must know itself unless we are to have an infinite regressus or an unknown term. The unity of mental states is no more conceivable with an absolute unitary substance in or beside the states than would be the unity of the states themselves, uncontained or unaccompanied.   And the persistence of the substance always identical with itself does not immediately account for the fact that all experiences seem to belong together, to be all my experiences.   When we have the immediate content all carefully taken up into the self as ordinarily pictured, we have all our problems over again in their original guise. The assumption that there is some advantage in the unitary is an analogy, a picture, and the details of the picture are not worked out sufficiently to be helpful.   If one is compelled to have recourse to an act of faith, one may as well solve all our difficulties at once, and assert that the mental stream knows itself, is of itself unitary, and always identical with itself.   Solution is no easier than it was when we first approached the problem on the known empirical level.   The solution ordinarily offered tends to hide difficulties, not to solve them.

If we are driven to the conclusion that there is nothing in the theory that would satisfy our logical need by putting a self of any character in or above the concrete mental elements, we have cleared the way for an attempt to find characteristics in the mental content that give rise to the demand and serve to make conceivable the processes.   As I conceive it, the whole problem of the self and its relations arises from the fact that structure and function do not correspond, that there are certain characteristics of the action and general accomplishments of mind that cannot, by any analogy, be ascribed to the structures that have been assumed to exist in mind.   The broad general accomplishments of mind do not harmonise with the asserted capacities of the structures upon which most stress has been laid in the more usual descriptions. We may for a time keep structure and function divorced, and assert functions for which no structure is assignable, but this at best is a temporary expedient. Before our problem is complete, structure and function must be brought together and made parts of a single whole. The hypothesis already considered attempts to set up a conjectural structure that should take over the functions not assignable on analogy to the elements directly and scientifically analysed out. This we have seen to be unsatisfactory, and probably such construction always will prove unsatisfactory, because there is no possibility of testing its truth. In fact, it is made *ex hypothesi* incapable of accurate observation. The result is that a premium is set upon poetic vague imaginings rather than upon careful observation or even logical self-consistent reasoning from the premises accepted. While then the first falls short in the attempt to develop a structure that shall be adequate to the function assigned, the structures ordinarily analysed out for structural psychology also will not explain the function that we find mind capable of when viewed in the large. The classic attempt of Hume to explain experience by discrete ideas is the man of straw for all-comers, and deservedly has been much buffeted about. If one holds to any similar view, the only consistent course is to deny the logical need of a self and to assert that we shall keep to the empirical level, with no attempt to go beyond to satisfy logical needs or to explain mental functions. This we already have seen is by general consent unsatisfactory. It would be a sad commentary upon modern investigation were there no results since Hume that throw light upon the problem from the concrete factual side. It behooves us, then, constructively to turn to the known nature of mental processes to see what there is that will illuminate the deeper connections of mental states.

In beginning the investigation, let us accept two general principles. First, that one may expect to find no direct evidence of self, but that the need for unity and identity of mental states is a real need, and that the problem of how mental states are known is a real problem. These needs must be satisfied, if possible, even if we have recourse to construction on the basis of fact. Keeping these guiding principles before us, let us turn to an examination of the results of modern psychology. If we ask what there is that gives first permanence and then unity, we may find a clue in the fact that an experience once present does not vanish as is assumed ; but there is some evidence that it persists as a dynamic force in consciousness from the moment of its first entrance to the end of life. That an experience may have an effect when there is no possibility of definite recall seems one of the striking results of many of the memory experiments treated above. So Ebbinghaus and many others have found, you remember, that many associations years old, of which there was no trace in the ordinary sense of spontaneous reinstatement, could nevertheless be brought back to consciousness with surprisingly few repetitions. In fact, there are some respects in which these older, long-deposited connections and experiences are more effective than those more recently acquired. One need not assume with the older men that an experience is never lost, but we can assert on definite evidence that there are secondary after effects of mental processes long after possibility of return as a specific process has ceased, and we have found reason to assume that consciousness is always in some degree different because of any experience, no matter how remote in time that experience may have been. Not only, however, is it possible to prove that these old impressions exist, by the fact that they can be reinstated with greater or less difficulty, but it is also probable, as I have attempted to show in more detail in earlier chapters, that they are active in some degree in the control of later mental operations of widely different character. Similarly, we have found reason to believe that all the operations of mind are an expression of these earlier experiences. Attention, association, memory in all forms, action, reason, feeling,—all go back for their explanation to these accumulated experiences.

In every mental act, then, we may find an illustration of the fact that experiences do not vanish entirely, and moreover that they always seem in some degree to exert an influence upon other and later mental states. These effects taken together seem sufficient to give two of the necessary presuppositions of experience, unity and identity. We have unity in mind, because all experiences, past and present, interact in the control and constitution of every apparently discrete act. Not merely, as Professor James insists in his chapter, do two or three succeeding states unite in a single one, but in some degree or other all experiences, no matter how far separated, in time combine into a single element in each moment's experience. The unity grows with each added element, is enriched by each new phase of multiplicity. It is, moreover, dynamic, not static, since it not merely takes up into itself each added element, but directs and controls what shall enter at any moment, and the response that shall be made to it. There is continuity too, not the continuity of a passive, unchanging onlooker, but of the active, all-absorbing kind. The first elements are retained for ever, and are constantly growing with each later experience. Not one element identical among many changing elements, but we may say with the Eleatics that the apparent differences are but phases of the one identical whole. The change is in part real, but in greater part it is merely a new expression of elements that have been present from the beginning. It is an identity from which nothing is ever lost, and persists with, if not through, growth. This unity and identity is not only constructive, but actual. The persistence and mutual interaction of experiences seem to carry with them a recognition of self-unity and self-continuity. For this we have best evidence in the much quoted instances of alternating selves. If we may be permitted in advance of the author to interpret the case of Miss Beauchamp, it is found to be in perfect harmony with our assumption that where earlier experiences are joined in a single unitary process, there is a unitary self. If we examine each of the dissociated selves, we find for each different experiences, different accomplishments, different organizations of older associations. One remembers within but one single group of experiences. This means primarily that associations are found or retained between certain elements of experience, not all. There is dissociation, which prevents recall from one system to another, but still permits recall within any given system. The dissociation is not complete for early acquisitions—language, the names of familiar objects. All the associations that pathology in general assures us are more fundamental persist from one to the other. But for our argument what is most important is that the entire character of the self changes with the change in the effective group of experiences. The habits of mind, interests, desires, actions, all are distinct from one group of experiences to another. So BI, BIV, and Sally are bundles of different forms of knowledge, and have a character in harmony with that knowledge. BI keeps the refinements of the family in tastes of all kinds and in knowledge. She has keen knowledge and appreciation of people and their opinions. As a consequence, we may assume, she has bookish cultivated interests, is too keenly alive to the opinion of those about her, and responds in reasoning and in action correspondingly. BIV seems to have taken over fewer of the refinements of the total self; her knowledge is of the more practical kind, and her appreciation of social demands and the rights of others is slight. With these different memories goes a character of thought and action entirely distinct. There is a selfishness and stubbornness at once indicative of strong instincts, and of slight guidance by accumulated social comprehension and knowledge. Her interests and knowledge are at one with the memories that predominate. Sally again is all primordial instinct, with very little control by accumulated knowledge. She seems to have kept none of the later and more complicated attainments of the original self ; her life is the life of a child, application of any kind is difficult, for there is no developed knowledge to restrain or control the impulse of the moment. Of these three persisting and recurring characters, she is least developed, least worth keeping alive as a member of society.

This is what one would expect on the basis of the hypothesis that the mental experiences, recent and remote, control later actions and serve to unify them with themselves, and with the earlier experiences. Where all parts of early experience act on each new element, there is unity in the self and constant self identity. Where the earlier experiences are divided into separate systems, the self lacks unity, there is no longer identity from moment to moment, but unity and identity only within the one partial system. One system seems to itself and to the observer an entirely distinct self from the other. The nature of the control each exerts in every form of mental act is different from that exerted by any other, and harmonises with the nature of the experiences that group to constitute it. There is a break from system to system, not only in memories, but in the self feeling, and in the self as an active, directive agent.

Nor do we need to look to these pathological cases, relatively rare, for our only evidence. In every individual some degree of dissociation is present with its corresponding different self or phase of self. In one's own home acts and feelings may be different in many respects from those in the home of an acquaintance. As one thinks or speaks in a professional capacity one's self is different from the self as one thinks and feels in a social capacity. If we look to the cause, we find different experiences clustered about the core of the state, and controlling the course of the action. Hypnotism, hysteria, and all forms of dissociation will furnish other evidence of the same general principle. Few physicians can be trusted to keep their impersonal scientific attitude when treating members of their own family, and I imagine few psychologists carry their theories of thought and action to the extent of interpreting the play processes of their lighter moods. When the dissociation disappears, the control is again in terms of the total experience, and the whole self reasserts itself. With reappearance of continuous memory, there again comes control by all factors that can be recalled. Control is apparently always exercised by all those processes that are sufficiently connected to render associative recall from one to the other possible. Nevertheless, always, whether in partial separation of the selves in the normal individual, in the more profound dissociation of hypnosis, or of alternating personality, there is some greater or smaller mass of controlling experiences that is common. A man's business and his friendly attitudes towards life and morality may be different, but there are always some limits that he will not pass, there are always some parts of his experience that are common, and these constitute what we may call his real self. In hypnotism, too, the most fundamental experiences still guide, and the somnambulist is not altogether unmoral or immoral. In smaller degree the same remark applies to the dissociated or alternating personalities.

Even the subconscious or unconscious selves, as they have been traced in much completeness by Professor Jastrow, are not distinct from this dominating unity. They are but new groupings of the same elements that for a brief time may hold independent sway, and during that time new, or at least long-forgotten experiences may co-operate in the control of thought and action, but also and more noticeably the elements or systems usually dominant are not for the moment in control.

Much has been made in recent discussions of these unconscious or subconscious mental states, and even of subconscious selves. There seems little reason to assume, however, that the phrases are much more than figures of speech which cannot be taken with full literalness. As has often been pointed out, an unconscious mental state is a contradiction in terms, and even more truly is an unconscious self a self-contradiction. To be conscious and to be mental are identical. We may use unconscious in one of two senses. It may mean states that are physiological, but not accompanied by consciousness. In this sense there are probably unconscious physiological links in most trains of association. We may also designate by the term nervous processes that reveal themselves in the modifications that they produce in consciousness although they themselves are not conscious at the moment. In the latter sense we may speak of the nervous processes as experiences not now conscious, and by this we mean to deny that there is any consciousness that can attach to them now, although they are resultants of earlier conscious processes, and themselves work changes in the consciousness of the moment. We are not aware as we select a tool of our profession from an indiscriminate mass that it is our early training that impels to the choice, we are conscious of the object alone. In this use all attention may be said to be the outcome of the unconscious. But the unconscious in this sense is not a separate personality, it exists only in and for the conscious. In that sense too it may be said to be part of the conscious self, for the conscious self could not be what it is without it. It is just the presence of these unconscious processes that makes the conscious personality what it is.

As ordinarily used, however, subconsciousness or the unconscious designates the better organised, and apparently more independent groups of experiences. So in hysteria there is frequently found, in fact Freud asserts there are always found, systematised but unconscious experiences that exert an important influence upon consciousness, are in fact responsible for the course of the disease.[5] This system of ideas goes back ordinarily to some emotionally toned event in the life of the individual, and is sufficiently strong to dominate all actions that are in any way related to it, but is usually not conscious in itself. In Janet's phrase it seems to be detached from the personality. It is not completely controlled by other elements in experience, and the actions it induces are not rationally appreciated. Nevertheless, the course of conscious thought and action is governed by it, and until the individual is freed from the obsession his actions are not normal.

Some authors, like Freud and the late F. W. H. Myers, would go farther and assert that every individual, no matter how normal, has a similar subconsciousness that plays a large part in the control of his everyday thought and action. Freud would have us believe that these subconscious processes are dominant in dreams,[6] and that they are then known for themselves, or more truly that we recall distorted fragments of the real dream on waking. In addition he would assert that many of the flashes of brilliancy that we exhibit in ordinary conversation originate in the subconscious. The subconscious is responsible for our witty remarks, writes our poetry for us, in fact deserves the credit for most of our commendable performances. This, of course, suggests Mr. Myers's conclusion, reached on other grounds, that the subconscious is the source of most works of true genius. We would be assumed, on a theory of the kind, to have two selves on different levels. The conscious self is duplicated by a subconscious, organised as is the normal consciousness, and presumably self-conscious.

It seems to the writer that theories of this type have developed on the assumption that the operations of mind are much more open to observation than they are in fact. Even in our most fully conscious moments we are aware of but a fraction of the causes that are at work in ruling our mental procedure. We have very slight prevision of the states that are to succeed those present in mind at any moment, and none whatever from direct observation of the causes that are at work in determining what elements shall succeed, and how the choice shall be brought about. In this respect a flash of intuition, or some act of genius, is on the same plane as the most ordinary decision or flight of fancy. This, of course, follows immediately from the discussions that have preceded. We are conscious of but a point in the mass of interacting experiences or remnants of earlier experiences. The great bulk of the whole group of forces is revealed only in the fleeting fractional process that is conscious at the moment. But the roots of that element lie deep below the surface, and without the hidden sources the consciousness of the moment would not be what we see it to be. If one were to regard all else than the spot of light, the centre of the attentive consciousness, as subconscious, that must constitute the surpassingly greater mass as well as the more important part of the whole. These other parts of the ordinary mental act are, however, not detachable from the central part of consciousness, nor do they reveal themselves in any other way than in the effect that they exert upon consciousness. They cannot exist apart from consciousness, and consciousness could not exist as it does apart from them.

In exactly the same way whenever any of the detached elements organise and become dominant, they are self-conscious, but conscious only at one point, although that point reveals the operation of all related parts. Still there is no evidence that the elements not in the focus of consciousness are organised, and themselves individually conscious at the same moment that they contribute to the dominant consciousness. Rather must we think of them as nervous dispositions, which have their effect, to be sure, but are not accompanied by any independent consciousness apart from their effect upon the whole. This is further substantiated by the fact that there is never immediate evidence of two consciousnesses simultaneously present. There are two possible exceptions to this statement. The most striking is Sally in the Miss Beauchamp case. She asserted that she had a memory of herself as separately organised at all times, no matter what self might be dominant at the time in question. We might regard this as a fault of memory on Sally's part, or we may interpret it as due to the fact that her experiences were connected with B1's, and so the memory was persistent when the other self was dominant, and her particular organisation was lacking. Experiences that were organised in one way to constitute B1 might be organised in another way to constitute Sally, and when recalled by Sally might very easily give her the impression that she had been in existence at the moment they entered the common nervous system. This assumption is rendered less plausible, however, by the fact that she also was in simultaneous existence with B1v, and had very few common memories with her. Then again the automatic writing seems to indicate for Sally, and for many other cases, that there is some trace of a subconscious personality when the primary personality is dominant. It is not very unusual to be able to receive answers from a pencil held in the hand when the person is absorbed in reading or some other occupation, and is not aware of the question or of the answer that is written by the hand. Tests of this kind with Sally confirmed her statement that she was often in existence when one of the other members of the family was dominant and held very positive views on topics under discussion views that were in direct contradiction to those held by Miss Beauchamp. Even if we give full weight to these facts, the simplest explanation is to regard the cerebral cells as responsible for the actions, rather than to assume a completely organised personality that exists more or less permanently in the lower strata of mind. In automatic writing the hand would then be controlled by the nerve cells that would ordinarily control it, and the words that were written would also be represented in the same anatomical elements that were effective in ordinary life. The difference between the automatic writing and normal writing lies in the way the nervous elements are organised, and the principle of organisation is again the same in both cases. In automatic writing there is a tendency for the two forms of arrangement to exist side by side. Giving the greatest weight possible to the facts we have mentioned, there is not enough to make the subconscious a distinctly different form of consciousness, nor even a consciousness distinct from the dominant mind. The elements are identical in both, the laws of action and interaction are identical, the difference lies merely in the tendency to combine in distinct ways. We may quite easily say with Freud that attention is controlled from the subconscious, for the elements that constitute the subconscious are also those that may at another time constitute the fully conscious and always control attention.

I presume the processes that are at work in post-hypnotic suggestion are typical of the subconscious. Dr. Ach has given us direct evidence that the post-hypnotic suggestion may act to control association and action in exactly the same way as mood or question. In his experiments upon the influence of the task in determining the direction of association, two sorts of reactions were possible. One was with complete freedom. Two numbers were shown, and the subject was free to add or subtract. In another series some definite task was set, as a requirement to add or to subtract. On one occasion one of the subjects was hypnotised, and told that in a designated series when the numbers were shown he must always add. In the series, whether the same day or the next, the post-hypnotic suggestion was followed without exception, and when questioned there was no reason assigned as to why the reaction had been performed in this way rather than in the other. In this case the post-hypnotic suggestion that is typical of the action of the unconscious in all of its forms operated in exactly the same way as a mood or purpose. It became part of the individual's experience, and appeared later to exert an effect upon attention or action just as would some bit of practical wisdom that had been acquired in a fully conscious moment. And the fact that the reason for the action could not be given does not serve to mark it off from the ordinary process, because it is seldom possible to recall the particular event or events that are responsible for the mood.

While, then, in general and in the abstract we must admit

that Freud is warranted in his assumption that the subconscious may and does have an influence in the determination of attention, we cannot mean by the subconscious
what he implies. The subconscious is nothing mysterious,
no new and detached realm of mind, but merely a mass of
experiences of the same general character as those that we
have been considering throughout the volume. We cannot mean by the subconscious a new level of mind ; we can at
most mean an organisation of the old experiences in a
slightly new way. This new unity is ordinarily easily
broken, and then will recombine with the original systems,
and acts upon them and is recalled by them as are any of
the other elements of experience. The facts that have received so much prominence in these theories of the subconscious are not the expressions of any entirely new set
of processes, or of entirely new laws, but are rather new
combinations of the same familiar experiences acting by
the same old laws, but organised for the moment about a
new centre.

Usually the elements that constitute and control thought
or action merge their influence with the general mass, and
count in the total according to their relative strength.
Nothing that is conscious escapes forming part of their
unity ; the larger the unity, the greater the number of
elements that compose it, the fuller the consciousness,
the more adequate the knowledge. A sensation or thought
detached would no more have consciousness than a particle
of matter without other elements in the universe would
have weight. In a system of this kind not only do we
have both a dynamic unity and a persistent effective self
identity, but the unity is conscious of itself as one, so long
as the unity is unbroken and the elements are conscious of
themselves as distinct when the unity is dissolved. It is
not a mere logical construction, but it is a self-evident
interpretation of observed fact.

It has been frequently urged as an objection against the
possibility of psychology that it is impossible to observe

mental states without altering them in the very process of observation. Since the mind observing itself is not the same as the mind observing external objects, and since it cannot be both observing something external and itself at the same time, we would be prevented from obtaining any knowledge of the action of mind. If we consider the nature of attending to the objects of the natural world and compare it with the methods of observing mental processes, we shall see that the difference between them is not great enough to warrant the assumption that we can know one and not the other. In both we have a process of attention that leads to interpretation and classification under general heads or types. We attend in one way when we observe the process as external, we attend in another way when we regard the object as a mental state. What makes it possible to attend to the same state successively in two ways is the fact that a state remains for several seconds in consciousness with slight change, a fact that has been designated as the memory after-image by Fechner, the primary memory by James, the perseverance tendency by G. E. Müller, and which depends upon the inertia of the nervous system. We attend in one way for the object, and then as we introspect attend to the remnant of the object in another way and obtain another interpretation.

When we perceive an object of any kind or give it meaning, we refer it to older established types under the influence of some general problem. When, for example, we see a colour, we refer it to some earlier standard, and we see it and make the reference because we have the particular question asked, What is that colour? or because our mood or the task involves recognition of the colour. In brief, we perceive an object as an object when we attach a meaning to it, and that consists in identifying it with a previously developed standard, an earlier crystallisation from experience.

In the same way when we attempt to know our mental

states as mental states, we look at them under the influence of a question, a different question, to be sure, and refer them to other earlier developed types or crystallisations of experiences. When we say that there is a bare sensation of pressure, we are interpreting this particular concrete experience by other similar impressions, are taking it up into the system of knowledge growing from numerous experiences of separate series of pressure and of the nature of their excitation by mechanical stimulation. We apply an interpretation or standard that has been found to harmonise large groups of similar experiences. A bare sensation or image is from this point of view not a datum ; it is merely another meaning that may attach to any experience. Whether the meaning is one of common sense, of an objective science, or of subjective science, depends upon the purpose one has in mind at the moment and the resulting type to which the experience is referred. Obviously each is an interpretation, one is as abstract as another. The bare image is no bare image, but a psychological interpretation of what was at the last moment interpreted under the influence of a question of everyday common sense. So to know mental states as mental states is not a different kind of knowledge from knowing things—it is merely knowing the same thing in a slightly different way. It is a matter of taking up the given, whatever it may be, into a different system of experiences from before, of attaching a different meaning or different type. So far as immediacy and abstractness are concerned both are on the same level. And even the process of knowing is not different. It is in both cases not a transfer from one level to another, or a process of bringing in elements of different grades, but merely one of making a reference to other elements previously organised into a type. If we attend in one way we have a vaulted sky, if in another a bare sensation, blue.

To know the self as self is, so far as it is possible at all, a process of the same kind. It is but to analyse out from one experience those phases that make that experience like all other experiences, a selection of the aspect that is common to all experience. The process frequently repeated gives rise to the idea or type of the empirical self to which each concrete mental process adds something. Even when we pass to the problem of the self as a dynamic active force, we are working along the same general lines. True, the experiences have not crystallised so definitely or completely that the type is unmistakable from the given, or that it seems to be a datum of consciousness as does the perception of the table. Still the construction comes by looking at the concrete with a definite question in mind, and gaining from numerous processes a common characteristic that, when combined with other interpretations of different phenomena, harmonises with them and can be made typical of all action.

So for example I have been endeavouring in this chapter to group the facts that are involved in knowing the self with a large mass of related facts. If I have succeeded in uniting the picture of the self with other bits of knowledge already developed into a system, we have a knowledge of the self in what seems to me the only possible way of knowing anything. To take some one concrete act, if any act is concrete, and to bring it into connection with a wide mass of similar phenomena that interpret it on the one side, and on the other take it over into themselves to enrich them, is to know. Similarly the self as developed socially is an interpretation, and as we know it in any of its physical or ideational aspects, we are selecting phases and grouping them with related phenomena. The data that are interpreted we find first, probably, in the constant mass of sensations, strains, bodily feelings, persistent visual impressions, etc. etc., that James and others have been so happy in routing out from the complex. About these group the socially recognised differences from other individuals, and from the mass there precipitates an awareness of the self as a meaning. In the interpretation the self does not stand out with all the distinctness of the desk I see before me.

It is more confused with the impression of body, more vague, more shadowy, but it originates in the same way. The difference in substantiality is probably due in part to the fact that it will not stand the pragmatic test, will not serve as the end of action, or will not give support in any physical way when trusted to. Even if the perception were more shadowy, if it were a mere logical interpretation of what is known, we should have the same principle. In short, we may say that instead of the mind knowing mental states, mental states know the mind. Knowing, whether of external objects, of sensations as sensations, or of the self, is a process of selecting some phase of the momentary experience, under the influence of mood, purpose or question, and amplifying that phase by earlier experiences that have crystallised into types. Knowing is a process that comes out of experience under the influence of experience and by the addition of experiences. And one form of knowing is no more complicated, no more mysterious than another.

To perceive an object, to introspect an image or bare sensation, and to know a self are all alike in that each is a different rearrangement of an entire experience about a common focal point, a different way of attending to the same experience, and the different ways of attending are due to different questions in mind that lead to different interpretations, to different types. We have come round to Münsterberg's statement that all knowledge is interpretation, with the difference that I believe that all knowledge is essentially interpretation, and that, far from falsifying experience, interpretation is the very life of experience. No experience would be possible without it, and the greater the amount of interpretation, the greater the number of elements that interact in any mental process, the fuller the consciousness, the more adequate the knowledge, the nearer the approach to the goal of truth.

The physical side of the self will necessarily be discussed later in connection with the physical side of attention. Suffice it here to say that what on the mental side is an organisation of experiences is on the physical side an organisation of nervous elements. We can parallel the mental by the physical at every point, in fact the mental derangements already considered have forced us at earlier stages of our argument to change at times from the mental to the physical in our picture. Further details here would merely duplicate the later chapter.

Taken together, the self and attention are so closely related as to be scarcely distinguishable. Conditions of attention and what we know as the self are for practical purposes identical. The self is an organisation of experiences as a dynamic whole. It is our word to express the fact that each man is different in his actions from every other man, that his experience is a unit, and that he feels it to be always identical with itself. The same process of interaction that is responsible for the unity and persistent identity of the self, and that makes it possible for the mental states to be known as mental states is also the factor that we have seen to be at the basis of what we know as attention. In short we may say that attention is merely the self active in controlling the entrance of ideas, just as will is the self active in the determination of action, and reason is the self exerted in the ordering of thought. It is essential merely to note that all operations arise and are determined from within, not from without experience. The self is not some part of experience, nor is it something above or beyond experience; but it is simply the whole or the sum-total of experience. When we say then that the self decides to what we shall attend, we do not mean that decision is controlled by some experience other than those previously discussed; we desire to designate those same conditions regarded from a slightly different point of view.

SUMMARY

1. The idea of a self has usually been introduced to explain the fact that mind shows unity and self-identity, and that mental states do not exist merely but are known.

2. These facts cannot be satisfactorily explained on the assumption of a mind apart from the states, but are perfectly explicable if we regard the interacting mass of experience as the self.

3. Unity comes from the mutual interaction of all elements of experience past as well as present.

4. Persistent self-identity finds its explanation in the fact that no experience is ever entirely lost, and that new experiences are never entirely new but are new arrangements of old experiences about a new element.

5. Mental states, like external objects, are known by being taken up into existing types earlier crystallised from the experience.

CHAPTER XIV

THE ANATOMICAL BASIS OF ATTENTION

WE have now considered the facts usually grouped under the head of attention and the related phenomena which seem to be susceptible of explanation in terms of the same general theory. It devolves upon us now to search out a theory for the facts we have been considering, to see how far they may be brought together under some more general principle, and to discover any related facts that shall throw new light upon those already noticed.

We may divide all the many theories of attention that have been developed in the history of psychology into three great groups. One considers attention from the side of the activities of the nervous system; a second group brings attention into very close connection with apperception in some form or other, and would treat it as one phase of this general centre of mental activity; and a third makes some one characteristic or accompaniment of attention fundamental, and would explain every aspect from that one feature. These groups are of course not exclusive. Some writers have considered different phases of the problem and have developed at least two of the theories in a single work. The physiological theory is a natural accompaniment of either of the other two, and there are also cases in which the first two have been combined.

We must begin with an examination of the physiological theories of attention, but before we can enter upon the details of the discussion we must consider for a moment the more general question of the relation between body and mind, which is presupposed in any "explanation" in psychology ; and then pass to a discussion of the anatomical substrate of attention. Both factors must enter into the discussion of each point, and unless we have some agreement as to what part each is to play confusion is sure to arise. A full treatment of the relation of body and mind is out of place here, and would take much more space than we have to devote to it. But as there can be no satisfactory conclusion reached without reference to both the physical and the mental antecedents of attention, and as there is always likely to be confusion and misunderstanding when there is not a definite picture of the relation, it seems necessary to give a brief statement of the generally accepted theory of their connection.

Daily experience reinforced by all that we know of mental pathology, comparative neurology, and cerebral physiology makes certain that there is a very close relation between the mental and the bodily states. Anything that affects the brain is at once seen to have an influence upon the thinking processes. A sharp blow upon the head produces unconsciousness, and all similar accidents have their corresponding mental effects. Diseases of the brain are accompanied by mental disturbances, and there is a very definite correspondence between the part of the brain affected and the nature of the mental perversion. In the animal series we find that the signs of intelligence increase as the nervous system grows in relative size and becomes more complicated in structure, and finally it is possible by physiological experiments on animals to show that modifying the action of the nervous elements produces movements which ordinarily are the result of conscious states. The fact of connection is certain, but when we attempt to think the nature of the relation more definitely we at once become involved in difficulties of all sorts, which up to the present time seem to forbid us to bring the relation under any of the usual categories.

In the first place we can hardly think of one as cause,

the other as effect, for both the mental and the physical processes seem to go on simultaneously while we think of the cause as preceding the effect. Again, if we regard mind and body as separate things we can only regard them as causally related if we restate some of the fundamental hypotheses of the natural sciences, the doctrine of the conservation of energy in particular. If physical processes cause mental states, there must be energy used up in the process, and this energy can no longer be regarded as within the series of physical relations, and hence is an incalculable factor from the standpoint of the physicist. There seems, then, no escape from considering the mental processes as identical in kind with physical processes, a conclusion which lands us in materialism. On the other side, if we assume that the mental processes can exert an influence upon physical states, we have again creation of physical energy in an incalculable manner which is also opposed to the same fundamental hypothesis. We can escape this only by accepting the materialistic hypothesis as above, or by assuming that mental processes are the type of all processes, and so that all seemingly physical processes are at bottom mental.

Many attempts have been made to retain interaction and the doctrine of conservation of energy at one and the same time. The method has for the most part been an attempt to find some way in which mind may conceivably influence physical processes without exerting force upon them. One of the most ingenious and frequently quoted is the suggestion of Sir Oliver Lodge, that it is possible that mind merely controls the direction of energy but does not add energy to the physiological processes. In spite of the scientific distinction of its author, it seems doubtful if there is ever any control of the direction of a force that is not due to another force. Change in the direction of motion of a projectile or of a stream would be regarded as just as certain evidence of the action of some force as would change in its velocity.

This and similar theories, of which there have been many, are all attempts to make nothing out of something by making that something very small, but a violation of a general principle cannot be excused on the ground of insignificance, and if you make the offence trifling the gain for the theory is similarly small.

We seem compelled then either to give up the doctrine of the conservation of energy, to abandon all distinctions between the bodily and mental processes, or to deny that there is a causal relation between body and mind. Of these possible solutions modern psychology has chosen the last. There would be no difficulty in modifying the conservation of energy hypothesis to suit the case if there were any positive facts that demanded it, but the objections which we have to meet do not rest upon positive facts but upon difficulties in picturing an unknown relation. Again, there might be no objection to identifying the physical and mental sides of phenomena. In fact modern metaphysics very decidedly inclines to that solution of the problem in its most fundamental aspects. But whatever we may decide as to the fundamental truth of the relation between the two, there can be no doubt that on the more concrete psychological plane there is an easily recognisable distinction between the chemical change which takes place within a nerve cell and the sensation which accompanies it in our mind. A fundamental unification of the two phenomena, although demanded by many philosophical considerations, can never disturb the fact that these two things are different experiences.

To avoid these many difficulties all use of the term causality in the discussion has been abandoned, and psychologists have very generally accepted the doctrine of psycho-physical parallelism. They assume that the mind and brain work on side by side, but they do not assume that either influences the other—that there is any interaction between the two series of events. Mental processes are explained by a reference to preceding mental states, and physical processes by the earlier bodily states, but there is no distinct assertion as to what the nature of the relation between them may be, although it is added that the same physical process always accompanies any given mental process, and vice versa.

Thè positive empirical facts which have led to this conclusion are easily stated. It depends in the last analysis upon the fact that no man has ever seen a bodily process pass over into a mental process, and in all probability never will see such a passage. Every man is immediately conscious of his own mental processes as they run their course, but knows nothing directly of his brain, of the changes that go on during the same time in his nervous system. He can see a rod come into contact with his hand and immediately after feel a sensation of pressure from the skin, he can see a morsel of food vanish in the direction of his mouth and have a continuous series of tactual sensations from fingers, lips, and tongue, but he knows nothing more of the process until the sensations of taste come into consciousness. He knows nothing of the nervous processes which intervene between the time he sees the rod touch the hand and the entrance of the sensation of touch, or between the contact of the food particle with the tongue and the coming of the sensation of taste.

When, on the other hand, the anatomist and the physiologist attempt to supply the link, to trace the connections between the sense organ and the conscious sensation, they can but follow the path of the nerve to the brain, trace the connections in the cortex of the hemispheres and the motor paths which lead back to the muscles. They can nowhere pierce the veil that shuts them off from the sensation and from consciousness. Magnify the present powers of observation a thousand-fold, and even devise experimental means that should permit one to study the brain cells during their operation and to watch the changes which go on in them while the mind is perceiving external objects or following a train of thought, one would still be unable to discover what connection exists between the mental picture and the chemical changes in the cells. The physiologist would know the mechanical side, the man whose brain was being examined would know the mental side, but neither could know both at once. So far as we can predict to-day it will be for ever impossible to have the two sides, physical and psychical, in the same consciousness at the same time. And granting by a stretch of the imagination that this difficulty be overcome, and by some ingenious contrivance it should become possible for an individual to watch his brain cells in action and to think at the same time, to receive impressions from the external world and at the same time to study the mechanism by which he receives them, there would still be two isolated conscious experiences, and the process of transfer from one state to the other would even then be hidden from view. Unless this process of transformation could be studied for itself, there could be no adequate representation of the relation between body and mind. At best the two series of processes would be but two disjointed groups of experiences which could never be united.

Moreover, so far as is known there is no relation in any way like the relation of mind and body with which it can be compared. It stands in our experience as a fact *sui generis*, and will not fit into the forms of causality as we see them in the world about, but so far as we can learn must stand alone. The reasoning processes of the human mind are such that if it is possible to refer one fact to a similar fact or group of facts we seem to have it explained, but this particular relation can find no explanation even in analogy. The picture of an object and the cerebral states which we know or can know seem doomed to stand in isolation in our experience, although other facts assure us that they never exist the one without the other. It is this apparent paradox that the two series of phenomena are constantly given together but with their form of connection unknown, which drives us to the hypothesis of psycho-physical parallelism. It is justifiable so long as it remains merely a statement of known fact, and makes no assertions positive or negative as to the nature of the connection between the two series of events.

For our purpose, an acceptance of this doctrine means that we shall everywhere seek an explanation of the physical facts within the physical series, and of the mental facts within the mental series. Furthermore, we shall attempt to connect the mental facts with the corresponding physical facts, but shall not regard one as in any case the cause of the other. This involves treating attention from two distinct sides, but always endeavouring to point out the elements in the two series which are concomitant. The pointing out of concomitants will not imply that we are dealing with causes, even if we do not definitely deny in so many words that there is a causal relation, but will merely be an attempt to complete our knowledge of each side as best we may from the facts at our disposal.

As a further preliminary to the discussion of the physiological theories of attention we must attempt to give a brief statement of the structure of the nervous organs which are involved in the process, a phase of attention which we have so far entirely neglected.

Roughly speaking, the nervous system is to-day generally thought of as made up of a vast number of separate cells, each an organism complete in itself, although dependent upon the body as a whole for its nourishment and protection. Our understanding of the nature of the nervous system is very largely confined to knowing the arrangement of the various organisms and appreciating their mutual relations. We know next to nothing of the processes which go on in the elements themselves. That there is some complex chemical change in the nerve cell while it is in action is certain, and we know too that there are electrical phenomena associated with the action of the nerve cells. Much, too, is known of the ways in which

Q

nerves may be excited, but after all, so far as inner action is concerned, the nerve cell is almost entirely a sealed book. Still less is known, as has just been said, of what the relation may be between the neural processes and the mental states which correspond to them. We must be satisfied at present then with what explanations can be derived from a study of the paths which the various nerve impulses follow from the sense organ to the brain and from the brain back to the muscles, with a slight knowledge of the different parts of the brain that are involved in the several processes.

The elementary cells of which the nervous tissue is made up are of very different sizes and shapes, but they have several characteristics in common. Each element consists of a cell body and two or more processes or prolongations of greater or less length. The cell body is the vital centre of the element. It contains the nucleus of the entire cell, and through it the other parts receive nourishment. The nerve fibres all grow out from this cell body originally, and when separated from it in any way they at once die. The processes vary greatly in length, from a millimetre or so to half the length of the body, but they do not vary in the closeness of their vital connection with the cell. Even the outermost part of the nerve fibre, the longest as well as the shortest, is absolutely dependent upon the central body for its life. We may crudely picture the nervous system as made up of a mass of living organisms with interlacing tentacles which connect with the outside world on the one side and ramify throughout the body on the other, and unite into masses in the brain and lower centres. They serve to bring each element into connection with many others.

From one standpoint we can think of the function of the nervous system as a process of transmitting stimuli from the sense organs to the muscles. In the more complicated processes the intermediate steps in the transformation may be much more important than the contraction of the muscle that results, but there is in every instance, even in purely sensory attention, some motor discharge. There are in general three levels at which sensory impressions may pass over into motor effects. The first and simplest of these is the spinal cord, the seat of reflex action. Next come the secondary centres of the medulla, the corpora quadrigemina, the thalamus, etc., and finally the connections which are made in the cerebral hemispheres. The difference between the nervous action at the different levels is mainly in the degree of complexity, in the number of stimuli that may be summed up in the motor effect. In the cord there are only a few impressions concerned, mainly those from skin and muscle, and the corresponding movement is simple. Nearly all of the senses may be concerned in the movements which originate in the lower centres, and the movements are correspondingly more complex and better adapted to the circumstances of the environment at the moment. In the cortex the movements are the resultant not only of the stimuli which are affecting the senses at the moment, but of those which have been active in the past as well. It is here that the activities of the cells are accompanied by consciousness in the fullest sense of the word, although it is not at all unlikely that the lower centres also contribute a part to the total consciousness. For our present purposes we may disregard the lower levels of nervous activity, or think of them only as the means by which the external stimuli are transmitted to the cortex.

The problem in connection with the cortex itself deals with the centres for the various senses, and with association paths which connect them. Probably the most satisfactory account of the architecture of the sensory areas of the cortex which we have to-day is contained in the two works of Flechsig, " Die Localization der geistigen Vorgänge " and " Gehirn und Seele." His conclusions are brought together in the accompanying diagram on page 228. From any diagram of the brain it will be seen that the motor area for the control of all the muscles of the body is situated in front of the central sulcus, from near the fissure of Silvius upward to the summit of the hemisphere, and

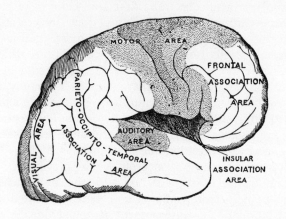

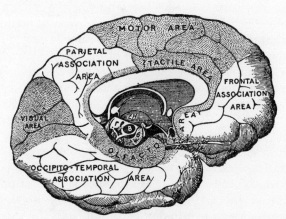

AFTER FLECHSIG, MODIFIED BY SCHÄFER

down for a space on the median surface where the two hemispheres come into juxtaposition. Within this area the muscles for the control of the different parts of the body have very accurately localised centres, an area for the thumb, another for the muscles involved in speech, etc. etc.

The sensory areas are more widely scattered, and are on the whole not so definitely known as are the motor centres. The tactile sensations seem to have their seat in the same general region of the cortex as the cells for the control of the movements of the corresponding part of the body. The area for hearing is located in the anterior portion of the temporal lobe. The visual sensations are received in the occipital lobe on both the external and median surfaces. Smell is placed in the temporo-sphenoidal lobe, and taste near it, although that is not so well made out. The various areas can be recognized much more easily from diagrams than from any description.

The main point for us is that the sensory and motor areas are widely separated in the cortex, and that the areas of the brain in which it is known that there are definite sensory or motor functions occupy a relatively small part of the entire cortex. What part the remaining portions might play has been long in dispute. The most satisfactory explanation at present is the one given us by Flechsig, that the function of all the areas is to unite the different sensory and motor areas with one another. There are apparently three kinds of connections to be distinguished in the cortex. A sensory area may be directly joined with a motor, two sensory areas may be united, and finally there are connecting fibres which form a bond of union between all parts of the cortex indirectly through a central associating area. The first form of connection is probably the simplest. The best instance is to be found in the connections which exist between optical and auditory centres on the one hand, and the motor centre for speech on the other. The fact is best brought out by the different forms of aphasia. In one form of this disease it is impossible to hear spoken words, and so impossible to repeat them. In another form it is impossible to read aloud written or printed words. The functions of the centre for sight are destroyed, and there is no visual cue for speech. When the motor centre is itself impaired there is the same effect produced, except that both visual and auditory cues fail to call out the speech movements, while it is possible both, to see and to hear. The same effects result from extensive degenerations of the connecting paths or of the intervening areas of the cortex as from the destruction of either the sensory or the motor centre. There must be extensive paths which join the two areas. Similar connections can be traced between the sensory centres and the motor centres for the control of any other part of the body, but the connection is not so evident since the centres which receive the impressions from the skin and muscles—which stand in the closest connection with the movement of the muscles—are found in the same area as the motor centres, so that the connecting paths are shorter and harder to demonstrate. This uniting of sensory and motor areas in the cortex is one of the functions of the portions of the brain which are neither sensory nor motor.

Another function is to associate one sensory with other sensory impressions. As we have seen throughout the book, sensations from one organ are constantly accompanied by those from another. To permit of this every part of the centre for one sense must be in connection with every other sensory area. This function Flechsig assigns almost exclusively to the region of the cortex between the visual centre in the occipital lobe and the area for the tactile, auditory, and olfactory sensations.

Another area in which no specific sensory or motor functions are developed covers the cortex of the frontal lobes. These, too, Flechsig found to be closely connected with the tactile area, and it is probable that they are also closely joined to the other sensory areas. The entire un-localised area of the brain is then occupied by these three association centres, which serve to make it possible for the sensory and motor centres to combine in any order.

A brief description of the method by which Flechsig has

arrived at these conclusions may serve to make the statements clearer, as well as to furnish a means of judging the accuracy of the conclusions themselves. It depends upon the fact that there is a progressive ripening of the fibres of the cortex in the child, which begins before birth and continues for a considerable period after. The nerve fibre in its complete form is made up of two parts, the conducting centre and an outer layer of fatty tissue, the sheath of myelin. In the first stages of the development of the cortical nerve fibres the sheath is lacking, and as the different tracts take on the sheath or myelinate at different times it is possible to distinguish the paths by the order of their myelination. The first to ripen in the hemispheres are the sensory fibres, and of these the tactile fibres appear first, and are followed in order by those of the olfactory, visual, and auditory tracts. The sensory are followed by the motor fibres, and these still later by the association fibres, which extend from part to part of the cortex. It was possible for Flechsig to make out accurately the place of origin of the different tracts by studying the brain of the child at different stages in its development, while the various tracts stand out very much alone in their development.

With this picture of the cerebrum as made up of a number of sensory and motor centres with connecting tracts of association fibres, we are ready to ask the question as to what part of the brain is likely to be the seat of attention. The answer is given most directly by psychiatry. Flechsig says of patients who suffer from lesions of the frontal lobes, with no other injuries that can be discovered in any other portion of the brain : " The patient now ascribes to himself every idea that in reality is to be referred to the external world, so that he thinks himself in possession of all conceivable goods, talents, and deserts. There is lacking the associative connection between the external perceptions and the idea of his own person, or, on the other hand, between the consciousness of his own personality and external perception, so that he forgets himself or does not attend to his surroundings (there is no 'active apperception.') There may be no obscurity in the ideas in the usual sense. The patient talks intelligently concerning many ideas, if he is not under the influence of an emotion, but he is not able to distinguish between the really experienced and the merely imagined, between the true and the false, the possible and the impossible. Along with this defect of the logical feeling (based upon imperfect memory) goes a lapse of ethical and æsthetic judgment which betrays him into actions that stand in irreconcilable opposition to his earlier character." [2] We see from this that attention, either in its effects upon perception or in its subtler effects upon the more complicated processes which we have noted to be dependent upon it, disappears or is woefully impaired when the frontal lobes are affected.

Similar testimony comes from many psychiatrists. In a list of cases of lesions of the frontal lobes reported by Dr. M. Allen Starr, there was a large proportion of cases in which there was a lack of interest in the surroundings, a general lack of memory, reason, and spontaneity of action. Operations upon the frontal lobes of monkeys have shown very much the same effects.

Injuries of the other association areas do not have this widespread effect. If the Island of Reil is affected alone we have merely a breaking of the connections between the auditory and speech centres, and, as has been seen above, an accompanying auditory aphasia or partial aphasia, paraphasia. Lesions of the posterior association centre in the temporal and parietal lobes are accompanied by a deterioration in the more rudimentary connections between the parts of knowledge rather than by a disturbance of the higher functions. There is a lack of recognition of the temporal and spatial relations, and a general disturbance of the ordinary associative connections. Objects are not recognised, and so cannot be correctly used. But there is no disturbance of the relations of the self to external objects or of the external objects to the self. What we denominated the objective conditions of association are impaired, but the subjective control remains normal, so long as the frontal association centres are not injured. Psychiatry then seems to point to the frontal lobes as the area which is at the basis of attention.

Other evidence that would tend to support the same theory was adduced by Professor Cunningham in his presidential address before the Anthropological section of the British Association in 1901. He pointed out that the most constant difference in the skulls of animals and of men consisted in the greater width of the skull of man in the region of the boundary between the frontal and parietal lobes, and the chief change in the brain of man as compared with the higher animals lies in the extension of the frontal lobe and the anterior portion of the parietal lobe downward until they cover in the Island of Reil. Part of this is undoubtedly the neural accompaniment of the great development of speech in the human species, but part of the increase must be ascribed to an extension of the frontal association centre.

It is significant in this connection that, next to speech, power of sustained attention would probably be chosen as the distinctive characteristic of the human race. It would point to the fact that increase in attention goes on side by side with the development of the frontal lobes. There is also scattered and less satisfactory evidence that men of genius have possessed brains which were particularly well developed in this same region. The brain of the astronomer Hugo Gylden, of the mathematician Sophie Kovalevsky, and of Helmholtz, have shown in this region "a marked exuberance of cortical growth." [1]

What evidence there is, then, from the comparative study of the brains of the different species and of different individuals goes to confirm the results of pathology in assigning attention to the frontal lobes. Impairment of the frontal lobes means impairment of attention, increase in the frontal lobes accompanies increase in efficiency of attention. These two facts, while they do not amount to an absolute demonstration of the correspondence between this region and activity of attention, do raise a very strong presumption that attention corresponds to the anterior association centre of Flechsig.

One other fact remains to be mentioned here in preparation for the physiological discussions of the next chapter. This is the result of the labours of Theodore Kaes [6 7] on the successive medullation of the more minute cortical fibres. His experiments carry on the method of Flechsig, but apply it to the connecting paths within the different areas, and extend the investigation over a much longer period in the life of the individual. He found that the course of development is much slower than was previously supposed. There is an increase in the number of completely developed fibres of fifty per cent between the ages of eighteen and thirty-eight, and the process is not entirely complete at fifty. Moreover, the order in which the different areas develop is in confirmation of the results of Flechsig. Kaes found that the central and occipital regions develop much earlier than the association centres, and that the anterior portion of the brain comes to maturity last of all. Certainly if medullation is an essential condition of function we should expect the association centres to appear later than the centres which they connect, and the most complicated association centre, the frontal, to ripen last of all.

We must leave over to the next chapter the attempt to construct a picture of the physiological action of the anatomical mechanisms here sketched.

SUMMARY

1. As a starting-point for a nervous explanation of attention we may accept the hypothesis of psycho-physical parallelism, that mind and body run along side by side, but with no assertable causal connection between them.

2. The anatomical seat of attention is apparently the frontal lobes.

3. The frontal lobes are not the seat of spontaneous energy, but are shown by Flechsig to be association centres that mediate between sensory, and sensory and motor, areas of the cortex.

CHAPTER XV

THE PHYSIOLOGY OF ATTENTION

WHEN all has been said that can be said from the anatomical side, we are still without an understanding of the way in which the structures act in making one object stand out clearly at one time and another at another. To know that attention is in some way connected with the frontal lobes, and that the different sensory areas, although situated in different parts of the cortex, are connected with the frontal lobes and with each other by association fibres, is still to know nothing of the physiological functions involved in attention. Even the discovery of Kaes that the association fibres develop as the man grows older, and thus increase the number of connecting paths between the various parts of the cortex, is merely suggestive of a theory of the action of the cerebral structures, and is not in itself an adequate explanation.

Our problem here is as to how a group of cells in the frontal lobe with its connecting fibres can make now the paper on which I write, now the inkstand, and again the words that I am striving to put on paper, stand out clearly before me, and monopolise my consciousness. Facts are not as yet known which will give an absolutely conclusive answer to this question, but there are many known physiological activities which raise a presumption in favour of one theory or another. It is our purpose in this chapter to state as many as possible of the facts that seem to have a bearing, and then to attempt to harmonise these physiological processes with the psychological observations that we have collected in the earlier parts of the book.

There are three ways in which one nerve element may affect another : (1) by direct transmission of the impulse, as when the excitation of a sense organ affects each successive neuron between it and the cortex ; (2) by another influence that tends to increase the activity of the second cell, but not to excite it if it is not already in activity ; and (3) by a similar influence that will decrease the activity of the cell below its normal. The first of these forms of influence is the simplest, and the one which is regarded as fundamental for all nervous action. What the nature of the transmission may be, or how it is possible for the activity of one cell to excite another to activity, are both matters of which we are as yet ignorant, but action always takes place by reason of some direct contact between the parts of the cells. It is improbable that this simple form of transmission should constitute the basis of the activity of the frontal lobes. For, in the first place, there is no original source of excitation in the frontal lobes that might serve to initiate the series of activities, and, in the second place, the frontal lobe does not itself excite the cells of sense, but merely increases their tendency to act when an immediate stimulus is given.

The other two forms of stimulation are much less direct, and consist simply in a tendency to influence in one way or another the action of a cell when excited from some other source. We must turn for the type of both forms of action to the relations between the different motor centres, and preferably those of the cord. Perhaps the simplest in-stance of the two processes are to be found in the knee jerk, which has been worked out in great detail by Jendrassik, [12] Dr. Weir Mitchell, [17] Professor Lombard, [14] and Professors Bowditch and Warren. [5] Every schoolboy knows that if he sits with his legs crossed, his neighbour can excite a vigorous kick by gently tapping the tendon just below the knee-cap. A careful study of this phenomenon has shown that the extent of this kick varies with the condition of excitation of the nervous system as a whole. The experiments show that the contraction of any other muscle in the body tends to increase the extent of the kick. Clenching the fist, talking, setting the teeth, in fact, any movement however remote from the part of the body in question, will serve to reinforce the movement, and in many cases will considerably more than double it. Another instance of much the same kind was worked out by Professor Loeb. Professor Loeb found that it was possible to exert a greater amount of strain upon a dynamometer with the right hand if not only the muscles of that hand were contracted but those of the left as well and all the muscles of the body. It was pointed out in connection with the strain sensations, and is also a fact of general observation, that when one exerts himself to the utmost in the performance of any bit of work, there is contraction not only of the muscles which are directly involved but of nearly all the other muscles of the body in addition. When gripping with one hand the other too is tightly shut, the muscles of the scalp are contracted, the teeth are set, and the whole body is braced, although none of these movements are of any direct advantage to the movement in question. Loeb showed that these other contractions were not mere useless grimaces, but that without them it was impossible to exert the full force of the right hand. If you check the contractions of the other muscles, you not only do not seem to be trying so hard, but you are really accomplishing less in the task that you have set yourself. Here, as in the preceding case, we cannot be concerned with the mere transmission of impulse from cell to cell, but must look to reinforcement as an explanation. Each motor cell, simply because it is active, will tend to increase the amount of activity of the other motor cells in the body, whether near or remote in their seat.

The evidence that under other circumstances the activity of one motor cell may tend to decrease or inhibit the activity of another is just as direct. One of the first instances of this kind of action to be made out was the effect of the

vagus nerve upon the heart. It is known that the contraction of the heart muscle would go on at a regular rate
much faster than the normal, were it not that it is held in
check by the activity of the vagus nerve. Stimulation of
the vagus tends to slow the heart, cutting the vagus or producing a partial impairment of its function, as in a fever,
will release the heart from the inhibitory control, and
permit it to assume its own rate, or to approximate to
that rate. There seem to be similar but less well-known
inhibitory influences exerted by the other functions of the
medulla upon one another. The respiratory rhythm seems
to check the activity of the vaso-motor centre at certain
points in its activity, and both the vaso-motor and the
respiratory rhythms affect the vagus centre, and through it
the rate of the heart.

There are also many instances of inhibition between the
voluntary motor cells. Bowditch and Warren found that
all the impulses which Professor Lombard and Jendrassik
had shown to reinforce the knee-jerk if they were received
at the same time as the blow which called out the kick
would inhibit the movement, if the stimulus preceded the
blow by 0·4 of a second or so. The primary effect of the
contraction of any other muscle of the body is to increase the
amount of the movement, but its secondary or delayed
effect is always to decrease or even to destroy the movement. Even more striking and important are the results
of Professor Sherrington [25, 26] and his students. They have
shown that with every stimulation of a motor area in
the cortex there go out two innervations. One will exert
an influence to contract a group of muscles, while the
other at the same time inhibits the activity of the
antagonists. The same stimulus, then, will at one and the
same time excite the muscles which bend the arm at the
elbow and decrease the tonus of the muscles which tend to
straighten the arm, and thereby remove any possibility of
interference of that group with the movement of flexion.

On the basis of these results we are safe in formulating

the general principle that any motor cell will by its activity increase or decrease the activity or tendency to activity of other motor cells, however remote the two may stand in the body, and, apparently, however devious the connection between the two cells may be. Whether it shall increase or decrease the activity will depend in part upon the temporal relations between the two excitations, and in part upon the paths that connect the two cells. What the other elements are which determine whether the effect shall be of reinforcement or inhibition have not been made out. We can still further extend this law of reinforcement and inhibition by making it include the effect of sensory cells upon motor cells. Professor Lombard found that music, a dream, a knock upon the door, or any sensation of sufficient force and suddenness, would reinforce the knee-jerk. Drs. Bowditch and Warren still further extended these results to show that a loud sound, a bright light, a puff of air against the skin, would act in the same way as the contraction of a muscle, would first reinforce and then inhibit the activity of the cells that control the knee-jerk. It seems that we can say that the activity of a motor cell is influenced positively or negatively by the activity of very many cells, both motor and sensory, in other parts of the body. These forms of influence seem as frequent, if less marked, as the direct effect of cell upon cell in transmitting a sensory stimulus from the sense organ to the cortex, or a motor innervation from the cortex or other centre to the cell in immediate control of the muscles. [5]

What the nature of this effect may be it is very difficult to say. It is probably carried by the same paths as the directly transmitted stimulation, and differs from the direct effect only in so far as that does not of itself excite the nerve cell, but only increases or decreases the tonus of the cell upon which it acts as shown in the effect of any direct excitation.

It seems probable that we must look to these facts of reinforcement or of inhibition as the basis of the explanation of the nervous processes which accompany the mental changes of attention. In fact the three physiological theories of attention which are now most current, all put the emphasis upon one or the other of these effects.

Beginning in the order of historical development, we find that G. E. Müller would make attention almost entirely a phenomenon of reinforcement; Wundt insists that it is entirely a result of inhibition; while Exner would combine the two, and regard it as both inhibitory and reinforcing in its activity. Müller [21] sees three ways in which attention may be regarded as a reinforcement. It recalls memory images which serve to hold the corresponding new impression in consciousness; it produces an adaptation of the sense organ which permits a greater accuracy of observation, and it also produces changes in the circulation in the sensory centre and makes the nerve more sensitive. The physiological side is not developed in detail, so that it is not quite clear that a certain amount of inhibition is not also provided for in the theory, but the main emphasis is clearly put upon reinforcement.

Wundt [30] is a little more definite in working out the physiological processes. He assigns to the frontal lobes the seat of the attention phenomena, and insists that it is due to an inhibitory influence which the cells there exert upon the other parts of the brain. At the time of attending to any one sensation all other processes are excluded, and this alone is permitted to come to its full natural strength. He admits that there is no physiological objection to assuming that there is reinforcement as well as inhibition between the different parts of the cortex, but, as we saw in the earlier chapter, he feels assured that attention does not increase the intensity of the sensation attended to, but merely its clearness, and as it is hard to see how reinforcement could avoid influencing the intensity, he inclines to the opinion that it is safer to regard the entire process as one of inhibition. The argument does not seem to be entirely valid, for, as was seen in chapter 1, it is by no

R

means satisfactorily established that attention does not increase the intensity of the sensation attended to, and, furthermore, it is barely possible that there might be an influence of reinforcement exerted by nerve cell upon nerve cell which would increase the efficiency of its action, and so the clearness of the corresponding sensation, and not increase its intensity. As was pointed out also in the earlier chapter, all the arguments which hold against assuming that attention increases the intensity of the stimulus would also hold against having it decrease the intensity of all the others. It is a relative increase in intensity which offers difficulty to the theorist, and this would be present whether obtained by increasing the one or decreasing the many. Further criticism must be left over until we have an opportunity to consider the concrete facts.

Exner [8] combines the two possible effects in a single theory. He points out that we find reinforcement and inhibition both going on together all through the nervous system, and sees no reason why we should not also use both in our explanation of the attention phenomena. He formulates his theory of the physiological processes in attention in the statement that one set of paths is made much more permeable, while the permeability of all the others is greatly decreased. As a result one set of processes is increased in its activity, while all others are decreased. He does not discuss the probable point of origin of the inhibiting or reinforcing stimulus.

We can of course decide between theories of this kind on the basis of such concrete facts alone as we can find in the literature. It is evident from the theories mentioned above that it is theoretically possible for either or both processes to be at work, and which is to be actually effective must be decided from the experimental evidence at hand. Fortunately there have recently been several pieces of experimental work that bear upon the problem and will go a long way toward deciding it.

The experimenters who have contributed to the solution

of the question have all been working more or less consciously to discover a measure of the attention process. There have recently been three methods suggested and used more or less extensively. The first would measure the attention by determining its effects in some concrete process which can itself be measured. The activity chosen was the discrimination of difference as it is ordinarily employed in the experimental verification of Weber's Law, or the quickness of reaction to some simple sensory stimulus. Both have been found to be very closely dependent upon attention, and any variation in the one can be taken to indicate a change in the other.

The second method is more indirect. It consists in measuring not the strength of attention itself, but the amount of distraction which is necessary to destroy the attention to any other process. The method is analogous to testing the strength of materials by measuring their breaking point. In practice it is probably not easily applicable because the only means of distracting attention is by attending to something else, so that the method in practice is reduced to determining the effect upon one attention process of attending to something else at the same time. And as any attempt to attend simultaneously results merely in an alternation from one thing to another, what we get in reality is a measure of the results of attending successively to two processes of different kinds.

The third method makes use of the fluctuations of attention. It will be remembered from chapter v. that a stimulus of very slight intensity does not persist continuously in consciousness, but alternately appears and disappears. Marbe discovered that the length of time a sensation would remain in consciousness depended upon the intensity of the stimulus which occasioned it. If the grey line on the Masson disc increased in distinctness it would be a relatively longer time in consciousness than before. It occurred to Mr. Taylor [28] that the time during which the line remained in consciousness, or the relative proportion of the time seen to the time not seen, might be made to serve as a measure of the adequacy of attention under any set of circumstances. When attention was at its best it would be seen for a comparatively long time, the ratio of the period of visibility to the period of non-visibility would be comparatively large, and would decrease with the adequacy of attention. This method is very easy to apply, and gives results that record very slight changes. Since Mr. Taylor published, Dr. Wiersma [29] has applied the same method to a study of the influence of fatigue and of drugs upon attention. After he had thoroughly confirmed Marbe's results as to the effect of the intensity of the stimulus upon the time of visibility, he showed that the period of visibility undergoes very marked changes in the course of even a five-minute experiment. There was in the case of one man a decrease in the ratio of the time of visibility to the time of invisibility from the beginning to the end of the period; in the other, first an increase in the ratio, due to practice, and then a decrease, as the result of fatigue. In both cases the method proved its adequacy as a measure of the efficiency of attention.

Each of these methods, with the possible exception of the second, has given us some results which will have a bearing upon the general question as to whether reinforcement or inhibition is the predominant influence in the physiological processes which accompany attention, and the results of the attempts to apply the second method have proved very valuable, although the method itself has not shown itself to be theoretically well founded. It will probably prove most satisfactory to violate the temporal sequence of these theories, and begin with the application of the third and most recent, and then come back later to consider the results of the earlier in its light.

Three men have published results that have a bearing upon the problem as to whether the attention process is one of inhibition or reinforcement, using the attention wave as a measure of the adequacy of attention. Dr. Breese [6],

the earliest, looked upon his results as an evidence of inhibition, of the effect of one stimulus to decrease the efficiency of
another, and did not connect it with attention at all.
Dr. Breese worked with the rivalry of stereoscopic fields as
the basis of his experiments. It will be remembered from
chapter v. that when two fields of different colours, or of
any other two different kinds that appeal almost equally
to attention, are brought before either eye, there is a
constant fluctuation between them—now one will appear,
now the other. If the two colours are complementary, so
that there is no possibility of fusion to form a third, the
alternation will come at very regular intervals, and the line
of division will be sharply marked. The colours chosen
were red and green. It was found that it was impossible
to control the rate at which the two colours succeeded each
other, but that it was possible voluntarily to keep one colour
in the field for a longer time than the other, and that the
period for one colour could be influenced in various other
ways. This is of course entirely in harmony with the
results obtained on the perception of the grey rings of the
Masson disc, and, since the time relations are the same,
would point to the vaso-motor rhythm as the condition of
the fluctuation. It would seem, then, that just as any
influence that increases the activity of the central cell
would make the grey ring of the disc remain in consciousness for a longer time, so the same factors would tend to
alter the time relations of the periods of alternation between
the two colours. This is in harmony with the work of Dr.
Breese. He found in the first place that one colour could
be held for a longer time than the normal by an act of will.
The red could hold the field for sixty-eight per cent of the
time, as against a normal fifty-three per cent, if one strove
vigorously to retain it. It was found, however, that the
essential part of the so-called act of will consisted of making
vigorous eye movements, and that when these were suppressed there was practically no difference to be noted
between the voluntary effects and the normal. It was

found also that the introduction of conscious eye movements had exactly the same effect, even when there was no effort to hold the colour, and that a drawing upon one surface which would tend unconsciously to induce eye movements would have exactly the same effect, would retain the field upon which the drawings were made. In the same way it was shown that varying the colours upon the surface, placing a patch of blue upon the red, or surrounding the red with a white border, made that colour remain a greater proportion of the time. Moving one field while the other remained at rest, or increasing the intensity of the light which fell upon the one, produced an identical result.

It is evident that we have to deal here with the effect of one sensation or stimulus upon another. Eye movements, motion of one field, etc., are all stimuli which call up other sensations, and these, by their simultaneous presence in consciousness, tend to make stronger one of two other rival stimuli which are otherwise very evenly balanced. Dr. Breese thinks of the entire process as dependent upon the activity of the new stimulus in inhibiting the one which seeks to enter consciousness, but it seems much easier to regard the process as a reinforcement. Of course the matter here reduces to a question of words, for it is as easy to think of one as inhibited as of the other as reinforced. Introspection, however, seems to show that the red is the positive process all through, and that the conscious endeavour so far as it is present tends to hold the red rather than to exclude the green. This is even clearer in some experiments which have been performed in the laboratory of the University of Michigan, but not yet published, which show that certain unpleasant stimuli tend to have exactly the opposite effect, and to decrease the period in consciousness of the field that is emphasized, and which is kept in consciousness by the pleasant or exciting stimuli which Dr. Breese used. Here, then, we would have a reinforcement of the green if we had previously had an inhibition, while if we think of both effects as working upon the red, we have an inhibition of that colour. We have inhibition and reinforcement in either case, and it seems simpler to think of the pleasant or milder stimulus as the reinforcing, and the stronger or unpleasant as inhibiting, than to reverse the ordinary relation, and regard the pleasant as inhibiting. This seems even more true when we consider the results of work upon the minimal stimuli, where the relations are those which would normally be expected.

Mr. Taylor used the grey rings of the Masson disc, but made the same use of them as did Dr. Breese of his stereoscopic slides, except that he regarded them definitely as a measure of the adequacy of attention under different circumstances. In this method, instead of having but two stimuli which can enter consciousness, or which are preeminently favoured, but favoured in equal degrees, there was one principal stimulus, the grey rings on the white ground, and when they disappeared, only the white ground was left, unless the mind wandered off to some unrelated stimulus. However, the results in both cases seem to show that, just as the rings are favoured here, and held in consciousness, whenever conditions permit, so one of the colours in the field of vision tends to be favoured, and all factors which increase the efficiency of the cerebral activity, tend to hold that in consciousness rather than the other. Mr. Taylor's experiments are different, too, in so far as he worked not with stimuli that were closely connected with the stimuli in question, but with those which were of only general influence.

His results show that the first effect of a moderate stimulus was to increase the relative time of visibility. A further increase in the intensity of the stimulation (an induction current was used as the stimulus) was to decrease the period of visibility, and to increase the time of invisibility. Dr. Slaughter [27] found in another investigation that straining upon a dynamometer had the same effect as a slight stimulation in increasing the period of visibility. Accompanying these effects upon the adequacy of attention were always some apparently almost independent effects upon the length of the entire attention wave. This we must regard, however, as the direct effect of the stimulus upon the vasomotor centre, which is apparently affected by a stimulus in the same way that the respiratory or heart rhythm is affected. It has nothing to do with the effect of the stimulus upon the adequacy of attention, and may vary independently of it,

We must then picture the effect upon attention as an immediate reinforcement or inhibition exerted by the excitation of the sensory cells in the area for touch upon the cells of the cortical area for vision. This process makes them more capable of function, and so capable of acting for a longer period of time than they act normally. The peculiar thing in the results of both Mr. Taylor and Dr. Breese is that the effect seems to be selective, and to increase pre-eminently the cells which are concerned in the action which is desired at the time. The grey dots are always affected rather than the white surface, the red field rather than the green. This means, of course, merely that the reinforcement or inhibition acts upon those cells only which are at work in making these two processes prominent. Probably part of the reinforcing influences go over to the secondary cells which are determining that the grey ring or the red field shall occupy the centre of consciousness.

We have an effect here that seems exactly parallel to the reinforcement and inhibition of one motor nerve cell by another in the cases discussed in the earlier parts of the chapter. Just as we think of the impulse that passes out of the cell which controls the left arm as producing an increased amount of action in the cell that controls the right arm, so we must think of the activity of one sensory cell in the cortex as increasing the activity of the other sensory cells merely because it is itself active, or in the case of the contraction of the arm in squeezing the dynamometer that the action of a motor cell has the effect of increasing the activity of sensory cells as well as of other motor cells. There is a possibility, of course, that the effect in this case is due to the sensory impressions which come in from the muscles, but there is no great difficulty in assuming that motor cells reinforce sensory cells, any more than that sensory cells reinforce the motor. Whether there be a reinforcement or inhibition seems to depend upon the strength of the stimulus in this case, just as in the case of the knee-jerk it depends upon the time relations between the two phenomena.

Professor Münsterberg [19] and Dr. Hamlin [10] obtained results by means of the first method, or by a combination of the first and second methods, which seem to be analogous to these, although both writers have given them another interpretation. They both found that the ability to discriminate between two slightly different sensations increased when the subject was attempting to do something else at the same time. Many different senses were investigated, and the distraction was given by asking the subject to perform operations in mental arithmetic, to learn nonsense syllables, or count the beats of the metronome. In every case it was found that, if there was attention to the judgment at all, there was greater accuracy while the distraction was operative than if there was no distraction. The simplest explanation that offers itself for these results in the light of the later investigations is that activity of the cells employed in adding, etc., reinforces the activity of the other cells, so that they are more adequate to their work than when they are in the normal state. The only difference between this and the preceding is that the two operations are successive, not simultaneous. The adding does not take place at the same time as the estimating of differences, but comes in the intervals between two judgments. But the activity has the same reinforcing effect that the electric stimulus which Mr. Taylor used had upon the simultaneous attending to the grey rings. Later experiments by Mr. Moyer [18] and Miss Birch [4] go to show that if the distraction becomes too great there is a reduced accuracy of judgment, which would correspond to the inhibition that Mr. Taylor found for the stimuli of a greater degree of intensity. Successive stimulations of two cells, then, may modify the action of each other either positively or negatively, just as does the simultaneous stimulation of the two cells. Taken together, the results of these experiments go to show that the activity of any one sensory cell in the cortex has a tendency to increase or decrease the activity of all other sensory cells which may be active at the same time, whether the two groups of cells be situated in the same sensory areas or in areas which are widely separated. The sensory and motor areas would, then, seem to be on exactly the same level, so far as the question of mutual interaction is concerned.

But still we have not solved the question of the physiological basis for the selective activity of attention. All of the effects which we have considered so far would affect the entire cortex alike; there would be reinforcement or inhibition, not only of one set of cells, but of all at once. We must find some physiological basis for the fact that the grey rings only are made more prominent by the electric current, or for the fact that it is the red field alone which is retained for the greater length of time, and that necessarily at the expense of the green. We must considerably extend our view if we are to obtain an explanation of this phase of the phenomenon, although it must be an extension of the same general principle, not the introduction of anything new in kind.

If every sensation has an influence upon every other sensation, it would only be natural to suppose that it would have a more marked influence upon the related sensations than upon those which are entirely foreign. And this is what we find on the side of consciousness. G. E. Müller lays great emphasis upon this aspect of the problem. In the terminology of the day he wrote, he said that mind holds one sensation before consciousness by calling up from memory other ideas which are related to it, and that these serve to retain it. Nicolai Lange, working with the fluctuations of attention, obtained very similar results. He noticed that if one looks at a figure drawn in ambiguous perspective, its form will change as one changes the secondary associated ideas in consciousness. The truncated prism which we mentioned in chapter v. as constantly changing from a concave to a convex figure, seems in the earlier changes at least to make the transformation in time with the coming and going in consciousness of associated ideas. If a receptacle of some kind was thought of the figure became concave, if a paper-weight was the object expected the form became convex. From the physiological side we should think of the process as a reinforcement of one set of nerve paths exerted by the cells at the basis of the one idea in the one case, and with the other in the second. As the idea changes, of course there would be a change in the nerve cells which are active, and corresponding to that a change in the other cells which would be reinforced. The idea of the receptacle would make the tendency to see the object as concave strongest, while the idea of the paper-weight would reinforce the cells at the basis which compel the perception of the prism as convex.

We can run through all the various subjective conditions of attention that we have considered earlier, and reduce each to some such selective process of reinforcement or inhibition. The first set of conditions, the conscious process which had just previously been in consciousness, would act by making the path which it had traversed more permeable for a short period after the excitation had died away. The tendency to act would not cease at once, but would die away gradually, and if one of several stimuli which presented themselves tended to excite that path, or set of cells, the corresponding sensation would be preferred over the others, and would become conscious, while the others would be excluded.

The second great group of conditions would find their explanation very much on the same basis as the effect of the related ideas in determining the way the figure in ambiguous perspective should be seen or interpreted. Not merely the paths directly traversed would be made more permeable, but the associated or connected paths would have their tonus increased, and would be more easily excitable by all stimuli which might appeal to them. These stimuli would be selected above all others that might be offered. There would be a spread of tonus or of reinforcing impulses to those cells most closely connected with the impressions in question, that would be of the same kind as the spread from the electric stimulus to the cells of the cortex as a whole. The only difference is that in this case the reinforcement is limited in its action, or at least it spreads most completely to certain elements, less completely to all of the others. In this instance, too, it seems quite possible to assume that there is not merely a reinforcement which spreads to one set of cells or fibres, but that there is an inhibiting influence that goes out to all the other cells in the cortex. This would be in harmony with the results of Sherrington for motor action, and would also be made possible by the known fact that there is an inhibitory effect exerted in certain cases by one cell upon another in the sensory areas.

At the next level of remoteness in the series of conditions of attention we would have to introduce a new principle, but one that is after all but an extension of those already considered. In the circumstances of the hour, the general setting of mind at the time, we have merely a whole system of paths connecting various nerve cells in a condition of tonus, of slight excitement, that makes anything which tends to excite any one member of that group take preference over all stimuli which are entirely unrelated.

Slightly more complicated, but still similar in kind, is the explanation of the influence which we found past experience, remote as well as recent, to play in any state of consciousness. This influence takes two forms. It is in part undoubtedly due to the fact that the earlier experiences tend to organise the cells affected into groups, and so to determine the paths along which any reinforcement from a given stimulus will extend. But, more than this, we may look upon the sensory area in the cortex as in a constant state of slight excitation, comparable to the tonus of motor cells which holds the muscles contracted as one stands erect. What Exner calls the tonus of the sensory nerve cells would be constantly exerted upon all the connected cells of the group, and would, within limits, control the nature of their activity. It would be an expression in kind of the nature of the influences that had acted upon that cell in the earlier life of the individual. It would be the same in quality as that which the cell undergoes when the earlier events are consciously recalled to memory, the difference would be but one of degree. Just as the original activity of the cell would recall, or tend to recall, other impressions, and its influence would spread as a reinforcement to an entire group, so the slighter activity would contribute its share in deciding what elements would respond at any given time. Where the activity is so slight, the corresponding influence would be small, but in the mass would play its part in determining every later activity. That every mental process will have its effect upon all later experiences we found to be a fact in an earlier chapter. We now see that the fact can be brought into harmony with what we know of the action of the nervous system.

The effect of the social influences which required separate treatment psychologically will find its explanation in the same physiological principle. They are themselves direct sensory stimuli, and the cells which they affected would bear the impress for all time in the same way that they retain and continue the influences of all other impressions. They are merely of earlier growth, and so more deeply rooted than the others, and therefore are of larger influence. Hereditary effects probably exist in the form of a liability to action of certain paths in preference to others. They too would serve mainly in the organization of the different systems.

It is very evident from the facts of attention that the

reinforcing and inhibitory impulses which we have been considering could not originate in any centre. In the first place, it is impossible to think that an isolated centre would have any motive for action, or that its action should be in any way in harmony with the circumstances of the moment. Furthermore, we have seen that the activity of attention is too closely related to concrete events of the present and of the immediate past to suppose that it is an irresponsible and unmotived action, as the reference to a centre of this kind would require it to be. Again, we have seen that the pathological facts would compel us to assign attention to the frontal lobes, and these, anatomy teaches us, are nothing more than association areas, areas not for the origination of activities of their own, but merely for transmitting and co-ordinating the activities of the other parts of the cortex.

If we discard the centre theory as obsolete so far as attention is concerned, we find that the facts of psychology and physiology can be brought together with comparative ease. We have only to think of the frontal association centre of Flechsig as providing the lines of irradiation for reinforcement and inhibition, as they spread from one sensory centre to another. When a sensory area in the cortex is excited, it probably not only calls up its direct associates in the centres for the other senses through the posterior association centre, but there is also a secondary effect of reinforcement or of inhibition, which spreads through the frontal lobes to more widely scattered areas and renders these cells more capable of function. In addition to the direct transmission there is a very much more widely spread effect that is mediated by the frontal lobes, where the different stimuli are received and whence they may make connection with all of the other areas, and where the many influences of inhibition and reinforcement may be co-ordinated before they go out.

We must also assume, in view of the psychological facts, that the various paths gradually become organised into systems which are closely related on the nervous side to what Stout calls apperceptive systems on the mental side. Apparently a group of associatory fibres becomes in the course of time so closely connected that when any general or specific stimulus arouses one part of the system the other parts are thrown into a state of greater or less activity. The instant that a locomotive engineer steps into his cab the group of impressions from eye, ear, and hand arouses a closely-knit set of paths that are thereby at once prepared to receive the sensations that belong to his profession, which would not be received under ordinary circumstances. Usually, of course, these systems are closely interconnected, the outer fringes overlap, and the same elements may be involved at different times in more than one system. In fact we must assume that all parts of all the systems are connected with every element of every other, and any excitation of one will affect all of the others; it is merely that the effect of the different elements of the same systems is more marked. Every cell that is active at any time influences all other cells, but its activity is exerted most strongly upon a certain group, and the influence decreases in amount as you get farther away, down to a vanishing minimum. In the normal man every act of attention is controlled in greater or less degree by the activity of every cortical cell. There is no isolation of part from part. In pathological cases, however, there is often an apparently total separation between systems, in which a system or group of systems becomes broken off from the others and controls consciousness without reference to any other group of experiences. These conditions must be discussed in detail later. They serve here to illustrate by contrast the closeness of the connection which exists between the elements of different systems in the normal man.

Again, we must assume that there are not only different systems, but different levels of systems, in the organisation of the nervous mechanism. Systems upon one level would control directly the systems at the lower level, just as the lower systems control the activity of the single cells. The larger, more general, systems would at any time be in comparatively slight activity, while the one subordinate system would be in a relatively high state of activity. These different levels would correspond in general to the different levels of conditions of attention which we have previously discussed at length. The physiological differences between a man's brain at one time and another, which makes him attend to different things, lie in the differing groups of nerve cells which are effective at the two times. The difference between two men while dependent in part upon the different experiences that each has been subjected to, depends in very much larger measure upon the way in which their nerve paths are organised, upon the connections that have been made between the elements of the experience.

Each system, looked at from its physiological side, as we are now doing, is made up of a certain number of sensory cells together with the associatory cells of the frontal lobes. The multiplicity of connections in the different systems is made possible by the millions of cells in the association centres, which may be regarded as the stations for varying the connections between cells and groups of cells. There is necessity for this possibility of innumerable connections, for each sensory element undoubtedly enters into many different systems, is combined at different times in its reinforcing action with practically every other cell. Each cell in the association centre would probably stand in connection with many sensory cells, and with many other association cells, and thus make possible the great variety of connections which we see must be provided.

The results of Kaes, mentioned in the preceding chapter, tend to show that development of these associatory paths goes on side by side with the increase in knowledge. Kaes found, it will be remembered, that while the association centres in the new-born child were entirely non-medullated, there was a much greater proportion of fully-developed fibres in the adult, and the medullation seemed to increase throughout life, or at least up to the beginnings of old age. It would be very satisfactory if we could assume that the action of the associatory fibres produced the medullation, but there is no warrant for this assumption in anything that we know of physiology. We must rest content with the fact that the development of the nervous system is progressive in this respect, and that there is increasing possibility of organisation with advancing years and experience.

One further question remains to be discussed, and one objection of a theoretical character to be met. The first is : " How does this reinforcement control the course of association ? " And, secondly, " Is this system of control which we have been developing anything more than the physiological basis of what is known in psychology as association ? " An answer to one of these questions will involve an answer to the other also.

Flechsig assumes that the associatory processes take place between the different sensory areas in the association centres of the parietal and occipital lobes, in the region between the visual centre on the one side, and the auditory, olfactory, and tactual centres on the other. Lesions of these centres are not accompanied by any loss of attention, disturbances of personality, or the like, but impressions and ideas simply fail to call up their usual associates. The interpretation of temporal and spatial relations is disturbed, right use is not made of the different articles which are seen or handled, and the direct associatory processes in general are impaired. Evidently what we have called the relations that constitute the mere objective physiological connections have their seat in this area, but we must look to the same area that controls attention to external objects for the subjective conditions of association, for the more general considerations which determine that an unusual association shall win against a more usual, a stronger, or more frequent. The reinforcing and inhibiting excitations

s

which arise in the frontal lobes would not be restricted to affecting the cells in their relations to the stimuli which come in from the external world, but would also make it easier for the excitation coming from another sensory cell to arouse this particular cell rather than some other which, from the closeness of the connection alone, would be aroused just as easily. This influence might exert itself either by making some link in the associatory chain more permeable than another possible path, or it might directly increase the excitability of some sensory area. In either case the explanation would be the same fundamentally as for the simple sensory attention discussed above.

The differences between this indirect reinforcing and inhibitory effect of one cell upon another and the physiological process at the basis of association are numerous and marked. First, the reinforcement is not the chief factor in exciting the cell to activity, but merely modifies the activity when it has been aroused in some other way. It is very similar in this respect to the difference between direct transmission and simple reinforcement between the different motor cells in the cord that permit of being studied directly by physiological methods. In the second place, the action of the cell that exerts the modifying influence need not be accompanied by consciousness, in fact in by far the greater number of cases it is not conscious at the time that it exerts its influence, while the direct incentives in the case of association are usually conscious. Thirdly, the cells at the basis of the activity of attention are very much more numerous than those which are involved in association. The reinforcement which affects any act of attention involves masses of cells in all parts of the cortex, which have been active at all times, past and present, in varying degrees—is an expression of slight activities in cells everywhere—while the association is directly due to a few definitely localised cells. Although the two processes of association and the reinforcement which is involved in attention are alike in that on the physiological side they depend upon the mutual action of cell upon cell, the differences are sufficiently great to require that they be distinguished by different names.

We are compelled to assume, then, from our present-day knowledge of the nervous action and from the psychological facts, that attention physiologically is due to the reinforcing and inhibiting effect of one group of nerve cells upon another group, which makes the group affected more easily excited by impressions coming in from the external world or from other cells in the cortex. The relative excitability of the cell depends upon its relation to other cells, either those which are active at the time, which have just been active, or which have been active in the past, and that the activity of these cells themselves is in turn to be explained by earlier excitations of other cells, as well as by the conditions of external stimulation at the time. Each stimulus is effective not merely during the time that its stimulation lasts, but helps in varying amount in the determination of all later activities of the cells which are in any way related to it.

We have been assuming throughout that there is both reinforcement and inhibition involved in the attention process, without, however, definitely deciding between the three theories which were mentioned at the beginning of the chapter. As we have seen, it would be perhaps easier to explain the attention process as one of reinforcement alone, but there are facts which make it certain that inhibition plays a part at times. A strong stimulus appealing to one sense tends to decrease the activity of attention in the other senses, and, as Sherrington's experiments show that every motor impulse from the cortex involves both reinforcement and inhibition, it seems necessary to assume that with each increase in the excitability of one set of cells there goes a corresponding impulse to decrease the activity of all other cells whose activity could in any way conflict with the effectiveness of the first. But there is certainly no room for the assumption of Wundt that attention is an inhibitory process alone. Not only do Bianchi's experiments on monkeys and pathological cases show that the frontal lobes do not exert a pre-eminently inhibitory influence, but we have positive experimental proof that attention may be a reinforcing process. Exner is in this respect considerably nearer the truth than any of the other writers who have proposed theories.

Another theory explanatory of attention from the physiological side uses the circulatory changes which go on in the brain during its activity as the principle of explanation. As was seen in chapter II., the contraction of the blood-vessels in all parts of the body is an invariable concomitant of the attention process. Mosso also proved that the volume of blood in the brain increased during the period of attention. On the basis of these facts Lehmann has attempted to construct a theory that shall explain attention in its details. His theory is that the action of any part of the brain depends upon its blood-supply, and that the portion of the brain which is best supplied with blood at any time will be predominant in its conscious activity. Attention for him would be entirely a matter of the state of the capillaries in different parts of the brain at any given time. If a certain area of the optic lobe should happen to have its capillaries dilated, attention would be directed to some visual impression; if some part of the auditory tract were favoured in the same way, an auditory impression would come to consciousness.

There are three objections to this theory. First, there is as yet great doubt as to whether the blood-supply of different parts of the cortex changes separately, without involving changes of a similar kind in all other parts of the brain. There is even some question as to whether the blood-supply of the brain varies independently of the other parts of the body. There could be no explanation of such selective action of parts of the brain, as would be necessary in attention, on this theory, unless the blood-supply of the different areas could change independently. And even if it could, it seems hardly likely that in an impression which involved sensations from several senses a few capillaries scattered here and there over the cortex would all chance to be dilated or contracted simultaneously, even if we could assume that it was possible for the blood-supply to be so minutely divided as to provide for the separate action of the small mass of cells that would correspond to seeing the point of the pen at which I look to make sure that it is clean, or to any similar minute and qualitatively simple object. Secondly, it seems hardly probable that the activity of the nerve cells should be so closely dependent upon an increase in the blood-supply beyond the normal. It seems plausible to assume that under ordinary conditions there must always be more blood about the cell than is needed for its momentary activity, and that increase in the amount of blood available would be in excess of the actual demand, just as increase in the proportion of oxygen in the air beyond a certain point is of no importance, because it is not absorbed.[20] And, thirdly, the reaction time for the vaso-motor system is so slow that it would be impossible for attention to follow the contraction in time.* There is a further general difficulty with the theory, which is that, granting its truth, it still is not sufficient to decide that we shall attend to one object not another at any particular time. There is nothing in the theory to tell us when the blood-vessels of the brain are likely to contract or to connect their contraction with anything else.†

That the variations in blood pressure are accompanied by changes in the activity of consciousness we have seen in

---

* Mosso asserts, *loc. cit.*, that in the case of a patient with exposed brain, he has seen the attention completely aroused before the change in the colour of the cortex indicated the beginning of increased blood-supply to the brain.

† In his latest work, " Körperliche Äusserungen Psychischer Zustände." vol. II, pp. 237 ff., Lehmann definitely abandons his vaso-motor theory and adopts one that makes attention depend upon the inter-relations of psycho-physical units. Since the vaso-motor theory as he presents it is a possible theory, and has been held at different times in one form or another, it seems well to permit the criticism to stand as first written before Lehmann's last volume appeared.

an earlier chapter, in connection with the attention waves, but, as was seen there, it is extremely doubtful if these are not produced by irradiations of reinforcing impulses from the medullary centres rather than by the direct changes in the blood-supply.

A subordinate physiological theory of which there is a first statement in G. E. Müller, " Zur Theorie der sinnlichen Aufmerksamkeit," p. 51, is that there is in attention an actual excitement of the sensory nerves, or sensory end-organs, that produces actual sensations when no stimulus is present, and increases the effect of stimulation when it is present. There are cases cited in which there is an after-image of an imagined colour, and sensations in the skin, as a result of thinking of some one point, so strong as to compel one to touch the spot, before there can be certainty that no object is in contact with it. Müller suggests generally that there must be a spreading of the nervous process to the lower sensory tracts, if not to the sense organ. The theory has recently been revived, apparently in ignorance of Müller's suggestion, by M. D'Allonnes, [²] in a form that makes use of the centrifugal sensory fibres that have been discovered in the optic nerve at least, and may exist elsewhere. The theory in this form is that the excitation spreads over these fibres to the sense organ, and there excites the same kind of process that is ordinarily excited by the external stimulus.

The theory seems unnecessary, even if we accept unreservedly the existence of the fibres in question. Every process before it becomes conscious must come to the cortex, and it seems as easy to assume that the intensifying process takes place there immediately as it is to take it out to the periphery and back.

SUMMARY

1. The physiological processes that are peculiar to attention are reinforcement, or facilitation, and inhibition.

2. Reinforcement may be defined as increase in the

activity of one nerve cell by the action of another cell or cells not in the direct line of transmission, while inhibition is a mutual opposition of two cells in their activity.

3. The subjective conditions of attention can all be paralleled by various forms of reinforcement ; the idea in mind by the vanishing effect of earlier excitations ; mood or purpose by an aura of excitation from some one centre ; education and the social factors by the tonic influence of remote areas exerted in a manner that reveals the nature of the earlier experiences.

4. It is probable in addition that there is an inhibitory influence that renders it more difficult than usual for other impressions to enter consciousness.

CHAPTER XVI

THEORIES OF APPERCEPTION IN RELATION TO ATTENTION

W E may begin the philosophical and psychological explanations with the apperceptive theories, as at one time and another every phase of the attention process has been treated under the head of apperception. While the word has at the present time fallen into disrepute because of the many different uses to which it has been put, and because in the minds of many it has become synonymous with wild and unbased speculation, its history is dignified, and, what is of greater importance for our purposes, its close connection with the more theoretical aspects of attention make its history serve also as a history of the attention theories.

The first to introduce the word apperception into the philosophical vocabulary was Leibniz. Leibniz used the term to distinguish the clear ideas from the vague perceptions. The importance of the distinction can be better understood from the outlines of his metaphysical system. The universe for Leibniz was made up of thinking units, absolutely isolated one from the other, but with the order of their presentations established in such a way at creation that they should always mirror the events in the external world. Each " windowless monad " gave a kinetoscopic reproduction of the changes in the world as a whole, but because of the operation of internal laws, not by virtue of any causal connection with the world.

The monads could be arranged in a series in terms of the clearness of their ideas. The dust particles had only the vaguest perceptions ; plants and animals possessed perceptions only, but they became progressively more distinct as the animals rose in the scale, while men were endowed with clear ideas or apperceptions which reached their maximum clearness in the ideas of God.

In the individual man there was the same distinction. One had *petites perceptions*, indistinct ideas, during sleep and the less vigorous periods of mental life. These passed over gradually into apperceptions in the more active moments of the mental life. Leibniz then placed most emphasis upon the use of apperception to denote the clear as opposed to the vague ideas.

There is an occasional passage which may be read to mean that he regarded apperception as in some measure dependent upon earlier experiences, as in the passage in the " Nouveaux Essais," p. 186 (Gerhart's ed.), where he says, " For all attention requires memory, and often when we are not so to speak warned and admonished to take notice of some of our present perceptions, we let them pass without reflexion, and even without observing ; but if some one directs our attention to them, and, for instance, bids us notice some sound that had just been heard, we remember it, and are conscious that we had some feeling of it at the time." From passages of this kind, and from statements that clear perceptions may be made up of many *petites perceptions* it would seem that Leibniz thought of clearness as in some degree the result of the interaction of many mental elements.

There is also throughout his work a recognition of the part which the disposition of the mind plays in the control of general mental processes, that could be quoted in support of our own theory. To Locke's famous dictum, " *Nihil in intellectu est quod non prius in sensu,*" Leibniz, it will be remembered, added, " *nisi intellectus ipse.*" In expanding the statement he is constantly likening the mind to a block of marble, with veins that foreshadow the figure which the sculptor is to carve. The mind, like the marble, has certain characteristics which make it easier for the resulting product to take one form than another, the resultant perceptions are in part dependent upon the nature of the mind, as well as upon the impressions of sense.

It must be emphasised, however, that the word apperception was, in spite of its importance for his general theory, never used to designate this state of preparedness, but was applied only to the resulting clear ideas. For the other uses we must look to later writers who have applied the term in ways which Leibniz would not have recognised, although in ways that were implied in his theory, and were in themselves closely related to his apperception.

Kant,* the next in the historical line of descent to make any considerable use of the term apperception, paid too little regard to the phenomena of the concrete consciousness, at least for the sake of the concrete conscious processes themselves, to make any very valuable contribution to the theory of apperception, from the psychological side. We might, by tracing out similarities and analogies, show that very much of Kant's system could be incorporated into a modern psychological system, and that the essential features would correspond to what we now designate as attention or apperception. In the first place, he insists that there can be no effective knowledge without the participation of the mind's own activity, and that an essential part of all knowledge comes from within. This process of addition or of transformation by inner activity was unconscious in perception and imagination, but became fully conscious in thought or thought forms. For this he adopted Leibniz's term apperception. He added transcendental, to indicate that it supplied the conditions for there being any object at all. He uses the term as descriptive of the final unifying activity of the self. The transcendental unity of apperception is above the categories of the understanding, and is the force that introduces final harmony

---

* The suggestion for this treatment of Kant I owe to Professor Muirhead.

into the processes that have already been partially unified by the categories and by the forms of space and time. It is the final expression of the self, the basis of the unity of consciousness, and the ultimate condition of the rationality of experience. It must be emphasised that while we may read these more modern psychological views into his system, and find confirmation for them in his doctrine, Kant himself explicitly denies the relevancy of psychological processes in the individual mind to the development of knowledge. Nevertheless, there are passages where he shows that the psychological processes were not so unimportant in his regard as he in general asserts them to be. The elements in Kant's theory that have made his discussion important for the history of apperception are, first, that he, like Leibniz, makes apperception the most complete and perfect form of consciousness, the most adequate expression of man's mind; and in the second place, his statement that this unifying activity is something which is entirely spontaneous to the mind itself, something that is enforced upon the materials of experience from above, and is not derived from the materials of experience.

The great prophet of apperception in the history of philosophy is Herbart. With him apperception becomes not an incidental phase of psychology, but is the fundamental principle of the entire system. If Kant's mind was a monarchy in which the lower was always subject to the higher, and all to the sovereign transcendental unity of apperception, Herbart described the mind as a democracy in which all laws were derived from the governed and all control was exercised by the separate elements themselves.

The universe for Herbart was composed of reals, elements not subject to change, but which by their interactions gave rise to all change. The human mind is one of these reals, and ideas arise originally from the attempt of the ego to protect itself against the other reals which constitute the external universe. Abandoning this point of view as he develops his more definitely psychological theories, he carries the analogy over to the relation between the different ideas in mind. Ideas, like the reals, are centres of force which by their mutual action and reaction produce and control consciousness. If two ideas of the same kind come together in consciousness they mutually help each other, and each persists in greater strength than it would have had alone, while if the two ideas are at any time in opposition they mutually tend to destroy one another, and the resultant is the force of the one minus the force of the other. All ideas influence each other in this way, and consciousness at any moment is determined in its nature by the balance between the conflicting and reinforcing ideas. In practice there are always many ideas in mind that claim recognition. These may, for convenience, be divided into two general classes : those already in mind, and those which are coming in or which seek to come in. The older ideas are always in the majority, and so become the dominant or active elements in determining consciousness, and are therefore spoken of as the apperceiving ideas. The newly-entering ideas are, on the whole, subordinate or passive, and are known as the apperceived elements or masses. Mind, then, is the resultant of the effects of the apperceiving and the apperceived masses. A new idea to receive recognition must be in harmony with the ideas already present, must be in some way connected with the earlier experiences of the individual. In Herbart's often-quoted instance, school boys who are listless and inattentive during the routine of class instruction become at once interested as the master begins to tell a story. The ideas already in mind hold no relation to the matter of the lesson, and so are hostile to it, but as soon as the story begins ideas are offered which stand in close relation to the daily life of the hearers—there are other ideas in mind ready to receive and facilitate the entrance of the new. As a consequence attention is awakened, the boys are alert, and the entire room still, except for the words of the tale. So in general what shall be perceived, what shall enter mind at any time, depends almost entirely upon the ideas which are already present. Of course, what are the apperceived ideas at one moment may become the apperceiving ideas at the next. The apperceived impression, therefore, is said to react upon the apperceiving mass in much the same way that the apperceiving reacts upon the apperceived. This aspect of the process is, however, subordinated to the other. The important part is that the course of the mental states at any moment is largely determined by the perceptions of the periods that had preceded it. It may be regarded as the essential feature of the Herbartian psychology, and is the point that has been most elaborated upon by his followers both in psychology and in pedagogy, and has been the most fruitful conception of his entire system.

Another point of considerable theoretical interest, and one which is characteristic of the later developments in psychology, is that feeling and will are made subordinate to the ideas, and grow out of their interactions in much the same way as the other mental processes. While with Leibniz, idea and will are on the same level, unless indeed the ideas were subject to the will, and for Kant the spontaneity of the mind dominates everything else, for Herbart all voluntary action, as all voluntary thought, is entirely subordinated to the ideas and their mutual interaction. Feeling, too, has no independent place, but depends entirely upon checking or reinforcing strains that go on between the ideas in mind at the time. In general, then, Herbart's system depended entirely upon the interactions and mutual relations between the elementary ideas which are in mind at any time. Everything else is derived from and is subordinate to them.

The last statement of a doctrine of apperception in any comprehensive form has been made by Wundt. In large measure Wundt combines the position of both Leibniz and Herbart, although the starting-point is almost entirely derived from Leibniz, with suggestions of modifications by Kant, rather than from Herbart. The fundamental mark

of apperception for Wundt is the clearness of the idea.   We
find in consciousness at any moment that certain processes
are clear and distinct—stand out for themselves against
the others, which serve only as a background.   These ideas
are fully in consciousness, are apperceived, while all others
are merely perceived.   To repeat his well-known metaphor,
consciousness is like the field of vision.   There is a clearest
point in the centre in which everything is sharply defined,
and the details are all well marked.   About that clearest
point is a region of gradually increasing vagueness of outline,
until we reach the limits of the visible area.   Similarly in
consciousness we have a point of greatest clearness, and
about it a large area of indistinct ideas.   The point of
clearest consciousness can be made to wander over the whole
of the field in very much the same way that the eye can
be moved over the field of visible objects in the external
world.   An idea that is confused at one instant may become
distinct the next, and at the same time the idea that held
the centre of consciousness becomes less clear, and finally
disappears from mind altogether.   Entrance into the field
of vision in consciousness is perception, while entrance into
the field of clearest vision of consciousness constitutes apperception.

So much of Wundt's theory is purely Leibnizian.   The
next phase to be considered is in one aspect more nearly
Kantian, in another more Herbartian.   This deals with the
problem of the conditions of the clearness of the ideas.
When speaking in general terms, Wundt talks almost as if
there were a faculty or force of apperception, something
behind and superior to consciousness, which brings about
the change in the clearness of the impressions.   There is in
the brain a definite centre of apperception, and in consciousness a force very closely related to will, that in and of itself
chooses certain ideas for elevation to the high places of
consciousness, and equally arbitrarily rejects others.   It
is very much like the self-conscious unity of apperception
of Kant, which gives the final form and order to the various

disconnected elements of mind, and is in so far something entirely inexplicable, a factor in experience that must be assumed without any further discussion of its nature, origin, or laws of action. This is the theory which comes out most clearly in his latest works and in those passages where he makes no attempt at an analysis. Closely related is his recent tendency to go over to a doctrine that would make the will fundamental in consciousness as it was for Fichte, Schopenhauer, and von Hartmann. He recognises, however, that this is but a concept, and as such has no place in psychology. His endeavour is to keep to concrete consciousness, but to insist that concrete consciousness is more like what we ordinarily know as will than anything else.

There is another phase in the discussion of the problem of apperception as condition which partakes much more of the character of Herbartianism than of Kantianism. This would make apperception, or the coming of ideas to clear consciousness, due rather to the previous experience of the individual. Wundt makes this side of his doctrine most prominent when discussing the conditions of attention. In that connection he insists that one of the factors which decide which idea shall come to mind is to be found in the ideas that were in mind just before the act of attention, and in a more general passage he states that apperception is determined in large part by the previous experience of the subject. If we attempt to combine this view with the one above, it would seem very much as if we were to think of apperception as a bearer and communicator of experiences. Apperception in that case would not be the unconditioned determinant of attention, and so of consciousness, but would itself be in part determined by experience, or might be said to act as an intermediary between the experiences of the past and the mental processes of the present. Apperception as a whole, then, would seem to be the permanent, fundamental conscious process. It is the basis which persists throughout the changes of consciousness, and the source of whatever spontaneity we grant consciousness, but it is not entirely unconditioned, for it is itself subject to the experiences of the individual, and so must conform to them. Through the modifications which the experiences exert upon apperception they also must be regarded as influencing the mental processes.

The sign or the accompaniment of the activity of apperception is the " feeling of activity." As regards the meaning of this feeling also there are two interpretations of Wundt's position possible. In the earlier works, where more stress is laid upon its analysis, it seems to be made up entirely of strain sensations, but in his " Grundriss der Psychologie " he leans very strongly to the view that this feeling is in part at least *sui generis,* and is to be regarded as the immediate coming to consciousness of the workings of the will, or of apperception used as a name for the causes of the changes which go on in consciousness rather than for the changes themselves.

For Wundt apperception has a very large place in consciousness. Although it is primarily the term for the coming to clear consciousness of certain ideas or groups of ideas, it becomes soon the condition of this change, or the something which stands behind and produces the change. From this meaning its use is extended to the process that controls the course of ideas. As passive apperception it is at least a permissive factor in directing associations, and in the active form it governs the " apperceptive combinations," which include judgment, reason, and some of the higher forms of imagination. On the other side apperception is made the fundamental fact in the feeling processes. Feeling, for Wundt, is nothing more than the coming to consciousness of the activities of apperception. Apperception is also closely related to will, if we are not to regard apperception as the genus under which will and attention are the two species. In the earlier works this view is taken, while in the later, " will " tends to become the more general of the two terms. Wundt's uses of the term apperception include all of the activities that we have ascribed to attention.

Since Wundt there have been two diverging lines in the development of the theory of apperception. Professor Münsterberg, in his earlier and more experimental work, charged Wundt with implying in the term apperception a mental faculty, a metaphysical something that was beyond the range of our experience and about which we could know nothing. To this Wundt replied that he did not use the term to designate any " metaphysical completion of experience," but merely applied the word to certain definite and well-marked phenomena of consciousness, and that the line of distinction between it and all other conscious processes was sharp enough to warrant the ascription of a separate term. It must be confessed that there is one line of statements in Wundt's earlier works which would warrant Münsterberg's objections. But, as has already been pointed out, these may be in large measure explained as due to the necessity for using a shorthand expression in referring to a process which has already been analysed in another connection. In all the passages in these earlier works in which there is any attempt at description or analysis there is no doubt that it is the actual concrete mental processes which are referred to.

In the later works of both writers, however, it is clear enough that there is an element brought in which they do not now so definitely call apperception, but which covers very much the same phenomena, and which is definitely asserted to be something behind the conscious states and more permanent. Wundt meets the necessity for something that shall be more stable by asserting that the persistence of effects in consciousness can be most easily understood if we regard mind as, in its essentials, like will in the popular use of the term. This fundamental extra-conscious force becomes then the bearer of all other conscious states, and the basis of explanation for everything that cannot easily be explained from empirical data. Professor Münsterberg has shifted his position with equal completeness, and, whereas ten years ago he contended that one could never

T

explain anything in consciousness by an unknown element
outside of consciousness, he now insists that all consciousness
is but the manifestation of the unknown will which is never
seen and never can be recognised for itself, that mind in
all its phases is but the working of this meta-empirical
something and constitutes the only explanation of any state
which shall have the least claim to be final. This is the
exact counterpart of the apperception of Wundt as he interpreted it in his earlier polemic. Both have entirely
changed their original positions and both are united in
upholding what they previously condemned.

One other writer who has made notable contribution in
recent years to the doctrine of apperception is Professor
Stout. Dr. Stout's theory has entirely changed its character in the period that has elapsed between his earlier and
his later writings. In the earlier work, " The Analytic
Psychology," he held an essentially Herbartian position,
while in the later " Manual of Psychology " he has dropped
the term apperception entirely and employs the word
conation instead in a meaning not essentially different
from Wundt's earlier use of the term apperception. The
main advance that Stout has made over his predecessors
in the doctrine of apperception is in introducing the term
" systems of apperception." In brief, this consists in
picturing the different elements which by their interaction
were for Herbart the determining factors in mind as influencing each other as groups, not as separate individuals.
He pictures the different processes of mind as standing in
very much the same relation to each other as do the individuals in a society. Different men will combine for a
definite purpose without thereby losing their individuality,
or in any way impairing the possibility of entering into other
combinations at another time. From one point of view
a man may be a member of a political party, from another
he may belong to a certain church, while from still another
he may be a lawyer or a doctor. Membership in one organisation does not in the least interfere with any of the other

activities. But we cannot work actively in more than one connection at the same instant. " Brutus in the office of magistrate ceases to be a father. In like manner, mental elements which share in the activity of one mental system, are for the time being disabled from acting either in any other systematic combination or independently. When we are engrossed in writing or speaking about some serious topic, it does not occur to us, unless we are inveterate punsters, to play upon the words we use. When we are interested in a game of billiards, the idea of the billiard balls does not set us thinking about the trade in ivory and African slavery." Our mental states, like our social relations, are grouped in this way about certain points or centres of reference, and form, for the time being, more or less complete units. They may aid each other or oppose each other according to the nature of the systems to which they belong or to their own relations, but they always act as units towards each other, and in reference to the materials which are entering mind. When thinking about one set of objects everything is influenced by consideration of that particular kind of process ; everything which comes into mind must have some relation to that particular system. From this point of view Stout's theory of mind is different from Herbart's only in that he gives a more complex and complete organisation. But there are other differences which are even more fundamental between the two systems. In the first place, the groups are not, or may not be, made up of ideas actually in mind, but may include as well dispositions or traces left over in a vague form from some previous experience, which has long since vanished. Again, we are not able to think of the groups as consisting of isolated elements, but they merely constitute ways in which mind as a whole may act. An apperceptive system is not so much an aggregation of elements as it is a phase or aspect of the total activity of mind. Thirdly, apperception is not complete in itself as it was for Herbart, but we can only explain it if we consider it in relation to the active will element which Mr. Stout calls conation. Conation is defined very much as Wundt defines will or apperception in the active sense, as something which is not outside of, or superior to consciousness, but is merely a name for the fact that consciousness is always changing, or as he puts it, is moving towards an end. It is a term which is to cover the phases of consciousness which imply searching for some preconceived end, and is to include the mental states in which there is a striving successfully or unsuccessfully toward the attainment of some goal. Here we have the most complete statement which he gives us of an attempt to harmonise Wundt and Herbart. But it must be confessed that the exact relation between them is left rather indefinite and hazy. There is no very distinct line drawn between conation and apperception, nor any very close statement of the part which each is to play. They are rather affirmed side by side than reconciled, in spite of the fact that either alone is sufficient to explain the whole series of processes. It seems rather an attempt to keep spontaneity and at the same time to recognise the fact that everything in mind is capable of explanation. The position finally assumed gives one the impression that it has resulted from a tendency to vacillate from one view to the other, owing to a disinclination to give up either, rather than to be the consistent working out of a preconceived and well defined system. This becomes even more evident from the omission of the term apperception and the substitution of conation altogether in the "Manual of Psychology," the later work. There the pendulum seems to have swung entirely to the side of spontaneity, or at least the opposing view has been so far subordinated that the peculiar term has disappeared.

If we attempt in conclusion to bring the scattered threads from the history of apperception together into some consistent whole, we are met by the difficulty that the term has had at least three distinct meanings in modern philosophy and psychology. It is a name for a state of clearness in the ideas, for a form of organisation of mind which results in that clearness, and for something outside of the consciousness which is the condition of that distinctness. This last use as a condition of the change in the clearness of the ideas varies between a *deus ex machina* that is entirely outside of the mind or experience and an idea nearly identical with the second use of the term as a plan of organisation of mind.

It is evident that consistency requires that these different uses be combined, or that some of them be discarded if the word apperception is to be kept in psychological nomenclature at all. The first difficulty comes from using the same term for the cause and for its effects ; for the state of clearness of the ideas and for the conditions which induce that state. The only means of avoiding this ambiguity is by an agreement to use the term in one sense only. Historically any use can be justified, but since we already have the term perception, or clear perception, for the state, it seems very much better to retain the word as the condition of the clearness.

When we come to choose between the other two uses, between apperception as something meta-empirical, above consciousness, and as a word for a method of organising consciousness or of a set of relations within consciousness, we are dealing at once with a matter of fact and with a theory to explain the facts and a decision can not be so easily reached. There are three possible theories as to the nature of these conditions. Either we can say that past experience alone and directly accounts for the present clearness of the ideas in question, or that there is a something behind consciousness which arbitrarily decides which idea is to be clear and what others are to be excluded from consciousness, both without reference to anything else that has happened to the individual or to any other consideration whatsoever ; or thirdly, we can combine the two theories and assume that there is something behind which is the immediate determinant of the change in consciousness, but which is itself in turn dependent in part at least, upon the earlier experience of the individual.

Every one admits that nothing outside of consciousness can serve as an explanation of the events in consciousness, at least for psychology. But every one also seems to feel that the easiest explanation, if it only were an explanation, is to think of mental states as determined in some way by an external agent that we call conation, apperception, or will, rather than to think of it as self-determining. This is evidenced by the constant fluctuation from one theory to the other which we have seen on the part of the last three writers examined.

The only decision that can be reached is in the light of the facts of consciousness itself. All that we can say from that standpoint is that consciousness changes in certain ways and that the present changes bear a definite relation to the past changes and earlier states of consciousness. If we disregard entirely the non-psychological questions we can perhaps cut the Gordian knot by saying that apperception is the name for the fact that any event in consciousness is different in some degree from what it would have been had the preceding history of the individual in question been different, while everything else in his present environment remained the same. Apperception would then be merely the general term for condition of attention, the name for one relation between observed facts. For psychology, too, it is a matter of indifference whether we think of the earlier experiences as acting upon present mental states directly or through the mediation of an unknown third process. If we interpose a bearer which we picture as receiving the experiences, retaining them in some way, and then controlling the later conscious states in the light of them, we gain nothing but a metaphor. The *tertium quid* can never be directly perceived. All that we can know is that the first impression is received and that the others are modified by it. The remainder of the process is hidden, and little is to be accomplished by speculating concerning it.

SUMMARY

1. Theories of apperception in the history of philosophy have dealt with mental processes which are closely allied to attention—in fact, nearly every phase of attention has at one time or another been related to apperception.

2. The first use of the word apperception is in Leibniz, to indicate the clear as opposed to confused ideas.

3. In Kant apperception is the term applied to self-activity as the supreme determinant of mental operations, of the knowing process.

4. With Herbart we find the term applied to the determination of consciousness from within consciousness—as the word applied to the interaction of ideas, the forces that ultimately decide what shall enter mind.

5. Wundt in a measure combines the three preceding theories. Apperception is the process of clearing up ideas, but is also the supreme mental activity that produces the clearness, and is in this sense, in part, determined in its operations by earlier experiences.

6. Professor Stout, the last to make a contribution, is an Herbartian, with the addition that the ideas or experiences are organised and act in systems to control all mental processes.

7. Apperception then coincides in the main with attention, but must be regarded as a name for a process or group of processes, not as a thing, or a single force.

CHAPTER XVII

HISTORY AND CRITIQUE OF PSYCHOLOGICAL THEORIES OF ATTENTION

IN this chapter I shall endeavour to treat those theories of attention which are neither apperceptive nor physiological in their nature. Many of them, of course, have an apperceptive and nearly all have a physiological aspect, but in all, the predominant factors are to be found under neither head. There will be no attempt to follow any chronological order or to do full justice to all of the phases of any one theory. Our purpose is rather to find historical instances of the different possible forms that a theory of attention may take, than to give an exhaustive enumeration of the theories or to state completely those chosen as representatives of the different tendencies.

There is one general characteristic of all the theories of this group. They are alike in raising some part of the attention process to the rank of a general condition or cause. We find that attention has been said to be an intense sensation, that it is the result of interest, is due to feeling, is caused by movements of various kinds, and is produced by the direct action of the will. Each of these must be examined in the light of the facts, in the hope that we may be able to assign it its proper place in a more embracing theory. We have already mentioned most of these views in connection with our treatment in the earlier chapters, but not with definite reference to the validity of the explanations themselves. The previous examination of the facts should make it easier to deal with them in detail.

The first and simplest which we need to consider owes its first satisfactory formulation to James Mill.[7] It makes the intensity of the stimulus for the sensation and the strength of the association for the idea the only condition of its coming to consciousness and of its clearness when it becomes conscious. If an idea is intense or interesting— and interesting is for Mill the equivalent of being strong— it will succeed in getting into mind. In his formulation, attending to the idea and having it are identical. This is to make what we classified as the objective conditions of attention the only ones which need to be considered. If it were necessary to refute Mill's theory at this stage in the history of psychology, it could be done most simply by point- ing to the fact that weak ideas are frequently preferred to strong ones. If more emphasis is placed upon the statement that the interest of the idea is responsible for its entrance, and interest is interpreted in the ordinary sense and not as being another name for the intensity of the stimulus, as Mill seems to take it, we have again not furthered our explanation very much. As we saw in a preceding chapter, interest is not an independent attribute of an idea, but is simply another way of saying that a sensation is likely to be attended to. It does not at best help us out in explaining the attention process. In short, Mill has raised an occasional and even unusual condition of attention to the rank of a general explanation.

Ribot [9] is the most important representative of the view that attention is fundamentally a motor phenomenon. He enumerates the list of movements and the changes in movement which accompany every act of attention, and finally concludes from the frequency of the appearance that it is movement which is the ultimate cause of attention. He divides these movements into three classes : effects upon the vaso-motor system, respiratory effects, and changes in the voluntary muscles. Attention, he says, consists very largely in the accurate adaptation of the sense organ, in a checking of breathing and of all other movements that can in any way interfere with the perfection of attention, and finally of changes in the blood-supply which will send a greater amount of blood to those parts of the brain which are in a state of activity. Attention, Ribot tells us, is in many cases an inhibition, but in by far the greater number of cases it is an inhibition of movements rather than of cerebral states. Essentially, then, we would say on this view that what we call attention in looking intently at an object is nothing else than the fixed position of the body, the accommodation and converging of the eyes, the checking or momentary cessation of respiration, and the contraction of the smaller arteries which accompanies the entire process. True, he says, that this state is finally due to interest, but interest is a feeling or emotion, and this too is traced in its turn to movements or tendencies toward movement in some part of the organism.

Ribot's theory naturally gives rise to two questions. The first is a question of fact. Do the movements precede or are they even exactly concomitant with the attending? Granting this, and that they are also essential, will the movements in themselves suffice for an explanation? No one can deny that the movements are always found accompanying the attending process, and that they are very important. But our question is, Are they the most important, the fundamental phenomena? In the first place, it seems very doubtful if the movements can be said invariably to precede or even accompany attending. When we raise our eyes from the book to look at a clock we would be said to be attending during the interval which elapses before the eyes can adjust themselves to the new distance, an operation that takes an appreciable time if the clock be at any considerable distance. We have a blurred image in the meantime, it is true, but that occupies the centre of consciousness —is attended to as much as the clear image of the clock face that succeeds it. There must even have been an image of the clock in mind before we raised the eyes from the page, or the movements themselves would not have taken the proper direction. This standing in the centre of the field of consciousness in itself constitutes attention. Some such image must precede all movement of the eyes, as has been definitely stated in Wundt's law of eye movements. The same objection holds with even greater force in the case of the circulatory phenomena, particularly with reference to the contraction of the arteries. This reflex, like all reflexes of the sympathetic system, is relatively very slow. It takes from two and one half to three seconds for the contraction to begin to show itself after the stimulus has been applied. It is certainly absurd to say that attention lags as far as this behind the stimulus which calls it out. A trained fencer will have made and parried several thrusts before the blood-vessels would have time to respond to the first stimulus. On the whole it seems very doubtful if the temporal relations between the movements and the clearing up of the ideas is such as to warrant the statement that the one is the cause of the other.

Neither does movement seem to be essential to the attention in all cases. At least a very prominent movement may be lacking during the attention process without entirely changing its nature. Helmholtz, as was seen in an earlier chapter, found it possible to attend to different parts of the field of vision when it was impossible that his eyes moved. Here, certainly, the most constant and frequent accompaniment of visual attention was absent and attention persisted unchanged. It may be granted that there were undoubtedly other elements of the normal complex of movements going on, but if attention is movement and that alone, it would hardly seem that so important a factor in the usual complex could be missing without profoundly changing the entire process.

Again, even if we assume that the thesis is proved completely, what does it tell us of the nature of attention or of its real conditions? Does it make 1 any more possible to decide whether a given man in a given mood is likely to attend to one object rather than to another? Does it explain the differences in attention which we find in different individuals, and in the same individual at different times ? To all of these questions it can give no answer. There is nothing in the theory to say when these wide-spread motor disturbances are to occur, or which movement is likely to produce any particular kind of attention. Both of these problems must be faced before the theory can expect to have any great value as an explanation of the attentive phenomena.

The incentive to the theory seems to have come indirectly from the popular tendency to regard the activity which accompanies the attention process as its cause. In discussing the feeling of effort in an earlier chapter we saw that it can be analysed into strain sensations which arise from the contraction of muscles in different parts of the body. If we start with the assumption that the feeling of activity is the cause of attention, then we are logically driven to the explanation which Ribot gives of its origin. Movement, the real basis of the feeling of activity, would be the true cause of attention. We have shown at some length that this primary assumption is fallacious, and so Ribot's entire theory falls to the ground.

Of similar character, but stated in a form that makes it more difficult to advance facts either for or against it, is the *Aktionstheorie* of Münsterberg.[8] It might be called an incipient movement theory. Briefly stated, it is that each sensory nervous process becomes conscious only as it goes over into motor paths, although the discharge need not be great enough to produce movements. The vividness of a sensation depends upon the degree of excitation that it produces in the motor or efferent nerve paths. Most of the objections that were raised against the Ribot theory would hold as well against Münsterberg, with the exception that no one knows whether all sensory processes do thus produce centrifugal effects, and therefore we can know nothing of their time relations if the theory is valid. Like the former theory, however, it would, if true, give no explanation of the likelihood of attending in advance of the process, and there is no explanation in the theory as to why the vividness should depend upon the centrifugal effect of the stimulus. We may then pass it over as a degenerate form of the motor theory, with the remark that it is another instance of the author's taking back without evidence a theory that he himself banished from psychology on evidence. It will be recalled that Münsterberg gave the death-blow to the sensation of innervation in his " Willenshandlung."

A third theory of attention which has found very general acceptance in competent circles is that attention is conditioned by the feeling—that the pleasantness or unpleasantness of the stimulus decides whether it is to be attended to or denied admission to consciousness. Typical representatives of this theory are Bain in England, Horwicz and Stumpf in Germany, and Ribot in France, although, as we have already seen, the latter reduces the feelings in turn to movement.

Bain's theory is closely related to Ribot's so far as the statement of facts is concerned. He too insists that there is a motor element in every mental process, however abstract. The will acts through the motor element in controlling the entrance of the ideas. But it all goes back ultimately to feeling, for the will, whether exerted in controlling the ideas and the entrance of sensations, or in directing bodily movement, is entirely under the influence of the feelings. All will is derived from the fundamental fact of animal life that the pleasant is sought and the unpleasant avoided. The ordinary attentive consciousness is thus dependent only indirectly upon feeling, but there is another case which, although rarer, shows the immediate effect of the feeling. This is found in those cases of emotional excitement when the feeling accompaniments of the sensation control the course of ideas even in spite of the will. In either case the control of attention goes back to the fact that we seek the pleasant and avoid the painful. Feeling is the final determinant of attention. Ribot's theory is different from Bain's only in the part of the process which each makes of primary importance. Bain makes feeling act through will and movement, Ribot makes movement act indirectly through feeling.

Horwicz is even more explicit in making feeling the controlling process. "The attention, which we regard as essential to perception, actually follows the feelings, and the coming to clear consciousness of external stimuli is absolutely dependent upon the feelings." [3] The basis for this statement is again that the attention process is nearly always accompanied by a feeling, usually pleasant. Stumpf [11a] is as strenuous for identifying feeling and attention. But he means by his statement only that the conscious phase of attention is the feeling of interest and that interest in itself is always pleasant. He traces the conditions of attention to other factors than feelings, and describes its results in consciousness in very much the way that we do. In the second volume of his work he still further modifies that statement to make it apply to passive attention alone, and admits that the will can hold the attention upon disagreeable impressions in certain cases. [11b]

To decide as to the value of the feeling theory also we must appeal directly to the facts of consciousness. We must put the same questions that we put before. Do feelings precede the attention in time ? Are they essential to the attending process ? Should we have a satisfactory explanation of attention if we admitted that the attention process was always preceded or accompanied by a feeling of one kind or another ? In answering these questions we must distinguish two uses of the word feeling. One, the more ordinary, includes only pleasure and pain, the other means to emphasise interest as the most important element in feeling. The second problem we have already disposed of in chapter IV. The object attended to is always interesting, but it is interesting because it is attended to or is likely to be attended to, not attended to because interesting. We need not then consider that form of the feeling problem in this connection.*

* See note at the end of this chapter.

If we return to our questions with reference to the feelings of pleasure and pain, it seems very doubtful if we can answer any one of them in the affirmative. Feeling in the first place seems always to succeed attention rather than to precede it. We have feeling only toward objects that are already clearly in mind. We can be neither pleased nor displeased by a sensation that is not yet in consciousness. It is true that we frequently have a memory-image that is pleasing, and seek to bring back the original impression, but in that case attention has already been given to the memory-image, and our problem is as to why that attention could itself have been given. That evidently cannot be answered in terms of feeling, for the feeling succeeds the entrance rather than precedes it.

Moreover, not merely the presence but the nature of the feeling depends upon attention. If we are occupied with one aspect of an event or object it may be pleasing, while the same object from another point of view may be disagreeable. There is hardly a circumstance in life which cannot be made endurable if one will and can but look on the bright side of things. This influence of attention upon the nature of feeling can be seen very clearly in the differing views which are taken of the same event at different times. Quite frequently an event that is pleasing at the time it occurs becomes unpleasant later when viewed in another light. The new knowledge compels a new attitude to the facts, and with that a new feeling tone.

Again, feeling does not seem a necessary condition of attention, because we attend to many objects which are indifferent to us, or at least have only the feeling that comes with interest, which is not a feeling in the real sense, but only a phase of the attention process, as has been pointed out several times before. And as was instanced in an earlier chapter, attention is drawn by the unpleasant as well as by the pleasant. Suffering holds the mind equally with the happiest event or the most beautiful picture. If there were an immediate relation between feeling and attention it would seem strange that pleasant, unpleasant, and indifferent stimuli should have exactly the same effect.

There is finally a difficulty of the theoretical sort that seems to complete the chain of evidence against this explanation. This is that many writers have insisted that feeling in general, as well as interest, finds its ultimate basis in attention. Herbart and Wundt, to quote no others, are both convinced that feeling can only be explained in terms of attention or apperception. It would take too much space here to give in full their arguments for the view, but it depends in general upon the relations between the different aspects of feeling and attention, and upon similarities in the conditions of the two processes that can best be explained by the assumption that feeling is the secondary, attention the fundamental process. If, then, all the arguments of the people who stand for the causal relation between feeling and attention can be as well transformed to prove that attention is the basis of feeling rather than vice versa, and if the temporal and qualitative correspondences would show that feeling could not be the condition of the attention, it seems safe to regard the view as inadequate.

A fourth group of writers hold that attention is controlled directly by the will, that attention is but an expression of mental activity in some form or other. We have already been compelled to consider this theory in a modified form in the preceding chapter. One phase of the apperception question is identical with the problem of will. We find other types of the theory in Sully and Lipps. Each of these men represents a different conception of what the theory implies. Each endeavours to make it something more definite than the will of popular speech or its scientific counterpart the will of the faculty psychology. Each nevertheless is left with an indefinite idea of a force of an unknown kind. Sully [14] says that attention has the characteristics of our conscious active states in general, and that these characteristics are known by such expressions as " sense of exertion, effort and strain." This then, so far as he definitely analyses his process, would mean that he considers the strain sensations accompanying the attention process to be the cause or condition of the attending. We have already had occasion to point out that these sensations can in no sense be regarded as causes, but are rather the signs or the effects of attending. It is undoubtedly implied in the theory that there is an effective force in consciousness which is above the strain sensations and which acts to control the course of ideas, something that is much more positive than any shadowy conscious feeling, and this in spite of the fact that Sully distinctly states that he is making no assumption with respect to an " active, spiritual principle." *

With Lipps [6] the assumption of the spiritual principle is more definite, although he too endeavours to avoid the much-derided faculty of will. Lipps recognises the fact that the conscious sign of activity has nothing to do with the clearing up of ideas—is not in any sense the effective process in mind—but he states the determination in terms of the " unconscious self." As he puts it, attention is not due to the activity of will but to the activity the mind itself, meaning some unconscious force which lies behind mind in the ordinary sense. By this term the use of the word will is avoided, there is no breaking up of the mind into separate parts ; but it is nevertheless very difficult to assign any definite meaning to the word, or to obtain any clear-cut picture of the way in which the whole mind is active, as has been seen in chapter XIII. We have the old objection to oppose here to the use of an unconscious mind, that it is something that must lie entirely beyond the range of our knowledge, and to use it to explain conscious pro-

---

* It must be confessed that as an expression of Sully's most recent theory this account is unfair. In the " Human Mind," pp. 141 ff., he traces the conditions of attention to events in the earlier history of the individual in a purely empirical way, and gives will but an unimportant part in the control. And even that is always restricted in its action by the earlier developed educational influences or interest. The passage quoted from the earlier work may stand as an instance of the will theory of attention, but not as a fair account of Sully's most recent position.

cesses is very obviously an explanation of the known by the unknown, and in this case even by the unknowable.

The fondness of all of these writers, and of popular thought as well, for the term will or activity with the implication of something beyond consciousness, seems to be rooted in the anthropomorphic tendencies of the human mind. Just as primitive man tended to see himself writ large everywhere upon nature—thought of all objects, animate as well as inanimate, as if they were human beings or owed their actions to men concealed somewhere about them—so at a later stage, when he began to think of his mental life, and to seek for a cause of the phenomena that go on within him, he turned first to the same familiar objects for his explanation. When he struggled to lift a heavy weight he had a picture of himself over against the load and a mass of strain sensations coming in with every effort. As he felt the same strain sensations when trying to attend or to think closely of any thing, he assumed most naturally that there must be some man like himself within himself, who struggled to produce the changes in consciounesss just as he struggled to lift the weight. This picture, which undoubtedly is the result of a personification on the same level as that of the savage who sees human activity in every action of natural forces, has certainly become very firmly fixed in the popular thought of the day, and is by no means without its echo in the theories of psychologists. That it is only a metaphor, and a metaphor which is of very slight value as an explanation of the facts, is evident at a glance. If this individual, this second self, really existed within us, it would be as difficult to assign the conditions of his actions as it is to explain our own immediately. It would indeed be even more difficult, for he is by hypothesis entirely removed from observation, and is usually regarded as too high to be profaned by investigation.

It seems, when we go back to consider the facts and drop all metaphors, that the term " active will " means either some independent and irresponsible agent that stands behind consciousness, or the strain sensations in consciousness, or what Lipps calls the activity of consciousness itself, what Stout calls conation or Wundt, apperception. The first theory, since Herbart's attack on the " faculty psychology," has been recognised everywhere as an unfruitful hypothesis. The second we have already shown to be inconsistent with the facts. The third theory, which introduces an active mental force, requires more consideration. For the most part it is merely a combination of statements from the two previous theories. For Lipps it is practically identical with personified mind. Professor Stout's [10] conation is merely a statement of the fact that there is a felt current in mental processes, while the will or apperception of Wundt is but a claim that it is easier to picture mind in terms of voluntary processes. In last analysis, the first view would amount to the statement that there is a feeling of tendency in mind, an unanalysable feeling, but its causal efficacy is implied rather than demonstrated. It could be met just as well by a recognition of the subjective factors upon which we have put so much emphasis throughout the entire discussion. Stout's " tendency toward an end " means nothing more than that there is a change in consciousness and that some of the changes are foreshadowed in earlier states. We can only know that there is a tendency toward an end from the fact that the end is finally reached. This is merely to say that mental states succeed each other and that many of the conditions of the succession are to be found in earlier mental processes. The view that consciousness is itself active must be either another personification or a reference to strain sensations as an explanation of the changes. In each form of the theory we are dealing with a metaphor of one sort or another, and in most cases the metaphor serves rather to cloud the facts than to explain them. If we leave metaphor out of consideration, all that can be asserted is that the experience of one moment is different from what it would have been had the previous history of the individual and of his ancestors been different.

To attempt any explanation beyond this is to indulge in speculation, and in almost every case it would be more satisfactory to admit ignorance in the beginning.

The fifth and last theory of attention which we must consider is represented by Kohn [4], and is to the effect that attention and consciousness are identical. This is not far different from the conclusion that we have reached, in so far as it must be admitted that attention is involved in all consciousness, and that degree of attention and degree of consciousness amount to the same thing. This seems to be the main point upon which Kohn insists. If he means, however, to do away with the word attention we should be compelled to take issue with him. There are peculiar concomitant phenomena of the attention process, strain sensations, feeling of interest, etc., which are definitely marked off from the other conscious process and are bound to receive a distinctive name. We might agree that attention is consciousness regarded from one aspect, but as there are other aspects the name must be retained to avoid confusion. It is as important that the different points of view from which consciousness is regarded should have names that will enable us to distinguish them, as it is that the different states themselves should be distinguished.

We may say then, in conclusion of our examination of the various theories of attention from the side of consciousness, that each has picked out some more or less important concomitant process or some aspect of attention and regarded it as the explanation of all the remaining parts or aspects. Attention is always accompanied by movements that result from attention. These Ribot has emphasised and made the cause or condition of attention. Attention is followed by interest, and this fact Stumpf has made central and a cause. Frequently, feeling precedes or accompanies attention. Horwicz has generalised this fact to make of it a cause. Attention involves clear and distinct ideas, and sometimes results from the intensity of the external stimulus ; Mill assumed that attention always depended upon the intensity of the stimulus. The various forms of the will theory tend towards a personification of the conditions of attention as a whole, or for Lipps toward a personification of the unconscious elements in the conditions, and these are then designated by a single word as the cause of attention. And finally Kohn makes attention the equivalent of consciousness as a whole, because of the important place that attention holds in consciousness. They are all right, but all incomplete. Attention is not any one of these things alone, but it is all of them taken together, and more. Attention as a state is the clearness of some one idea with its resulting analysis or synthesis. Attention as a cause is an expression of everything that the man has known and experienced, and accompanying and colouring the whole are the feelings of interest and effort, together with the movement processes that make known the degree of attention to others. We cannot regard any feeling or sensation of the moment as an explanation of even the simplest attention process. To understand it we must trace it back to the impressions received in the earliest periods of life, and to the dispositions with which the man is endowed at birth.

NOTE.—To prevent misunderstanding, it may be well to explain that in this chapter "interest" has been used in the second of the senses discussed in chapter IV, as the pleasant feeling that accompanies attending. In the first use, equally general, interest is the equivalent of condition of attention, and would therefore be cause, attention effect. The word in this sense seems superfluous in psychology, for it is practically identical with attention in one of its frequent applications.

CHAPTER XVIII

ATTENTION IN PATHOLOGY AND IN DEVELOPMENT

MUCH evidence in favour of the physiological theory which was advanced in an earlier chapter is to be found in the phenomena connected with the degeneration of attention and allied processes in certain pathological cases. There is very frequently a dropping out of some of the normal factors in the control of attention which serves to make clearer the nature and to emphasise the importance of the effect which they ordinarily exert in mind. These disturbances range in extent from the temporary lack of restraint which we see in dreams and in the ordinary waking suggestion to the most complete derangements of all mental phenomena found in insanity. We can of course mention but a few, and shall attempt to select those which throw into highest relief the conditions of attention that we have been discussing, rather than attempt a general treatment of the changes of attention in mental diseases.

Perhaps the most striking of all these cases, and those which bring out most clearly the relative independence of the systems of control, are the so-called alternations of personality. A favourite theme for the modern novelist is the man who contains within himself two separate selves, who changes from one individual to another, with loss in the one state of all memory of the other and with a corresponding change in his mental attitude and habits of action. The classic instance is Stevenson's Dr. Jekyll and Mr. Hyde. Many cases very similar to this have been subjected to careful scientific study. So, for example, Dr. Azam [¹] found a woman who during a period of forty years would alternate from one state to another. She forgot in one state all that had happened in the preceding, and had a different disposition and a different attitude toward life while in each condition. There is not only a discontinuity in memory, but there is also a different character. The woman was essentially a different person in each stage. During her normal state she was serious, almost sad, and very industrious, but in her second self was always cheerful, although less industrious. Her memory was perfect from one period to another of the same self, but there was no remembrance in self number one of impressions received in self number two. Change of character in some degree is associated with loss of the particular memory processes in all of the cases that have been carefully studied. Of course it is difficult to trace many of the more minute differences which would be interesting for our purposes, but the more profound changes in emotional tone and in the general attitude to the duties of life are well marked and always reported.

From the physiological facts that have been considered in the last chapter, the explanation would be comparatively easy. We need resort to no fanciful assumption of a separate mind associated with the spinal cord, or say that there are separate minds for each hemisphere or for any other isolated part of the nervous system. All can be explained on the hypothesis that there is some breaking up of the associatory paths in the cortex, such that one system of associated experiences is very largely cut off from the others. The result is that the part of the experience which is received while the partial brain alone is active will not be recalled when the brain is working as a whole, and vice versa. There are no direct paths open between the two systems of connected nerve cells and so there is no possibility of recall as well as no possibility that the experiences received in the one state will influence the activity of those received in the other. That there is not complete separation between the two parts is shown by the fact that the more deeply

seated earlier associations still persist. The patient recognises the names and uses of familiar objects, can still speak
in the normal manner ; it is merely that the recently acquired and more unstable connections disappear. The
paths which connect the partial system with the whole are
merely impaired, not broken, and, as is usual in all such
cases, the earlier associations remain while the newer and
less firmly fixed disappear.

The degeneration may sometimes extend further. In a
case reported by Dr. S. Weir Mitchell, quoted by Professor
James [5], the discontinuity between the two systems became
so complete that the patient was compelled to begin her
education anew and to build up her knowledge from the
beginning as does a child. Even in this case, in which the
breaking down of the connections was probably as complete as in any case which has been reported, there were
nevertheless traces of the persistence of the old connections,
for learning went on much more quickly than it had at first,
and the complete recognition of objects and their uses had
not disappeared. Moreover, the effect of the earlier experiences was not completely destroyed, but returned with
a sudden rush after a period, and the patient became a
normal woman again.

By far the most interesting and instructive case of multiple personality so far reported is that of Miss Beauchamp,
reported by Dr. Morton Prince. [9] This was a young woman
of college education who developed a divided personality
as the result of an emotional shock that acted upon an hereditary nervous instability. The self divided first into two
selves, then later a third developed, and there could be
distinguished a dozen or more that were less well developed.
The three most marked were known as BI, BIV, and Sally.
The one that first made itself known to Dr. Prince was BI,
a studious, morbidly conscientious person of poor health.
Then Sally appeared, first as a sub-self or hypnotic self
that never had an independent existence, never had " her
eyes open " or normal control of the motor mechanism.

Even in that condition, however, she announced that she was always conscious of BI's thoughts. Later she developed more fully, and would alternate with BI in the control of the bodily activities. She was a childlike individual, thoughtless, mischievous and vengeful, was not studious, had few of the accomplishments of the other, but possessed much better health and physical strength. Later, without warning, BIV developed with still a third character. She was thoughtless of others, a stronger person than BI in every way, except for her extreme selfishness. BI and BIV remembered only their own experiences; Sally was familiar with the thoughts of BI but did not know those of BIV, although she was aware of the external perceptions of BIV and of her actions. What added to the dramatic interest of the case and to the discomfort of the participants was that the selves were nearly always at odds owing to the differences in their tastes, and each was usually trying to get even with the others for some fancied disregard of her own rights. After living the separate disjointed lives for several years, BI and BIV were finally amalgamated into a single self with memory of the past of each, and Sally was put out of existence. We cannot, of course, go into the details, interesting as they are.

The important fact for us in all the cases is that with the impairment of the direct associations there is also a diminution in the adequacy of the indirect control which we have ascribed to the reinforcement and inhibition between the separate cells and areas. With the vanishing of the memories of a certain period there is also a corresponding change in the self. Emotionally, socially, and in every other respect there is a decay; the person is no longer the same as before the change. From that, too, it is probable that the different controlling series of experiences may be regarded as relatively independent in their action. For while in the normal man the elements are constantly being varied in their relations, uniting first with one set of elements and then with another, and all systems modify each other in some degree, in the abnormal states which we have been considering the interconnections between certain of the systems seem to be broken, and one system or group of systems will temporarily take the place of first importance in the control of consciousness to the exclusion of all others. Under these circumstances the direction of thought and action is in terms of a partial experience, and is therefore inadequate to the reality of things in general and does not even do justice to the knowledge of the individual in question.

There are many less striking degrees of abnormality which show the same general laws. Closely related to double personality are the cases of fixed ideas which are found so frequently. These vary in degree from the " crank " with his head filled with some one project which is not altogether feasible, to states in which the whole consciousness is dominated by one group of ideas, which alters the entire view of the universe through its control of all other mental processes. Every one is familiar with the man who can think of but one topic and who is reminded of everything by that topic, and who, moreover, has all of his mental processes determined in the light of that one dominant idea. Everything that enters the senses is transformed by it, and if there is a choice between perceptions he will see only those which are in harmony with the interpretation that he has already decided upon. The one circle of ideas rules his attention, his associations and perceptions, his actions. Every mental process is determined by it. This state of mind grows to be permanent in many cases, and is often accompanied by loss of sensibility in several domains, by loss of power of movement, and other profound mental disturbances. It passes over by indefinite stages into the state of double personality discussed above. The same physiological explanation will serve here as in the preceding case. There is an abnormal and permanent domination of consciousness by one system of associations at the expense of all others, and a resultant loss of mental balance and perspective. Other experiences do not play their full part in determining the course of ideas, and the one-sided control means general loss of efficiency in all directions and a complete misinterpretation of all perceptions.

Hypnotic phenomena offer many examples of a very similar condition. Whatever may be the ultimate theory of hypnotism, there is undoubted evidence that there is a weakening of the control normally exerted by the experiences of the past and a tendency for some one system to become for a moment dominant to the almost complete exclusion of others. The system which shall gain the ascendancy is determined by the circumstances of the hour, usually by some word or sign from the operator who has induced the state. When the system has once gained the ascendancy every other idea is subordinated to that. Only those objects are seen which are in harmony with it, and only those actions are performed which correspond to it. It is possible to reproduce artificially in this way the phenomena of double personality. During the hypnotic state the subject can be made to take on a consistent character, or several of them successively, which are entirely different from the normal self of the daily life. A hypnotised person has been made to assume in succession the part of a general, a thief, an empress, and in each case would not only act the part assigned so far as he knew it, but would for the moment adopt the whole manner of thought and action which the character impersonated ordinarily has. For the instant every other influence is excluded from consciousness, and the avenues of sense are closed to any experiences which might reveal the true relations of the individual to his surroundings. The hypnotic state is like the alternating personality also in that there is frequently memory from one hypnotic state to the other, although there is no memory in the normal state of events which occurred in the hypnotic condition and no memory when hypnotised of the events of the normal life. Again, these facts reinforce the old conclusion that it is possible for one system of experiences to become cut off from the others and to take complete control of the mind in disregard of experience as a whole.

We find very similar tendencies at work in a very much slighter degree in the normal life of many individuals. Quite frequently a man in the full possession of his senses will find himself temporarily so strongly under the influence of one idea that it is impossible for any other to enter consciousness. Under these conditions all statements, no matter how clearly heard, even if directly opposed to the interpretation that has been made, will be understood to confirm it in every respect. One who has absolute trust in the fidelity of a friend will see in a statement that undoubtedly proves treachery to every unprejudiced observer a new and convincing instance of his loyalty. Many are the men whose belief in themselves and in their good repute in the community is so strong that any derogatory remark which they may happen to overhear concerning themselves is robbed of its sting by a perfectly honest misinterpretation. Numerous instances can be recalled by each reader in which a passing remark, surrounding objects, or some event, will change completely the ordinary course of thought as long as the individual remains under its influence. These conditions are like all the others mentioned in this chapter in that the cause is to be found in an excessive development of some one system of ideas, until it for the time will overbalance all other ideas, and produce a warped mind that will induce a misinterpretation of events about. It is unlike all of the preceding in that it is temporary and not sufficiently accentuated to lead to any dangerous actions, or to mark the man off as in any way different from his fellows.

There are, of course, many instances of similar accentuation of one system, or of a general decay of all the controlling elements in various forms of insanity, but it would require a far more extended and more technical treatment than we have space to give to bring out those aspects which cannot be brought under the head of the different phenomena already discussed. And even then we should have but an amplification of the facts already treated.

One other perfectly normal and very common experience offers an excellent illustration of the results of the decay of mental control. This is the dream. The remarkable feature of the dream life is not so much the character of the material that is offered, as it is the incongruous way in which the elements are united. In most cases the entire matter of the dream can be traced to some scene or scenes in the waking life, and the sensations of which they are composed can be shown to be derived in their entirety from our daily experiences. But the course of the associations is entirely out of harmony with experience, and brings about an irrational, if not uncanny, succession of pictures. This is exactly what would be expected on the theory that association, like attention, is ordinarily governed by the experiences of the past life, or physiologically, that the trend of ideas depends upon the reinforcing and inhibitory action of the nervous elements, which in turn owe their effect at any moment to the way in which they have been stimulated in earlier experiences. During sleep a large portion of the brain is incapable of function. We need not consider here whether the inability be due to diminished blood-supply, or to some change in the cell or its connections. However it may be brought about, we can feel very sure that parts of the brain are taking no part in the activity of the whole, while in dreams, at least, parts are in a state of activity. In the dream the nerve cells which are at work are not entirely without control, but the control is exercised by comparatively few cells, is directed by but a partial experience ; and while the dream is true to the mental conditions under which it originates, it is not true for real life—for experience as a whole. The factors which direct the dream life are one-sided representatives of the man as a whole ; by far the greater part of himself has no influence upon the process, and the result is an unreal and unnatural train of thought.

All of the pathological phenomena mentioned, then, find a ready explanation in terms of the dissociation of certain systems, of the undue prominence of some one or more of such systems and the almost complete disappearance of others. As a result there is a general decay of control. From a dream to the most complete case of double personality all of the facts, so far as we know them, will fit into this theory—that the nature of consciousness, both as to the sensations which enter it and the associations of the ideas in their course, is to be explained by the fact that no element or group of elements is ever found in complete isolation in the normal individual, but that every nerve process, every experience, depends for its ultimate nature upon all the other nerve processes that are or have been in action, upon all the experiences to which the individual has been subjected at any time in his life. If any considerable number of these factors fail to exercise their normal function, the mind becomes abnormal, its processes are uncontrolled, and incoherent. The mental life is no longer a true picture of the events in the world without, and is not in harmony with the views of others as to the nature of the universe as a whole.

The problems of the development of attention, particularly the question as to the point of entrance of attention in the course of the development of the animal series, find their readiest answer in the light of the physiological theory. On that view we should have attention as soon as the different sensory elements of the nervous system begin to act one upon the other in such a way that the entrance of any stimulus would depend in part upon the earlier stimuli that had entered and upon the previous excitation of the organism by other external processes—when the reaction of the animal is no longer due to the nature of the stimulation and the inherited nervous mechanism, but is also determined in part by the various experiences which the individual has undergone in the course of its own life. In the animal series we could look for attention only when the nervous system had made considerable development; when the different sensory elements were at least closely connected by association fibres that could transmit the reinforcing and inhibiting impulses from one cell to the other. We should also expect that there would be no sharp line of distinction between the animals which showed traces of attention and those which did not. As the process of development is always a gradual one, there would be a shading over from the animals whose activities would find their explanations in the mechanical action of the nervous system to those in which we could trace control by the earlier conscious processes. The facts fully justify the expectation of uncertainty in deciding where to put the first sign of attention. There is not as yet even general agreement as to the facts upon which we must base our interpretation. Bethe and the others who would carry the explanation in terms of mechanical reflex to the furthest point find no traces of adaptation in any of the animals below the vertebrates, while others see striking signs of it in ants and bees and many other of the higher invertebrates.

The problem is still further complicated by the fact that the only method of judging the effect of attention or of any other mental process is by inference from their actions, and these are always susceptible of more than one explanation. Still we do find that in the lower forms the stimuli which are responded to are those which are of a nature to appeal to the animal on account of its hereditary structure, that the same stimulus appeals with equal strength at all times, and that there is no failure to respond when the stimulus is present. Further on there is a selection, certain stimuli are attended to in preference to others of equal strength which would have been responded to at another time. Often the failure to respond comes in spite of the fact that the stimulus in all probability has acted upon the nervous system. But the inhibition of the response is due to the action between nerve cells of exactly the same kind as that which is involved in attention. Perhaps the best instance

of such an inhibition in a comparatively low vertebrate is
the experiment of Möbius [7] repeated by Dr. Triplett [¹³] upon
the perch. It was found that if a minnow and a perch were
put in the same tank but separated from each other by a
pane of clear glass, the perch would at first make many
vain attempts to seize the minnow and would strike its
head against the pane in its struggles. In a comparatively
short time, however, it would discover that the endeavour
was useless and would give up the struggle. The most
surprising thing from the human standpoint is that when
the glass was removed and the two fish were permitted to
swim together in the same space, the perch still made no
attempt to devour its natural prey. Here, frequent experiences had overcome the inherited impulse, the normal
association of movement with visual impression was destroyed. This is an effect very similar to the inhibition
which the electric current exerted on the perception of the
grey lines on the Masson disc in Mr. Taylor's experiments,
except that it affects the motor connections as well as the
sensory. Probably, however, the effect of one sensory impression upon another would appear at the same time, for,
as we have seen, the control of the movement is in terms of
a sensory process of some kind, and one inhibition would
make its appearance at very much the same place as the
others.

Of course the difference in degree between attention at
these lower stages of development and that which we see
in man is so great as to amount almost to a difference in kind.
To take even a fairly highly developed animal like the perch,
we find that only one aspect of the experience with the
minnow has any influence upon the later action—its unattain-
ableness. In man other phases would have entered as well.
He would have seen that the minnow was only unapproach-
able as long as the glass intervened, or as long as it was at
the other end of the tank. Development of attention from
this standpoint consists very largely in the addition of new
elements successvely to modify the one element which

was prominent in the earlier forms. As more experiences play a part in the total determination, as the action is not in the light of one phase of the earlier experiences only, but takes more and more completely the entire nature of the earlier life into consideration, we have a greater adequacy of the attention, a truer conception of each separate experience which may be offered. The development of the nervous system which goes on from the lower animals to man renders possible this increased control by means of the increasing complexity in the connections between different parts of the nervous system.

Very much the same story is to be told of the development of attention in the child as in the animal series, except that the development of the child is very much more rapid, and that the child at birth has already reached a point of development that corresponds to a comparatively advanced stage in the development of the animal series. While in the animal the lack of attention is the accompaniment of a relatively undeveloped nervous system, of a condition of marked lack of connection between the various nervous elements, in the child the same mental insufficiency is the concomitant of the incomplete state of the nervous elements. As was pointed out in an earlier chapter, at birth the fibres of the cerebral cortex are not yet enclosed in their sheath, and are as incapable of function as a mass of bare copper wires would be of carrying separate electric currents if the different wires were in contact from place to place, although probably not for the same reason. Not merely the associatory fibres of the cortex are lacking, but many of the sensory centres as well. Although the influence of cell upon cell in the lower centres is being exerted in directing the actions of the child to a greater extent perhaps than in the lower animals that we have considered to possess a small degree of attention, there is little or nothing of activity in the cortical cells which are to accompany attention in the adult. Attention, then, in the sense in which we use it in regard to man's mental processes, is largely lacking in the child at

x

birth, and probably enters at about the third month. Preyer mentions an instance in which the child seeks an object with its eyes on the eighty-third day, which was for this child the first sign of spontaneous attention. In the child as in the animal series, we are dealing with a course of gradual development, and it is impossible to fix the exact period of the appearance of attention in the one case as in the other. As has been said, if we should use the strict physiological criterion which has been applied to animals, we should probably be compelled to ascribe the beginnings of the phenomena to a period very shortly after birth ; if, however, we take the ordinary meaning of the term as applied to adults, consider the presence of an anticipatory idea as the criterion, we should see the rudiments of the process at about the third month ; but if we emphasise the side of social control, the first signs of the determination of ideas by the wishes of the other individuals about it, the first appearance would be put much later, probably after the time of learning to speak.

In any case, unless care is taken to understand the sense in which the words are used, there will be unlimited opportunities for misunderstanding, and little hope of a final decision. The most important thing is to see that the same general laws apply to the lowest mind as to the highest, that attention is nothing more than the inter-action of different nerve-cells and experiences in the control of other cells and experiences, and that in the lower animals few cells are involved, in the higher many. If this principle is accepted there is little importance to be attached to the question as to where attention first makes its appearance.

SUMMARY

1. The degenerations of mind are nearly all accompanied by weakened or deranged attention.

2. Two forms of change may be noted in insanity : the general instability of attention that forbids any concen-

tration as in mania, and distorted attention that gives rise to fixed ideas as of paranoia.

3. Closely related to attention are the dissociations of personality that result from a division of the experiences into two or more groups with different forms of attention for each.

4. Attention may be said to make its appearance in the race or in the individual whenever the nervous system develops to the stage where remote earlier experiences may modify the influence of the immediate stimulus.

CHAPTER XIX

GENERAL CONCLUSIONS

IT is now time to bring together the scattered threads of theory, to attempt to summarise briefly the more theoretical conclusions, and to fill in any omissions in the discussion which may have been necessary from the standpoint of the separate chapters.

We seem to be compelled to define attention from the standpoint of its conscious characteristics, from what Professor Titchener calls its structural side, as an increased clearness and prominence of some one idea, sensation, or object, whether remembered or directly given from the external world, so that for the time it is made to constitute the most important feature of consciousness. This central position of the process in question we have seen to depend upon two general factors, the present environment on the one side and the entire past history of the individual on the other. These two together are of course co-extensive with the known universe in the case of the ideal man. Man's experience is not alone composed of the comparatively few events which have brought him into direct contact with nature, but through tradition and books he has summed up within himself the entire experience of the human race as a whole in all times and places. On the other side, too, through heredity, it would be possible to trace some small number of the conditions which have to be taken into consideration in explaining any act of attention back to the acts and surroundings of his predecessors in the course of evolution. While no single man reaches this ideal condition, it is yet true for every man that the elements which may be said to determine his attention are not to be found in any chance movement of the body at the moment, in any feeling of pleasure or of effort that may accompany or precede the attending, but are to be found in the entirety of the preceding life of the individual and indirectly in the race history of mankind in general.

Moreover, it does not seem necessary to assume a particular bearer of these experiences under the name of will, conation, or apperception. An assumption of this kind can at most call up a picture, and the picture in last analysis is not adequate to the facts. We know nothing in our experience but a sense of effort, a change in ideas ; we can discover from an examination of other consciousnesses or in the actions of other men no facts that demand a picture of this kind. The most we can learn is that the consciousness of a given moment is different from what it would have been, if the individual had not been subjected to some of the earlier experiences which he has undergone. If you care to call any one of these concrete processes or facts " will " or " apperception," very well ; but it is also essential that you keep in mind what the term implies, and do not assume that there is something behind the facts which acts as a bearer of the effects which are retained from one experience and exerts them upon another. Of such separate entity we have no evidence, and to assume it is to complicate rather than to simplify the problem. Certain phases of consciousness we shall undoubtedly continue to call will, and there is great convenience in the use of the term in that sense ; but this can no more be taken to justify the separate existence of the entity apart from consciousness as a whole, than the use of the word memory to designate the fact that we remember justifies the assumption of a distinct mental being which retains old impressions. All are parts or phases of consciousness, not separate existences or consciousnesses distinct from the one mind.

One other question which comes up for mention here is

the old problem of the " freedom of the will." Whether we are to regard the mind as free or not depends entirely upon what we mean by the term. The whole long controversy reduces very largely to a confusion of words. If you mean that the man as he is at the moment is free to do as he pleases, man undoubtedly is free ; if you mean that any man can at any time act without any reference to present circumstances or past conditions, if you intend to assert the freedom of absolute irresponsibility, then only a negative answer can be given. No man but a lunatic would act entirely at variance with his past experiences and his reason, and if any man should attempt to act freely in this sense it would be sufficient ground for his incarceration. If you grant that a man ordinarily is and must be controlled very largely by the forces which have worked upon him in the past, and then ask if there are not still some other elements which combine with them in controlling his activity, the answer must be a confession of ignorance. No man has been and no man probably ever will be able to trace out all of the factors that are at work even in any one act of attention. There must always be a large part of every conscious process unexplained. Whether you insist that the remainder is to be explained as the first has been, and assert that if we could know more of the past life of the individual and of the influences to which he has been subjected, and had more accurate means of tracing the connections between them and the present mental processes, everything could be explained in the same way ; or whether you insist that part of these conditions in some way arise spontaneously in the individual, must be decided not by facts, but by the general temper of your own mind, and by the interpretation of life which appeals to you at the time.

Practically every one regards himself as a source of energy, as a force which can exert itself without reference to anything else in the universe. On the other hand, nearly every one tends to look at others as subject very largely to other men and things in his environment. The teacher is given to thinking of his students as so much material to be worked up into the finished citizen ; the lawyer of his jury as subject to suggestions which shall make the case take on a form favourable to his client ; the physician must ever keep before him the fact that the mind is dependent upon its bodily conditions and upon the preceding events in life ; while the judge tends more and more to treat the criminal as if he were the victim of unhealthy social surroundings rather than as the voluntary evil doer. Evidently, then, the answer to this question cannot be solved at present as a matter of fact, but rather must be left to be answered in harmony with the mental attitude of the individual. The answer will vary with the individual and at different times for the same individual. There is every practical advantage in treating every other man as if he were subject to natural laws, the product of his surroundings and of his previous actions, and of acting toward yourself as if independent of everything external, past as well as present. It must be added, however, that this freedom which we ascribe to ourselves is believed only, not proven, and that we can obtain no scientific conception of such free action.

If we once accept this general view of attention, we must in large measure abandon the old systems of classification. There can be very little meaning given to passive and active, sensorial and intellectual, voluntary and involuntary attention. Classified from the standpoint of the conditions, we have only the more objectively conditioned attention and the more subjectively conditioned—attention which depends upon the strength or size of the external object, and attention which depends upon interest or the mental condition at the moment. But these conditions never or very rarely occur in entire separation. Occasionally there comes a noise so loud or a light so bright that attention is drawn to it without reference to the state of mind at the time ; and again, there may be a preoccupation so great that no degree of external stimulation seems to disturb the train of thought ; but the ordinary attention is the resultant of both objective and subjective conditions in which one set tends to predominate slightly over the others. There is not a sharp, clearly drawn line, but a merging of one kind into the other. Most of the other classifications rest upon distinctions which are either unimportant or which disappear entirely when viewed more than superficially. The division into passive and active attention is based upon the absence or presence of strain sensations. It is the most satisfactory of any, because the characteristic chosen is one that can be easily recognised and plays an important part in the popular idea of attention. The difficulty with it is that the strain sensation is not an essential part of the entire process, and, furthermore, that it is not even an accurate sign of attention, for the strain sensation does not accompany the most adequate attention or the least adequate attention, nor is it confined either to the subjectively or to the objectively conditioned attention. We have seen that strain sensations are absent during the moderately adequate attention, attention to the external stimulus for its own sake; and also during the most adequate and effective attention, attention subjectively conditioned, after it has become most complete. It is only at the time of transition from the objective to the subjective conditions, or when there is a struggle between two sets of subjective conditions, that the sense of strain is present in any very marked degree. This is also usually a period of decreased attention efficiency. That there is a great difference in attention which is not due to the mere presence or absence of strain sensations is shown by the fact that the authors who divide attention into the passive and active forms also have other criteria of classification in terms of the conditions. They then subdivide into the passive attention proper or the objectively conditioned and the secondary passive which comes after the warming-up process is complete. This secondary classification shows the inadequacy of the strain sensation to serve alone as the criterion. If, however, it were possible to retain the distinction and at the same time to indicate the more essential differences, it would be very desirable to do so; but as the strain sensations are in themselves fortuitous accompaniments, and correspond neither to the conditions nor to the degree of attention, it seems impossible to retain any part of that classification without complicating the terminology to a degree which would more than negative the original gain.

The division into sensory and intellectual attention would apply only to the nature of the mental processes affected by attention, and not to the conditions or to the results. It, again, is a division that has had various meanings in the history of the science. Sometimes it has been used as synonymous with the active and passive; again, as corresponding to the objectively and subjectively conditioned. Both these meanings we have already considered. The only other use that can be made of it is to distinguish between the effects of attention upon sensation and its effects upon remembered or recalled impressions. The conditions we have seen to be the same in both cases, and there is little or no difference in the material which is acted upon or in the way in which it acts, except that in the latter we have the effect in controlling the course of associations as well as in facilitating the entrance or retention of mental processes in mind. This one effect does not seem to be sufficient to justify the use of the new basis of division.

As a result of the whole investigation, then, we are left with but one kind of attention so far as conditions are concerned, and judged from the results there is but slight difference between the various effects under different circumstances. Attention is a unitary process, and while there are two sets of conditions that bring it about, these merge into each other so closely that only the extremes are clearly distinguishable.

It is easy to show that many of the more complicated mental processes involve at basis the same factors, are very similar to attention in many of their characteristics. Using attention as a type, it is possible to bring many of the other mental processes under that head and to make it serve as a basis for the classification of states of mind. We have seen, for example, that attention influences recalled impressions in practically the same way that it influences their original entrance. When a memory image is once given in consciousness it will be retained very much as a perception received immediately from the external world. Furthermore, attention largely determines which of the many possible associates of any impression shall become actual. In this sense it selects the memories offered by association just as it selects the objects of sense that shall be permitted to enter. By attention in this sense we mean again from the side of the conditions, the effect of the sum-total of previous conscious states, as united in the purpose of the moment, the general trend of the preceding thought, the character of the man, his profession, and further back the complete series of earlier experiences and inherited tendencies which make him what he is. His thought about any subject, no matter what the starting point, is an expression of himself in the fullest meaning of the term. His associations, then, are not the result of a few isolated experiences as the English Associationists would have us believe, but are an expression of his entire life history, of the man in the fullest sense.

In the same way the perception of an object as an object, apperception in the Herbartian sense, is an expression, in fact, in very large measure a product of the earlier experiences of man. The entering sensation serves as little more than the occasion for starting up a whole mass of earlier perceptions, and these constitute the object that we say we see or feel. What the associates are to be depends very largely upon the circumstances of the moment, the earlier life of the man in question, and of the history of the human race as a whole. If it were not that mankind in general had been subjected to the same influences, there would be no agreement in the perceptions of different men, the world would be different for each, and there would be no possibility of discussing any external fact with the chance of arriving at the same conclusion. It is the common heredity, social as well as biological, and the common environment which give the worlds of different men such great similarity, not the fact that the external stimulus is the same for all. What the extreme Herbartians say about the importance of previous impressions is an under-estimation rather than an over-estimation of the truth, although we may not agree with them as to the way in which the result is accomplished.

Attention is equally important in memory as in association. What is remembered at any moment is dependent on the objective and subjective setting at that moment. The ease with which an event is recalled is largely due to the interest with which the impression was received in the first place, and to the way in which it fitted in with the other elements in consciousness at that period, upon the mental systems which were dominant then. Moreover, the attitude which will be taken toward the thing remembered on its return will be determined by the same conditions that go to make the perception what it is. An impression received in one way at its first entrance may take on an entirely different aspect when it reappears. New interpretations may be given it, new meanings put upon it, until it can no longer be recognised as the same object or image, and all because of the new knowledge which has been received between the times of the first and second entrance. In every possible way, then, memory is influenced by attention, and its conditions as a whole are very similar to the conditions of attention.

Many of the problems of voluntary action are also solved when once we have an understanding of the nature of attention. The prime condition of action of any kind is to keep an idea earlier associated with the movement clearly in mind. The idea of movement has exactly the same relation to attention as any other idea. Its coming up is usually dependent upon an association, and the association here as elsewhere is very largely determined by the conditions which control attention. Of course, there are certain questions relating to the motor side, the physiology of nerve and muscle, which are peculiar to action alone, but the mental side is completely determined when the idea of the movement becomes dominant. So choice is but the result of a conflict between two different systems of experience, between two ways of looking at a given set of circumstances. When one system wins and the mind is given over to its complete control, the corresponding movement decided upon, the action is determined beyond recall. Action, like thought and attention, then, is an expression of the entire earlier experience of the man, of everything that goes to make him what he is. It is impossible to set off action of any kind from the remainder of mind and regard it as unrelated to the rest. One cannot constantly think in one way and act in another. The action is an expression of the individual's thought, and that in turn of his character.

Reason itself is dependent upon the same factors. Reason is nothing more than thinking in the light of the entirety of knowledge. When an association is formed which is consistent with everything that the man knows at the time, you have an inference in the highest sense, and one which will be absolutely true for the individual at that time and in that environment. The adequacy of the reasoning will depend upon the number and nature of the impressions to which the man has been subjected, to his knowledge and the way in which it has been organised and brought to bear upon the particular experience of the moment.

Practically the same laws hold throughout all the mental processes. By far the greater part cannot be explained in terms of the conditions of the moment, but their roots are to be found far back in the mental history of the individual. Attention, perception, memory, action and reason, all alike, can be understood fully only in terms of the earlier life of the man, and their ramifications extend to the traditions of the society in which he has lived, and through these and the printed books which constitute so much of the environment of the civilised man, backward and outward to the limits of the experience of mankind in all ages and in all parts of the globe. These controlling influences of all mental processes are seen to arrange themselves into groups which are in part distinct, although each exerts an influence upon every other. A man is a different man, is moved by slightly different motives, in each of his social and civic capacities. He is a different man as a host than as a man of business; if he has several occupations he will take a slightly different view of the world while engaged in the duties of each. As a student turns from one subject to another, he tends to change his attitude towards all perceptions. He thinks and looks only under the influence of one particular system of knowledge. A group of facts that will be at work in determining his attitude towards a problem in physics is too often not serviceable in connection with a related problem in botany or chemistry, so that a statement which is perfectly intelligible when met in one text-book or lecture-room will seem to have no meaning in another. All the elements of knowledge seem to be marked off into systems, and it is usual for the connections to be less close between elements of two different systems than between elements of the same system. The state of mind at a particular time, then, will depend as much upon the system that is dominant as upon the nature of experience as a whole. A well organised mind is one in which the lines that divide the systems are well-nigh obliterated and all bits of knowledge, being fused together into one whole, are equally effective at all times in controlling the course of the mental stream. When the systems are small and rigidly distinct, much of the actual knowledge of the man will be almost worthless at all times, and he will necessarily take a biased and one-sided attitude toward all questions. In no mind are systems entirely merged; no man is capable of viewing all questions with entire fairness, or even in the full light of his own knowledge. It is the mark of greatness to approximate it. Genius consists, more than anything else in the ability to view familiar experiences from some unusual standpoint, in being able to approach a fact with a wider system of knowledge ready to interpret it than other men. Most advances in the realms of science and art are due to working out new connections between old facts rather than to the discovery of new, although, in many cases, the discovery of a new fact is necessary before the old can be observed from a new point of view.

The anatomical and physiological facts in connection with attention and the more complicated mental functions seem to harmonise with the theory that has been advanced. The one striking feature of the cerebral hemispheres is the richness of the associating fibres—the fact that every part is connected with every other part, both region with region, and elements of one region with other elements of the same region. Nowhere do we find anything like a dominating centre in any single part, but rather the structure is such that all parts of the hemispheres are united into one complex whole. Furthermore, the chief development of the cortex after infancy consists in the ripening and coming to maturity of these various association fibres. We have only to assume that the action of one set of nervous elements has a reinforcing or inhibiting effect upon other related elements, and to assume in addition that the action of a nerve-cell at one time will have an influence upon the action of all other cells at all future times to bring the physiological and psychological facts into agreement. The first assumption is strongly supported from the existence of analogous relations between motor cells, and while the latter is less strongly supported by known laws, it is not very different from the general principle upon which all explanation of memory is based, that a bit of nervous tissue undergoes a change with each activity which makes it more liable to act in the same way for ever after. It is only necessary to assume this fact, and that all nerve cells are always in a state of tonic activity which exerts an influence upon all related cells, and so contributes its share in controlling the action of all parts of the brain. That there are such systems of associations on the nervous side is supported from the side of pathology by the fact that groups of experiences tend to become detached from the whole, and either act alone in the control of consciousness or deprive consciousness of their influence for the time being. This would hardly be conceivable were there not an actual physical loosening of the associating bonds which could increase to complete dissociation.

What, then, from the psychological side is an action of each experience upon every other, is from the physical side a modification of the brain tissue affected in such a way that there is not only a present effect, but that these tissues will be for ever different because of that impression, and because of that earlier impulse will always exert a different impression upon whatever part of the cortex may be at that time in action. On both the mental and physical sides there can be no separation of the effects of different stimuli, no discussion of the action of one part without considering all other parts and the past history of the organism.

CHAPTER XX

APPLICATIONS TO EDUCATION

ABOUT the facts of attention centre many of the problems of the teacher. We may find it profitable to consider the conclusions for educational practice that follow from the results so far attained.

The first problem that meets the teacher, and that which most concerns us, is how to hold the attention of the child. If this can be satisfactorily accomplished everything else will be comparatively simple; the battle from the practical side is won, and all that remains is to decide what shall be taught. The solution of the problem that is usually offered is the adjuration to be interesting, to teach nothing that will not interest the child. But this does not take us very far. As has been seen earlier, it means nothing else than a reaffirmation of the end to be accomplished, is a command to hold the attention. To interest and to hold the attention are one and the same thing. We are then forced back to our original question, What is likely to hold the attention of a particular child? The only answer that can be given is in terms of the earlier history of the child. Anything will be interesting that the child already knows something about, and which is neither too old nor too new, which can in some way be attached to the pupil's earlier experiences and at the same time is new enough not to seem commonplace. Furthermore, the new material must be presented in such a way that the connections with the older elements shall come out prominently. The first condition of being interesting, then, is a knowledge of your child. This knowledge, to be effective, must be sympathetic, not merely statistical, although a statistical knowledge of what children in a given community or at a particular age are likely to know may be helpful if well assimiláted and vivified by a first-hand knowledge. It involves knowing something of the home life that the child has had; ideally it involves a personal knowledge of the child and his parents for some time back, but this is, of course, a condition which cannot be realised in the ordinary schools with their large classes and exacting duties. Still, every teacher must know what the children of the particular neighbourhood can be expected to know at the different ages, from observation, from statistics, from the memories of what he himself knew at that age. Furthermore, he should be able to make allowance for the different temperaments, for the various earlier surroundings and other circumstances that make the separate children peculiar each to himself.

But even after this knowledge is complete, everything depends upon the skill of the teacher. The application of the knowledge is as important as the knowledge itself. A person of keen sympathies can hardly fail utterly in the schoolroom, assuming a knowledge of what is to be taught; whereas without this sympathy and tact the most complete knowledge of child-life, and even of the theoretical principles of teaching, will not prevent a lamentable failure. But what is called tact is very often nothing more than a knowledge of children derived from keen personal observation, while the knowledge that is found useless in regard to children is often nothing but ill-digested masses of facts not really understood. It is doubtful if there could be intimate knowledge of child-life and conditions that would not result in sympathy and tact.

It has been suggested that it is possible to tell what the interests of a child will be at any time on the assumption that the order of development of the child's activities and interests will follow the development of the activities of the race as a whole—that the child will have its pastoral stage,

Y

its stone and iron age, just as the race had them and in the same order, This theory may serve as a guiding thread in the conduct of experiments, but it cannot be assumed as a general law in advance of trial. It is at best an analogy, based upon the fact that the body tends to follow in its development the course that the animal series pursued in evolution, so that the mental history of the child will take the same order as the history of the human race. Even granting the analogy to hold in its entirety, there would be difficulties. The physical development of the child does, it is true, tend to take the same line as the development of the species, but there are many short cuts, many stages that are not reproduced in the individual growth. Practically it would be impossible to tell in advance of experiment what stages would be omitted, what brought in.

But to decide what shall be taught a child in terms of his interests alone is only one side of the question. The aim of education is not to interest the child, but to mould the child for useful participation in the life of the community, to bring him into contact with the experience of the race as a whole in such a way that the essentials of human knowledge shall become part of the influences which guide and direct his thought and conduct for the remainder of his life. Society sets the end that the teacher must attain, pleasantly and agreeably to the child if possible, but attain at any cost. If, the, then culture-epoch theory of education or any other method fails to attain this end, and to attain it with a minimum expenditure of time and the maximum of efficiency, it is in so far to be discarded. Undoubtedly many of the steps which the race has lived through are not needed for an understanding of present-day conditions, or at least for an understanding of those phases which are most important to the average child in preparation for the active work of life. The test which every scheme proposed must meet is, does it effectively put the child in possession of those portions of traditional knowledge which shall most thoroughly prepare him for life in the community, taking into consideration the time that he is likely to have to devote to his preparation ? The ultimate test of a system is its product, but when the test must be long delayed, as is the case necessarily with education, it is essential to keep in mind the general aim and to measure the means by their apparent adequacy to those results.

Another difficulty in making interest the sole measure of what shall be taught is, that while interest is simply another name for the probability that a certain statement or body of principles will hold the attention of the child, it does not take into consideration the entire set of conditions that ordinarily work in the determination of any attentive process. Probably the attention that is ordinarily called interest is induced merely by those factors which are derived from earlier experiences and heredity, and omits consideration of the social factors, which are just as numerous and effective and accomplish the same result as the others. It is only so far as the child is made to feel the social pressure, to recognise the demands which society makes upon him and take them as his own ideals, that he can be said to be acquiring an education. These alone will enable him to persevere after the guidance of teacher and text-book have been removed, and they must also be trusted even in the stage of preparation at times when he is not directly under the eye of the teacher. The child must begin to feel the responsibilities of life as soon as he is beyond the kindergarten, to understand the social rewards which come with success of any kind and the social punishments of failure. All these will, of course, appeal but vaguely to the child at first, but with growing knowledge they will become more clearly and definitely conscious. Unless impressed early, they will never come to complete maturity.

The child, then, must always be conscious of his duty so far as he is conscious at all of the incentives which lead him to work. He should never be permitted to plead lack of interest as an excuse for neglecting his tasks. Much of his attention will, of course, be given naturally and pleasantly, with no idea that he is working. This is the ideal condition, for the young child at least. But he should never consciously be permitted to feel that the end of his endeavour is his own pleasure. Interest as a standard of attainment is too uncertain, and would necessarily carry with it an emphasis upon the nearer rather than the more remote advantage. It gives prominence to the momentary rather than to the permanent good. Only the pressure of the community, of society as a whole, can be relied upon to keep his attention long fixed upon one subject. Every appeal of the student to his own interest as a standard of educational value results in a weakening of the influence of society and a softening of the moral fibre. It is a neglect of this phase of the subject which seems to be responsible for the widespread feeling that modern educational methods, with their insistence upon interest as a criterion of what shall be taught, are in some respects a step backward rather than forward. And a use of social pressure, of an appeal to duty as a means of exciting interest, is not inconsistent with the theoretical laws of attention. Regarding the problem from the standpoint of the conditions of attention, these social factors undoubtedly furnish a very large and important element in the determination of every act. They constitute the balance wheel, the elements that make for continuity and persistency. It is only an entire misunderstanding of the nature of the attention process that would exclude them from its practical control. They are just as important as the conditions which we ordinarily call interest in governing attention, and it is quite as justifiable to make use of them in practice.

In a word, then, the attention of the child must be held to all those elements of knowledge which are essential to his individual progress at that particular time. Any influences which can be regarded as the natural determinants of attention must be used, if it is necessary, to accomplish the purpose of education. If the teacher can succeed by choosing those aspects of the subject which are related to past experience and so are interesting, well and good; if not, he is justified in calling to his aid the effect of social pressure as contained in the sense of duty. From the practical standpoint it seems that the end of education will be most satisfactorily reached if the student constantly feels that he is striving for the accomplishment of an ideal which he has set himself, while the teacher regards it as his function to make every step in the acquirement easy and interesting and relies as little as possible upon the aid of social pressure. Here, as was seen in the theoretical problem of the freedom of the will, we have two opposing attitudes toward the same question, each of which seems unavoidable, but each will be held by a different person. Fortunate indeed is the teacher who can keep both sides of the controversy clearly in view, and not confuse the two mottoes in practice.

A still stronger objection to an insistence upon interest as the only criterion of what shall be taught comes out when we think that extra application now may be the means of new interest in the future. Many subjects can be acquired without effort only at the expense of an enormous waste of time at the beginning, while the conquest of a few general introductory ideas in the early stages, at the expense of pain and forced attention, will quickly bring a large return in future pleasure, and will produce a healthy interest in the subject at a later period. Here again, if pressure of an extraneous kind, from the feeling that it is disgraceful to fail, or from insistence upon the fact that the particular subject is necessary for the accomplishment of a more remote purpose, which in itself appeals to the student, it is perfectly possible to develop an interest for the more advanced phases of the subject. In fact, to be interested in a subject means merely that there have been earlier experiences which were related to that subject, and each new experience lays the foundation for new interests. Bits of knowledge are not only to be thought of as acquired through interest, but as the basis of future interests in other subjects. It is certainly as laudable to consider the future acquirements that the knowledge will make possible as it is to think only of what present facts will be interesting.

The general educational principle that a study of the laws of attention seems to demand is a reconciliation of the two tendencies that are now striving for the supremacy in educational theory. In the first place, a knowledge of the child, however perfect, will not determine what the child shall be taught. That can be decided only in the light of social conditions and the needs of the times for men of a certain kind and training. On the other hand, the requirements of society can have nothing to say as to how or when the knowledge it demands is to be imparted. Child study can reveal the laws that tell us how and when certain knowledge shall be offered. The standards and demands of the community alone can decide what it is that shall be taught.

From the theory of attention many subsidiary principles may be drawn in regard to the other processes that the teacher must deal with. Perhaps most closely connected with it are the processes which are concerned in perception. Perception, as we have seen before, is not complete when the sensation is attended to. But there must be added to the sensation a mass of associations which have been acquired in earlier experiences. The sensation as it enters is met by a group of returning impressions, and the nature of the resulting idea is largely determined by the mood of the moment. It is only when what is seen is supplemented in this way that anything can be understood, and the nature and degree of the understanding will vary with the number and kind of the bits of previous knowledge which the child has already acquired. There can be no real interest, no making the new knowledge part of the old, without these associates.

But there may be interest and even continued attention when the wrong associates are present, or when they are so few that the resulting understanding is imperfect and partial. It is necessary, then, that the new object be seen in all its useful relations to the earlier facts. The egg for Professor James's child was only a potato, because it could be associated with nothing but the one smooth white object. It could not be fully understood even from a child's standpoint, unless its relations to the hen and the chicken, its similarities to other articles of food, were known and noted, and of course it could not be fully understood in the absolute sense, or even in the scientist's sense, unless considered in the light of related chemical compounds and of an untold number of facts in biology and physics. In fact, in ultimate analysis every bit of knowledge is in some way connected with every other, and a complete knowledge of any one bit would involve connecting it with every other. Of course, it is impossible to thread the entire universe of knowledge for each new impression, but it is equally absurd to leave the child without aid in connecting the new fact with the knowledge already possessed. The links which shall be made with the other facts must be selected with reference to the measure of development which the child has already reached, and to the purpose of the lesson in hand. But the connections must be made and made judiciously, for only in so far as it is connected with others is the new bit of information really known or likely to be of any use.

An effective and rational exercise of this principle is implied in the modern term correlation. In spite of the fact that a formal and unintelligent application of the doctrine has frequently brought discredit upon the term, teaching which does not bring about correlation is not education in any real sense. Properly used and connected, every fact should throw some light directly or indirectly upon every other fact, and the acquisition of each new bit of information renders easier an understanding of each succeeding statement, at the same time that it modifies and enriches the understanding of the knowledge already acquired when it comes up for reconsideration.

Almost the same conditions hold for memory as for perception. Proper perception may, in fact, be said to be the only condition of memory. The only phase of memory which does not depend upon the physiological structure and so can be modified by training, is recall, and recall depends upon the closeness with which each fact has been connected with every other element of knowledge which is likely to be in mind at the time that this particular fact is needed. If each new perception is seen in relation to all analogous objects it will have many associates, many cues for recall, and will be available for immediate use whenever occasion requires. If, on the contrary, it is associated with a few other ideas only, with those that were present accidentally when it came to consciousness, it will be easily forgotten. Principles which are alone considered in the light of the other parts of the particular lesson in which they are learned will have no connections with the concrete events of life, and will prove short-lived and unfruitful. There are few if any separate conditions of memory. A thing really understood is seldom forgotten. The only rule for memory which has any practical value is *Understand*.

Training reason is merely another phase of the same process. To reason is but to form associations under the influence of the entirety of experience. This means first to know and then to have the knowledge so connected that each association is controlled by everything that the man has learned, and is not swayed by a few considerations to the exclusion of others. The first desideratum here is knowledge, the second to use that knowledge. And use of knowledge depends only upon a proper co-ordination of the separate isolated elements. To teach a child to reason, then, is, on the one side, to teach him to see truly, to observe all of the relations of objects, and on the other to have all that he knows ready to test each statement that he hears and to govern each thought which is formulated in his own mind. The difference between a man who merely knows and a man who reasons is the difference between a mere accumulation of unassorted facts and an organised body of knowledge ready to re-act on any and every occasion.

There cannot be reasoning without information, but

relatively few facts, if systematised and constituting a unified whole, frequently make their possessor vastly more efficient than many a man of greater erudition. Reason, then, has the same basis as attention, as clear perception and adequate memory.

Much is said in educational circles to-day of training the will and the feelings as well as the intellect, and it may be well to digress from our more particular subject to point out the results of our discussions when applied to that field. The earlier chapters have made action almost entirely dependent upon attention for its control. The cue for a movement was seen to be always an idea, and the same conditions control the entrance into consciousness of the idea which calls out the movement as any other idea. The training of will, from this standpoint, is accomplished then with the training of attention. A man whose knowledge with reference to any circumstance is complete will always act properly if he acts at all. Of course, the knowledge which controls action is not restricted to merely formal disciplines. One must know human nature and the relations of the individual to society in ways so delicate that they have never been formulated in words. These experiences one can acquire only by living the life of the community, by understanding the thoughts and feelings of others. But this experience every man has opportunity for, and all that can be done to help him is to point out the elements in his environment which he overlooks. Over and above that, every bit of knowledge which affects his relations to mankind or to the world without will serve to direct his action. Full knowledge so co-ordinated as to be always effective would mean perfect action.

One fact which seems out of harmony with this statement is that we often find men who have full knowledge of what to do under all circumstances, who never accomplish anything, or at least fall far short of their best knowledge and even of their intentions. The difficulty in these cases is either that their knowledge is badly organised and so never available until too late, if at all, or more frequently they do not feel the full force of social pressure. They have not been forced to see that society demands action from them under these particular circumstances. It is, after all, an ignorance of certain principles, due to lack of training during the earlier years, which has often resulted in bad habits of action, and which it is very difficult to overcome by the knowledge of later acquirement. Nevertheless, failure to act when action is necessary, like improper action, has its ultimate seat in ignorance of the full and true relations of man to man and of man to his physical environment.

From the discussion in chapter XII it appears that feeling has certain obvious similarities to the other processes mentioned above. It can be said in general that the feeling which one has for any object or process depends upon two factors : the knowledge which one has about the object, and upon the way in which one happens to be looking at it. Both of these are evidently very closely related to attention, if not absolutely dependent upon it. Perfect knowledge, with that knowledge effective at the moment, would imply correct feeling, as it implies correct acting. Training of the feelings cannot be an isolated process, but must depend upon training in general—upon the acquirement and proper organisation of knowledge.

BIBLIOGRAPHY

GENERAL

1. P. Janet, "Attention," *Dictionnaire de Physiologie*, I, p. 831.
2. O. Külpe, "Attention," *Monist*, p. 33. October, 1902.
3. N. Lange, *Psychological Investigations: Laws of Perception and Theory of Voluntary Attention* (*Russian*). Odessa, 1893.
4. G. E. Müller, *Zur Theorie der Aufmerksamkeit*. Leipzig, 1873.
5. J. P. Neyrac, *Physiologie et psychologie de l'attention*. Paris, 1906.
6. A. Pilzecker, *Die Lehre von der sinnlichen Aufmerksamkeit*. Munich, 1889.
7. Th. Ribot, *Psychologie de l'attention*. Paris, 1889 *et freq.*
8. Rageot, *Les formes simples de l'attention*. *Rev. Phil.* LVI, p. 113.
9. J. Paulhan, *L'activité mentale et les éléments de l'esprit*. Paris, 1889.

I have not cited the general treatises on psychology, each of which contains a discussion of attention, but will refer to the more striking treatments in connection with the different chapters.

CHAPTER I

1. J. Dissard, "Influence de l'attention sur la perception des sensations," *Rev. Phil.*, XXXIX, p. 454.
2. O. Külpe, "Ueber den Einfluss der Aufmerksamkeit auf die Empfindungsintensität," 3e *Int. Congr. der Psychologie*, p. 180.
3. O. Külpe, "Zur Lehre von der Aufmerksamkeit," *Zeitschr. f. Phil. u. Phil. Krit.*, CX, p. 7.
4. A. Lehmann, *Die Hypnose*, p. 21 ff. Leipzig, 1890.
5. H. Münsterberg, "Increase of Intensity Produced by Attention," *Psych. Rev.*, I, p. 39.
6. H. Stumpf, *Tonpsychologie*, I, p. 70 ; II, p. 290. Leipzig, 1890.
7. W. Wündt, *Grundz. d. phys. Psychologie*, 5e ed., III, p. 339. Leipzig, 1903.
8. Ch. Richet, *Essais de psychologie générale*. Paris, 1887.

CHAPTER II

1. Binet et Courtier, " Circulation capillaire de la main," *L'Année psych.*, p. 87. 1895.

2. Binet et Henri, *La fatigue intellectuelle.* Paris, 1898.

3. Binet et Vaschide, " Influence of Intellectual Work upon Blood Pressure in Man," *Psych. Rev.*, IV, p. 54.

4. E. B. Delabarre, " L'influence de l'attention sur les mouvements respiratoires," *Rev. Phil.*, XXXIII, p. 639.

5. Ch. Féré, *Sensation et mouvement.* 2e ed., Paris, 1900.

6. Heinrich, " Sur la fonction accommodatrice de la membrane tympanique," *Bull. Imp. Acad. de Sci.*, pp. 105-11. Cracovie, 1900.

7. W. Heinrich, " Die Aufmerksamkeit und die Funktion der Sinnesorgane," *Zeitschr. f. Psych. u. Phys. d. Sinnesorg.*, IX, p. 342.

8. Heller, " Zur Blindenpsychologie," *Phil. Stud.*, XI, pp. 226, 531.

9. J. Jastrow, " A Study of Involuntary Movements," *Amer. Jour. of Psych.*, IV, p. 398.

10. A. Lehmann, *Körperliche Äusserungen d. Psychischer Zustände.* Leipzig, 1899.

11. Meumann und Zoneff, " Ueber Begleiterscheinungen psychischer Vorgänge in Athem und Puls.," *Phil. Stud.*, XVIII, p. 1.

12. W. Ostmann, " Die Reflexerregbarkeit des M. Tensor Tympani.," *Archiv F. Anat. u. Phys., Phys. Abt.*, p. 70. 1898.

13. W. Ostmann, "Ueber die Betheiligung des N. facialis beim Lauschen," *Archiv f. Ohrenheilk*, LIV, 209-15. 1902.

14. L. Patrizi, " La grafica psicometrica dell attenzione," *Archivio di Psichiatria*, XVI, pp. 100–107.

15. J. F. Shepard, "Organic Changes and Feeling," *Amer. Jour. Psych.*, XVIII, pp. 522–84.

16. Sommer, "Dreidimensionale Analyse von Ausdrücksbewegungen," *Zeitschr. f. Psych. u. Phys. d. Sinnesorg.*, XVI, p. 275.

17. H. C. Stevens, " A Plethysmographic Study of the Attention," *Amer. Jour. Psych.*, XVI, p. 409.

18. N. Vaschide, " L'Influence du travail intellectuel prolongé sur la vitesse du pouls," *L'Année psych.*, p. 356. 1897.

19. Vaschide et Lahy, " Les données experimentales et clinques de la mesure de la pression sanguine," *Arch. Gen. de Med.*, p. 71. December, 1902.

CHAPTER III

1. Arreat, " L'Hérédité chez les peintres," *Rev. Phil.*, XXXII, p. 155.

2. B. B. Breese, " On Inhibition," *Psych. Rev.*, Mon. Sup., III, 1.

3. F. Galton, *Hereditary Genius.* 2nd ed. London, 1892.

4. G. S. Hall and H. H. Donaldson, " Movement Sensations on the Skin," *Mind*, X, p. 557.

5. H. Helmholtz, *Phys. Optik*, pp. 605, 890. Leipzig, 1896.

6. Külpe, " Attention," *Monist*, p. 38. October, 1902.

7. Külpe, " Versuche über Abstraktion," *Bericht des I. Kongr. f. exp. Psych. Giessen*, pp. 56–8. 1904.

8. Karl Pearson, " The Inheritance of Mental and Moral Characters," *Biometrica*, p. 131. 1904.

9. Woods, *Heredity in Royalty*. New York, 1906.

CHAPTER IV

1. John Dewey, " The Psychology of Effort," *Phil. Rev.*, VI, p. 43. 1897.

2. Janet, *L'Automatisme psychologique*. Paris, 1889.

3. W. MacDougall, " The Physiological Processes in the Attention Process," *Mind*, N.S., XII, p. 473.

4. H. Münsterberg, *Die Willenshandlung*. Freiburg, 1888.

5. G. F. Stout, *Analytic Psychology*, I, p. 224. London, 1896.

CHAPTER V

1. J. R. Angell and A. H. Pierce, " Experimental Researches on the Phenomena of Attention," *Amer. Jour. of Psych.*, IV, p. 528.

2. F. G. Bonser, " A Study of the Relations between Mental Activity and the Circulation of the Blood," *Psych. Rev.*, p. 120. 1903.

3. Breese, " On Inhibition," *Psych. Rev.*, Mon. Sup., III, p. 1.

4. J. Mck. Cattell, " Ueber die Tragheit des Netzhaut und des Sehcentrum," *Phil. Stud.*, III, p. 121.

5. J. Mck. Cattell, " Psychometrischer Untersuchungen," *Phil. Stud.*, III, p. 486.

6. J. Mck. Cattell, " Aufmerksamkeit und Reaction," *Phil. Stud.*, VIII, p. 403.

7. A. H. Daniels, " The Memory After-image and Attention," *Amer. Jour. of Psych.*, VI, p. 558.

8. G. Dietze, " Untersuchungen über den Umfang des Bewusstseins bei regelmässig auf einander folgenden Schalleindrücken," *Phil. Stud.*, II, p. 362.

9. Knight Dunlap, " Some Peculiarities of Fluctuating and Inaudible Tones," *Psych. Rev.*, p. 308. 1904.

10. H. Eckener, " Untersuchungen über die Schwankungen der Auffassung minimaler Sinnesreize," *Phil. Stud.*, VIII, p. 343.

11. Erdmann und Dodge, *Ueber das Lesen*. Halle, 1898.

12. S. Exner, " Die persönliche Gleichung der zweiter Theil," *Pfluger's Archiv*, XI, p. 406.

13. C. E. Ferree, "An Experimental Examination of the Phenomena Usually Attributed to Fluctuations of the Attention,"*Amer. Jour. of Psych.*, XVII, p. 81.

14. C. E. Galloway, " The Effect of Stimuli upon the Length of Traube-Hering Waves," *Amer. Jour. of Psych.*, XV, p. 499.

15. M. Geiger, " Neue Complicationsversuche," *Phil. Stud.*. XVIII, p. 347.

15a. Goldscheider u. Müller, " Zur Physiologie u. Pathologie des Lesens," *Zeitschr. f. klin. Med.*, XXIII, p. 131.

16. R. Hammer, " Zur Experimentellen Kritik der Aufmerksamkeitsschwankungen," *Zeitschr. f. Psych. u. Phys. der Sinnesorg.*, XXXVII, p. 363.

17. Alice J. Hamlin, " On Least Observable Differences between Stimuli," *Amer. Jour. of Psych.*, VI, p. 564.

18. W. Heinrich, " Ueber die Intensitätsänderungen schwacher Geräusche," *Zeitsch. f. Psych. Abth.*, II, 43, p. 57.

19. W. Heinrich u. L. Chwestek, " Ueber das periodische Verschwinden kleiner Punkte," *Zeitschr. f. Psych. Abth.*, II, 43, p. 59.

20. J. P. Hylan, " Fluctuations of Attention," *Psych. Rev.*, III, p. 56.

21. J. P. Hylan, " Fluctuations of Attention," *Psych. Rev.*, Mon. Sup., III, 2.

22. J. P. Hylan, " The Distribution of Attention," *Psych. Rev.*, pp. 373, 498. 1903.

23. P. Janet, *Nevroses et idées fixes*, I, p. 77.

24. N. Lange, " Beiträge zur Theorie der sinnlichen Aufmerksamkeit und der activen Apperception," *Phil. Stud.*, IV, p. 390.

25. A. Lehmann, " Ueber die Beziehung zwischen Atmung und Aufmerksamkeit," *Phil. Stud.*, IX, p. 66.

26. K. Marbe, " Die Schwankungen der Gesichtsempfindungen," *Phil. Stud.*, VIII, p. 615.

27. J. F. Messenger, " The Perception of Number," *Psych. Rev.*, Mon. Sup., V, No. 5.

28. H. Münsterberg, " Schwankungen der Aufmerksamkeit," *Beitr. zur experimentellen Psychologie*, II, p. 69. Freiburg, 1889.

29. E. A. Pace, " Zur Frage der Schwankungen der Aufmerksamkeit nach Versuchen mit der Masson'schen Scheibe," *Phil. Stud.*, VIII, p. 388.

30. E. A. Pace, " Fluctuations of Attention," *Phil. Stud.*, XX, p. 232.

31. M. L. Patrizi, " Il tempo di reazione semplice," *Rev. sperim. di Fren.*, III, p. 11.

32. M. L. Patrizi, " La graphique psychometrique de l'attention," *Arch. Ital. de Biol.*, XXII, p. 189.

33. Wilhelm Peters, " Aufmerksamkeit und Zeitverschiebung in der Auffassung disparater Sinnesreize," *Zeitschr. f. Psych. u. Phys. d. Sinnesorg.*, XXXIX, p. 401.

34. C. D. Pflaum, " Neue Untersuchungen über die Zeitverhältnisse der Apperception," *Phil. Stud.*, XV, p. 139.

35. J. W. Slaughter, " The Fluctuations of the Attention in some of their Physiological Relations," *Amer. Jour. of Psych.*, XII, p. 313.

36. L. W. Stern, *Psychologie der Veränderungsauffassung*. Breslau, 1898.

37. G. M. Stratton, " Ueber die Wahrnehmung von Druckänderung," *Phil. Stud.*, XII, p. 525.

33. E. J. Swift, " Disturbances of Attention," *Amer. Jour. of Psych.*, V, p. 1.

39. Tanner and Anderson, " Simultaneous Sense Stimulation," *Psych. Rev.*, p. 378. 1896.

40. R. W. Taylor, " The Effects of Certain Stimuli upon Attention Waves," *Amer. Jour. of Psych.*, XII, p. 335.

41. E. B. Titchener, " Fluctuations of Attention to Musical Tones," *Amer. Jour. of Psych.*, XII, p. 595.

42. Ubantschisch, " Ueber eine Eigenthümlichkeit der Schallempfindungen geringster Intensität," *Centrallblatt f. d. Med. Wissenscaften*, p. 625. 1875.

43. Ubantschisch, " Ueber subjective Schwangkungen der Intensität akustischer Empfindungen," *Pflüger's Archiv*, XXVII, p. 436.

44. Wiersma, " Untersuchungen über die sogennannten Aufmerksamkeitsschwangkungen," *Zeitschr. f. Psych. u. Phys. d. Sinnesorg.*, XXVI, p. 168 ; XXVIII, p. 179 ; XXXI, p. 110.

45. W. Wirth, " Zur Theorie des Bewusstseinsumfanges und seiner Messung," *Phil. Stud.*, XX, p. 487.

CHAPTER VI

1. Binet, " Attention et adaptation," *L'Année psych.*, VI, p. 248.

2. Consoni, " La mesure de l'attention chez les enfants faibles des esprits," *Arch. de Psych.*, II, p. 209.

3. Whipple, " Reaction Times as a Test of Mental Ability," *Amer. Jour. of Psych.*, XV, p. 489.

4. Oehrn, " Experimentelle Studien zur Individualpsychologie," *Psych. Arbeiten*, I, p. 92.

5. Kraepelin, " Die psychologische Versuch in der Psychiatrie," *Psych. Arbeiten*, I, p. 58.

6. Stella E. Sharp, " Individual Psychology," *Amer. Jour. of Psych.*, X, p. 329.

7. L. W. Stern, *Ueber die Psychologie der individuellen Differenzen*, p. 82. Leipzig.

CHAPTER VII

1. E. Claparède, *L'association des idées*. Paris, 1903.

2. O. Külpe, " Ueber die Objectivirung und Subjectivirung vom Sinneseindrücke," *Phil. Stud.*, XIX, p. 508.

3. Lalande, " Sur un effet particulier de l'attention appliquée aux images," *Rev. Phil.*, XXXV, p. 284.

4. F. Paulhan, " L'attention et les images," *Rev. Phil.*, XXXV, p. 502.

5. H. J. Watt, " Experimentelle Beiträge zu einer Theorie des Denkens," *Arch. f. d. ges. Psych.*, IV, p. 289.

CHAPTER VIII

1. W. C. Bagley, " The Apperception of the Spoken Sentence," *Amer. Jour. of Psych.*, XII, p. 80.

2. T. Flournoy, " De l'action du milieu sur l'idéation," *L'Année psych.*, I, p. 180.

3. L. Hempstead, " Perception of Visual Forms," *Amer. Jour. of Psych.*, XII, p. 185.

4. J. Jastrow, *Fact and Fable in Psychology*, p. 275. Boston, 1900.

5. W. B. Pillsbury, " A Study in Apperception," *Amer. Jour. of Psych.*, VIII, p. 351.

CHAPTER IX

1. F. Angell, " Discrimination of Shades of Grey for Different Intervals of Time," *Phil. Stud.*, XIX, p. 1.

2. F. Angell and Harwood, " Discrimination of Clangs for Different Intervals of Time," *Amer. Jour. of Psych.*, XI, p. 67 ; XII, p. 58.

3. Ebert und Meumann, " Ueber einige Grundfragen der Psychologie der Uebungsphänomene im Bereiche des Gedächtniss," *Arch. f. d. ges. Psych.*, IV, p. 1.

4. H. Ebbinghaus, *Ueber das Gedächtnis.* 1885.

5. H. Ebbinghaus, *Grundzüge der Psychologie*, p. 633. 2nd ed. Leipzig, 1905. (Probably the best comprehensive survey of the present status of the memory problem that we have.)

6. P. Ephrussi, " Experimentelle Beiträge zur Lehre vom Gedächtnis," *Zeitschr. f. Psych.*, XXXVII, pp. 56, 161. 1905.

7. Jost, " Die Associationsfestigkeit in ihrer Abhängigkeit von der Verteilung der Wiederholungen," *Zeitschr. f. Psych.*, XIV, p. 436.

8. Müller und Pilzecker, " Experimentelle Beiträge zur Lehre vom Gedächtnis," *Zeitschr. f. Psych.*, Erg. bd. I, p. 1.

9. Müller und Schumann, " Experimentelle Beiträge zur Untersuchung des Gedächtnisses," *Zeitschr. f. Psych.*, VI, pp. 81, 257.

10. R. M. Ogden, " Untersuchungen über den Einfluss der Geschwindigkeit des lauten Lesens auf das Erlernen und Behalten von sinnlosen und sinnvollen Stoffen.," *Arch. f. d. ges. Psych.*, II, p. 93.

11. C. Pentschew, " Untersuchungen zur Ökonomie und Technik des Lernens," *Arch. f. d. ges. Psych.*, I, p. 417.

12. Lottie Steffens, " Experimentelle Beiträge zur Lehre vom ökonomischen Lernen," *Zeitschr. f. Psych.*, XXII, p. 321.

CHAPTER X

1. N. Ach, *Die Willensthätigkeit und das Denken.* Göttingen, 1905.

2. J. H. Bair, " The Acquirement of Voluntary Control," *Psych. Rev.*, p. 474. 1901.

3. Ch. Féré, *Sensation et mouvement.* 2 ed., Paris, 1900.

3a. L. T. Hobhouse, *Mind in Evolution.* London, 1901.

4. Lehmann und Hensen, " Ueber unwillkürliches Flüstern.," *Phil. Stud.*, XI, p. 471.

4a. C. Lloyd Morgan, *Animal Behaviour.* London, 1900.

5. E. L. Thorndike, " Animal Intelligence," *Psych. Rev.*, Mon. Sup., II.

6. R. S. Woodworth, " The Cause of a Voluntary Movement," *Garman Commemorative Studies*, p. 351. Boston, 1906.

7. R. S. Woodworth, " Imageless Thought," *Jour. Phil. Psych. and Sci. Meth.*, III. 701.

8. R. S. Woodworth, *Le mouvement.* Paris, 1903.

CHAPTER XI

1. J. M. Baldwin, *Thought and Things, or Genetic Logic*, I. London, 1906.

2. F. H. Bradley, *Principles of Logic*. London, 1883.

3. B. Bosanquet, *Logic.* London, 1888.

4. J. Dewey, *Studies in Logical Theory.* Chicago, 1903.

5. A. Meinong, *Psychologisch-ethischen Untersuchungen zur Werththeorie.* 1894.

6. K. Marbe, *Untersuchungen über das Urtheil.* Leipzig, 1901.

7. W. B. Pillsbury, " An Apparent Contradiction in the Modern Theory of Judgment," *Jour. of Phil. Psych. and Sci. Meth.*, II, p. 568.

8. W. M. Urban, " Definition and Analysis of the Consciousness of Value," *Psych. Rev.*, XIV, pp. 1, 92.

CHAPTER XII

1. K. Gordon, " Ueber das Gedächtnis für affektiv bestimmte Eindrücke " ; O. Külpe, " Bemerkungen zu vorstehender Abhandlung," *Arch. f. d. ges. Psych.*, IV, pp. 437, 459.

2. Külpe, *Outlines of Psychology*, p. 260. London, 1895.

3. Meumann und Zoneff, " Ueber die Begleiterscheinungen psychischer Vorgänge in Athem und Puls.," *Phil. Stud.*, XVIII, p. 1.

4. Stout, *Manual of Psychology*, p. 234. London, 1899.

5. E. B. Titchener, " Affective Attention," *Phil. Rev.*, III, p. 429.

Wundt, *Grundzüge der physiologische Psychologie*, II, p. 353.

CHAPTER XIII

1. M. W. Calkins, " A Reconciliation between Structural and Functional Psychology," *Psych. Rev.*, XIII, p. 61.

2. C. H. Cooley, *Human Nature and the Social Order*, p. 136. New York, 1902.

3. J. E. Creighton, " Is the Transcendental Ego an Unmeaning Concept ? " *Phil. Rev.*, VI, p. 162.

4. G. S. Fullerton, " The Knower in Psychology," *Psych. Rev.*, IV, p. 1.

5. S. Freud, *Der Witz und seine Beziehung zum Unbewussten.* Leipzig, 1905.

6. S. Freud, *Die Traumdeutung.* Leipzig, 1900.

7. W. James, *Principles of Psychology*, I, p. 291. New York, 1890.

8. Jastrow, *The Subconscious.* Boston, 1906.

9. E. B. McGillvary, " The Stream of Consciousness," *Jour. of Phil. Psych. and Sci. Meth.*, IV, p. 225.

z

10. A. H. Pierce, "An Appeal from the Prevailing Doctrine of a Detached Subconscious," *Garman Studies in Philosophy and Psychology*, p. 315. Boston, 1906.

11. Morton Prince, *The Dissociation of a Personality.* New York, 1906.

CHAPTER XIV

1. Cunningham, Presidential Address, Section H, Brit. Assoc., 1901, p. 781.

2. P. Flechsig, *Gehirn und Seele.* Leipzig, 1896.

3. P. Flechsig, *Die Localisation der geistigen Vorgänge.* Leipzig, 1896.

4. P. Flechsig, "Einige Bemerkungen über die Untersuchungsmethoden der Grosshirnrinde," *Sitzungsbericht d. königliche sächs. Akad.*, XLV, p. 51, 1904.

5. S. I. Franz, "On the Functions of the Frontal Lobes," *Archives of Psychology*, I, 2.

6. Th. Käs, " Ueber Grosshirnrindmasse und über Anordnung der Markfasersysteme," *Neur. Centralbl.*, p. 889. 1895.

7. Th. Käs, " Ueber den Markfasergehalt der Hirnrinde," 3e intern. *Kongr. d. Psych.*, p. 195.

CHAPTER XV

1. K. B. R. Aars, " Notes sur l'attention," *L'Année psych.*, p. 215. 1901.

2. G. R. D'Allons, "L'attention," *Rev. Scientifique*, 5th series, VI, p. 680.

3. A. Bertels, " Versuche über die Ablenkung der Aufmerksamkeit," *Diss. Dorpat.* 1889.

4. L. A. Birch, " Distraction by Odours," *Amer. Jour. Psych.*, IX, p. 45.

5. Bowditch and Warren, " The Knee-jerk and its Physiological Modifications," *Jour. of Physiology*, XI, p. 25.

6. B. B. Breese, "On Inhibition." *Psych. Rev.*, Mon. Sup., III, 1.

7. Darlington and Birch, " On Distraction by Means of Musical Tones," *Amer. Jour. of Psych.*, IX, p. 332.

8. S. Exner, *Physiologische Erklärung der psychischen Erscheinungen.* Leipzig, 1894.

9. Ch. Féré, " Physiologie de l'attention," *Rev. Phil.*, XXX, p. 393.

10. Alice J. Hamlin, "Attention and Distraction," *Amer. Jour. of Psych.*, VIII, p. 1.

11. G. Heymans, " Untersuchungen über psychische Hemmung," *Zeitsch. f. Psych. u. Phys. d. Sinnesorg.*, XXXIV, p. 15.

12. Jendrassik, "Beiträge zur Lehre von den Sehnenreflex," *Deut. Arch f. klin. Medicin.*, XXXIII, p. 177.

13. A. Lehmann, *Die Hypnose*, p. 20. Leipzig, 1890.

14. W. P. Lombard, "Variations of the Normal Knee-jerk," *Amer. Jour. of Psych.*, I, p. 5.

15. W. MacDougall, "Physiological Factors of the Attention Process," *Mind*, N.S., XI, p. 316 ; XVI, pp. 302, 473.

16. L. Marillier, "Remarques sur le mécanisme de l'attention," *Rev. Phil.*, XXVII, p. 566.

17. S. Weir Mitchell, "Physiological Studies of the Knee-jerk," *Philadelphia Med. News.* February, 1886.

18. F. E. Moyer, "A Study of Certain Methods of Distracting Attention," *Amer. Jour. of Psych.*, VIII, p. 405.

19. H. Münsterberg, "Increase of Intensity Produced by Attention," *Psych. Rev.*, I, p. 39.

20. A. Mosso, *Fatigue.* London, 1904.

21. G. E. Müller, *Zur Theorie der sinnlichen Aufmerksamkeit.* Leipzig, 1873.

22. W. B. Pillsbury, "Attention Waves as a Means of Measuring Fatigue," *Amer. Jour. of Psych.*, XIV, p. 277.

23. Ch. Richet and J. Soury, "Cerveau," *Dict. de Phys.*, I, II.

24. G. Saint-Paul, *Le langage intérieur.* Paris, 1904.

25. C. S. Sherrington, "Experimental Note on Two Movements of the Eye," *Jour. of Physiology*, XVII, p. 27.

26. C. S. Sherrington, *The Integrative Action of the Nervous System.* New York, 1906.

27. J. W. Slaughter, "The Fluctuations of the Attention in Some of their Physiological Relations," *Amer. Jour. of Psych.*, XII, p. 313.

28. R. W. Taylor, "The Effects of Certain Stimuli upon Attention Waves," *Amer. Jour. of Psych.*, XII, p. 335.

29. Wiersma, "Untersuchungen uber die sogennannten Aufmerksamkeitsschwankungen," *Zeitschr. f. Psych. u. Phys. d. Sinnesorg.*, XXVI, p. 168; XXVIII, p. 179; XXXI, p. 110.

30. W. Wundt, *Phys. Psych.*, I, p. 320, 5th ed. Leipzig, 1902.

CHAPTER XVI

1. Herbart, "Lehrbuch der Psychologie," *Sämtliche Werke (Kehrbach)*,IV.

2. Herbart, "Psychologie als Wissenschaft," *ibid.*, V, VI.

3. Kant, *Kritik der reinen Vernunft*, pp. 400 *et passim.*

4. Leibniz, "Nouveaux essais," *Monadologie (passim).*
    Pillsbury, "A Study in Apperception," *Amer. Jour. of Psych.*, VIII, p. 315.

5. G. H. Stout, *Analytic Psychology.* London, 1896.

6. G. H. Stout, "Nature of Conation and Mental Activity," *Brit. Jour. of Psych.*, II, p. 1.

7. W. Wundt, *Grundzüge der physiologische Psychologie*, III, p. 331 *et passim.* Leipzig, 1903.

8. H. Münsterberg, *Grundzüge der Psychologie*, I. Leipzig, 1900.

9. H. Münsterberg, *Psychology and Life.* Boston, 1899.

CHAPTER XVII

1. A. Bain, *Emotions and the Will.* 4th ed., London, 1899.
2. Ch. Bastian, " Le processus nerveux dans l'attention et la volition," *Rev. Phil.*, XXXIII, p. 353.
3. Horwicz, *Psychologische Analysen.* Halle, 1872.
4. H. E. Kohn, *Zur Theorie der Aufmerksamkeit.* Halle, 1895.
5. O. Külpe, "Die Lehre vom Willen in der neueren Psychologie," *Phil. Stud.*, V, pp. 179, 381.
6. Th. Lipps, *Grundtatsachen des Seelenslebens.* Bonn, 1883.
7. James Mill, *Analysis of the Human Mind.* 2nd ed., London. 1878.
8. H. Münsterberg, *Grundzüge der Psychologie*, I. Leipzig, 1900.
9. Th. Ribot, *Psychologie de l'attention.* Paris, 1889.
10. G. H. Stout, "Nature of Conation and Mental Activity," *Brit. Jour. of Psych.*, II, p. 1.
11. H. Stumpf, *Tonpsychologie (a)* I, p. 67; (b) II, p. 276. Leipzig, 1883, 1890.
12. J. Sully, " The Psycho-physical Process in Attention," *Brain*, XIII, p. 145.
13. J. Sully, *The Human Mind.* London, 1892.
14. J. Sully, *Outline of Psychology.* London, 1884.

CHAPTER XVIII

1. Azam, *Hypnotisme, double conscience, et altérations de personalité.* Paris, 1887.
2. A. Binet, *Les altérations de la personalité.* Paris, 1892 ; Eng. Tr., New York, 1896.
3. G. Compayré, *L'Evolution intellectuelle et morale de l'enfant.* Paris, 1893 ; Eng. Tr., New York, 1896.
4. L. T. Hobhouse, *Mind in Evolution.* London, 1901.
5. W. James, *Principles of Psychology*, I, p. 381.
6. Pierre Janet, *The Major Symptoms of Hysteria.* New York, 1907.
7. Möbius, *Zeitschr. f. gesammt. Naturwiss*, XLII, p. 89.
8. W. Preyer, *Die Seele des Kindes.* 4 ed., 1895 ; Eng. Tr., New York, 1893.
9. Morton Prince, *The Dissociation of a Personality.* New York, 1906.
10. Th. Ribot, *Les maladies de la personalité.* 2 ed., Paris, 1888; Eng. Tr., Chicago, 1891.
11. Boris Sidis, *Psycho-pathological Researches in Mental Dissociation.* New York, 1902.
12. Sidis and Goodhart, *Multiple Personality.* New York, 1905.
13. Triplett, "The Educability of the Perch," *Amer. Jour. of Psych.*, XII, p. 354.

INDEX OF NAMES

INDEX OF SUBJECTS

PRINTED BY
WILLIAM BRENDON AND SON, LTD.
PLYMOUTH

CLASSICS IN PSYCHOLOGY

AN ARNO PRESS COLLECTION

Angell, James Rowland. **Psychology: On Introductory Study of the Structure and Function of Human Consciousness.** 4th edition. 1908

Bain, Alexander. **Mental Science.** 1868

Baldwin, James Mark. **Social and Ethical Interpretations in Mental Development.** 2nd edition. 1899

Bechterev, Vladimir Michailovitch. **General Principles of Human Reflexology.** [1932]

Binet, Alfred and Th[éodore] Simon. **The Development of Intelligence in Children.** 1916

Bogardus, Emory S. **Fundamentals of Social Psychology.** 1924

Buytendijk, F. J. J. **The Mind of the Dog.** 1936

Ebbinghaus, Hermann. **Psychology: An Elementary Text-Book.** 1908

Goddard, Henry Herbert. **The Kallikak Family.** 1931

Hobhouse, L[eonard] T. **Mind in Evolution.** 1915

Holt, Edwin B. **The Concept of Consciousness.** 1914

Külpe, Oswald. **Outlines of Psychology.** 1895

Ladd-Franklin, Christine. **Colour and Colour Theories.** 1929

Lectures Delivered at the 20th Anniversary Celebration of Clark University. (Reprinted from *The American Journal of Psychology*, Vol. 21, Nos. 2 and 3). 1910

Lipps, Theodor. **Psychological Studies.** 2nd edition. 1926

Loeb, Jacques. **Comparative Physiology of the Brain and Comparative Psychology.** 1900

Lotze, Hermann. **Outlines of Psychology.** [1885]

McDougall, William. **The Group Mind.** 2nd edition. 1920

Meier, Norman C., editor. **Studies in the Psychology of Art: Volume III.** 1939

Morgan, C. Lloyd. **Habit and Instinct.** 1896

Münsterberg, Hugo. **Psychology and Industrial Efficiency.** 1913

Murchison, Carl, editor. **Psychologies of 1930.** 1930

Piéron, Henri. **Thought and the Brain.** 1927

Pillsbury, W[alter] B[owers]. **Attention.** 1908

[Poffenberger, A. T., editor]. **James McKeen Cattell:** Man of Science. 1947

Preyer, W[illiam] **The Mind of the Child:** Parts I and II. 1890/1889

The Psychology of Skill: Three Studies. 1973

Reymert, Martin L., editor. **Feelings and Emotions:** The Wittenberg Symposium. 1928

Ribot, Th[éodule Armand]. **Essay on the Creative Imagination.** 1906

Roback, A[braham] A[aron]. **The Psychology of Character.** 1927

I. M. Sechenov: Biographical Sketch and Essays. (Reprinted from *Selected Works* by I. Sechenov). 1935

Sherrington, Charles. **The Integrative Action of the Nervous System.** 2nd edition. 1947

Spearman, C[harles]. **The Nature of 'Intelligence' and the Principles of Cognition.** 1923

Thorndike, Edward L. **Education:** A First Book. 1912

Thorndike, Edward L., E. O. Bregman, M. V. Cobb, et al. **The Measurement of Intelligence.** [1927]

Titchener, Edward Bradford. **Lectures on the Elementary Psychology of Feeling and Attention.** 1908

Titchener, Edward Bradford. **Lectures on the Experimental Psychology of the Thought-Processes.** 1909

Washburn, Margaret Floy. **Movement and Mental Imagery.** 1916

Whipple, Guy Montrose. **Manual of Mental and Physical Tests:** Parts I and II. 2nd edition. 1914/1915

Woodworth, Robert Sessions. **Dynamic Psychology.** 1918

Wundt, Wilhelm. **An Introduction to Psychology.** 1912

Yerkes, Robert M. **The Dancing Mouse** and **The Mind of a Gorilla.** 1907/1926